Deep Space Commodities

Tom James
Editor

Deep Space Commodities

Exploration, Production and Trading

palgrave
macmillan

Editor
Tom James
NR Capital & Deep Space Technologies
Singapore, Singapore

ISBN 978-3-319-90302-6   ISBN 978-3-319-90303-3   (eBook)
https://doi.org/10.1007/978-3-319-90303-3

Library of Congress Control Number: 2018943700

Cover image © Sky Noir Photography by Bill Dickinson/ Getty Images

Printed on acid-free paper

This Palgrave Macmillan imprint is published by the registered company Springer Nature Switzerland AG
The registered company address is: Gewerbestrasse 11, 6330 Cham, Switzerland

I would like to dedicate this book to all the brave and courageous men and woman all over the world who have given the ultimate sacrifice to help advance our understanding of our place in the Universe.
A huge thank you must go to all the great people from planet Earth that did take my calls and emails and agreed to contribute to this book. Thank you!
To my editorial and research team Simon Peter Roper in London, Aditya Kumar in India, Justine Butler in the UK and Siddharth Bansal in India, your patience and support was invaluable. Thank You!
Tom James
Planet Earth

Contents

List of Figures

List of Tables

DSI
Planetary Resources
↓
ConsenSys

Nextbigfuture.com

1

Deep Space Commodities and the New Space Economy

Tom James

The New Space Economy: Star Date 25 November 2015

Since the dawn of agricultural civilization eminent scholars from Babylon to Beijing have looked to the stars to find meaning. This would manifest in our species as an evolving curiosity not just to observe the stars in the sky, but to also explore that void beyond. In 1865 Jules Verne imagined shooting astronauts to the Moon, in 1901 H.G. Wells wrote of his own Moon landing – perhaps portentiously, Wells envisages the two pioneer astronauts as a businessman and a scientist. The popular imagination has since exploded with ambitions and dreams of space travel appearing in popular media, such as *Star Wars* and *Interstellar*.

What was science fiction then, may soon be very possible. I still remember as a young boy being taken to the cinema by my mother to watch the first Star Wars movie in 1977, and only four years later watching the American Space Shuttle launch live on television for the first time in April 1981. My mother still fondly remembers watching Neil Armstrong's first Moon walk live on television on 20 July 1969.

Since then however, there have been few momentous milestones in the world history of space travel. The Russian space programme has atrophied to the point of crisis, whilst the US and other states entered a technical plateau—

T. James (✉)
NR Capital & Deep Space Technologies, Singapore, Singapore

© The Author(s) 2018
T. James (ed.), *Deep Space Commodities*,
https://doi.org/10.1007/978-3-319-90303-3_1

making little progress on new rocket technology, costs or performance of space vehicles. This period would be marked by governments seemingly content to stick to whatever worked in the 1960s or 1970s.

Then 25 November 2015 happened—a turning point in the diary of the new space economy.

On this day, President Obama signed into law what is popularly referred to as the Space Act 2015. Its full name is the 'Spurring Private Aerospace Competitiveness and Entrepreneurship (SPACE) Act of 2015'. This update to US law explicitly allows US citizens for the first time to 'engage in the commercial exploration and exploitation of 'space resources' [including … water and minerals]'.[1] The consequence would be the renaissance of space exploration, driven by the vigorous competition of private firms competing against one another in a new space race.

Well-equipped for the costs ahead, with some of the private firms driving the space race having access to larger material and intellectual resources than most governments, we stand on the brink of returning to space—this time, to stay. With the annual space economy already sized in excess of US$330 billion dollars a year, it is a business that is increasingly attracting the attention and wallets of investors, entrepreneurs and Earth-based resource companies. This is no small feat, considering the enormous investment, risk and technical hurdles involved.

Earth, post-Space Act 2015, has already begun to change. I have personally witnessed the first-hand impacts on my day to day work in the Earth-based Energy and Commodity industry thanks to the lowering of costs in access to space and space technology. In fact, access to space satellite technology is now becoming a basic requirement in order to operate a competitive commodity exploration and trading business here on Planet Earth.

For example, we see satellite data companies feeding real-time data and analytics to where resources might be found and prospected. Satellites observe and analyse ship movements around the world, watching raw commodities (the life-blood of economies!) being mined, transported and stored around the world. Two firms already making big headway in this field are Ursa and Orbital Insights.[2]

The very real impact on the day-to-day Energy and Commodity industry here on Earth is certain, and has given me the drive to pull this book together on deep space commodities. I intend to examine the issues, challenges and

---

[1] H.R. 2262 (114th): U.S. Commercial Space Launch Competitiveness Act, Summary, 3 February 2017, https://www.govtrack.us/congress/bills/114/hr2262/summary#oursummary
[2] URSA Space company website for general reference: http://ursaspace.com. Orbital Insight company website for general reference: https://orbitalinsight.com

opportunities that the development of resources and technology in space can offer Earth-based investors, entrepreneurs and Energy and Commodity firms. Helping me, I have brought together practitioners, scholars and academia in the areas of space technologies, space law, natural resources development and astropolitics to offer their insight into the scenarios, conundrums and potential answers we will face as a collective species, as we venture into the unknown commercial, political and physical territory of space!

Space: The New Frontier of Innovation to Help Humankind on Earth and Its Future in Space

'Space: the new frontier of innovation', sounds like a great catchy news headline but the reality is the space race has always been a frontier of innovation. Yet when I start discussing space and the new space economy, I am interested that I am often first asked "What has the Space race ever done to benefit society here on Planet Earth?" It seems that for many people research and development into space travel and industry comes off as at best, blue-sky research, disconnected from any practical use, or at its worst, ivory-tower projects diverting valuable resources away from solving problems closer to Earth.

It's a good question to ask, given the fact many people on this planet struggle to subsist on a daily basis, finding it difficult to find fresh clean water or enough food to eat. I would caution against seeing this as a zero-sum game, however, where resources allocated to space exploration come at the cost of human living conditions on Earth. To use the example of clean water, water-purification technology developed for use on board space stations has been deployed world-wide in ground-based filtration systems in areas with low water-security, whilst NASA's research into space farming has led to advances in hyper land-efficient vertical farming on Earth, allowing for less land to be used to support more people, with less disruption and costs to the environment.

Benefits do not come only from technological advancements; the NOAA weather satellites, and now more advanced nano-satellites, can track devastating weather developments, or detect and help predict crop failures and potential famine risk many months in advance of the actual famine hitting. If you drive to work using GPS (Global Position Satellites) map technology to guide your journey, all this technology was developed for the space race, now reapplied for everyday life. These same GPS satellites also help to identify the location of lost ships at sea or deliver the locations of radio distress beacons.

The reality is that the technological by-products spawned by the space race are in fact too many to list here, but include many other life-saving technologies such as the MRI and CAT scan systems used in hospitals. The MRI scanners use super-cooled liquids created during the Cold War space race. The satellite dish was created to receive signals from satellites in space. Cordless tools were created for astronauts to use on space walks. The tyres you use on your car came into existence through cooperation between NASA and Goodyear Tires, who together produced a fibrous material five times stronger than steel. This was first used for parachute shrouds to aid the soft landing of the Viking Lander spacecraft on the surface of Mars. Goodyear then went on to use the material to create a new type of tyre with a tread that would last 10,000 miles longer than a conventional tyre!

Other everyday technologies we take for granted now that emerged from the space race include TV satellite dishes, smoke detectors and robotic technologies which have advanced artificial human prosthetic limb systems. You may even want to check the mattress you sleep on at night as NASA invented memory foam, which is commonly used for applications in chairs and cushions, and mattresses for a better night's sleep.

It is not the case that we must choose between saving lives and improving living conditions or committing to the space race. The technology, global communication and infrastructure gained from the space race and its application to terrestrial civilian use is a powerful force towards the uplifting of all humankind, providing indispensable assistance to Earth-based operations aimed at improving human living conditions.

So What Does the Future Hold?

At the heart of this book is this question: What does the future hold? In the past, space was exclusively the territory of governments with big budgets. In the present, this is rapidly changing as private corporations can take bigger risks and bring bigger budgets than governments can allocate for space development, and since 25 November 2015, they have had the official green light to go forth and boldly go where no corporation has gone before.

The Spurring Private Aerospace Competitiveness and Entrepreneurship (SPACE) Act of 2015 created an update to US law explicitly allowing US citizens and corporations for the first time to own what they find in terms of minerals and water in space. It does not allow ownership of any living organism they find. Plus, in order to try to avoid a direct conflict with some Cold War international space treaties the Act asserts that the United States does assert sovereignty, or sovereign or exclusive rights or jurisdiction over, or the ownership of, any celestial body by bringing this Space Act 2015 into existence.

However, whether this Act does violate the Outer Space Treaty is something scholars and lawyers are still debating and something you can read about in later chapters of this book, where the book explores the challenges and issues which the international community must work through in terms of ownership rights in space.

We are still waiting for any substantial legal case history to develop in terms of citizens fighting in court over ownership or rights over celestial bodies. I say there are no 'substantial' cases, as NASA has been sued a few times so far, but currently no one has won their case. In 1997 NASA was sued by three men from Yemen who claimed that NASA invaded Mars by landing their spacecraft there, that Mars was their inheritance and that they inherited the planet from their ancestors 3,000 years ago,[3] citing mythologies of the Himyaritic and Sabaean civilizations that existed several thousand years BC To the best of my knowledge this case did not progress further.

In 2001 NASA landed the NEAR Shoemaker spacecraft on Asteroid 433, called Eros, the first ever landing of a spacecraft on an Asteroid. This triggered a well-publicized claim in the US by Mr Nemitz that NASA had illegally parked on his asteroid and he sent NASA an invoice for parking and storage fees of their spacecraft on an asteroid he claimed was his property.[4]

The entire legal premise of this claim, which became known as the Eros Project was based upon the natural inherent rights of humans, common law recognition of private property ownership and rights protected by the United States of America constitution. Mr. Nemitz made a lawful claim, with attached legal and equitable claims that he was the owner of Asteroid 433, Eros.

Mr. Nemitz officially published his claim to Asteroid 433, Eros about 11 months prior to NASA landing its 'NEAR Shoemaker' spacecraft on Asteroid 433, his property. The claim was recorded and published by the 'Archimedes Institute', a not-for-profit organization. In addition to this lawful claim, he later filed official documents with the California Secretary of State under the Uniform Commercial Code to establish attached legal and equitable claims.

Within a few days of the NEAR Shoemaker spacecraft landing on his property, Mr. Nemitz sent a very reasonable invoice to NASA for parking and storage fees.

---

[3] BBC "Yemenis Claim Mars", 22 March 1998, http://news.bbc.co.uk/2/hi/despatches/67814.stm

[4] Eros Project general website for reference: http://www.erosproject.com

Citing their interpretation of the Outer Space Treaty of 1967, NASA refused to pay the parking fees. Several letters were exchanged between Orbital Development and NASA's head lawyer, the office of their General Counsel. In finality, NASA's lawyer stated at the time that his individual claim of appropriation of a celestial body (Asteroid 433 Eros) appeared to have no foundation in law. But with times changing, the passing of the Space Act 2015 and private entities seeking to make their physical presence in space known, maybe corporations or people like Mr. Nemitz will have a better chance of staking their claim in the future?

What Comes First the Chicken, the Egg or the Saucepan?

The new space resources economy will provide vast benefits for humankind. It will push disruptive technologies forward as we find ways to live sustainably beyond our planet, lead to improved Earth observations to help protect, preserve and improve life back on our home planet, and ultimately create new jobs, companies and opportunities.

This reality is understood well in the Middle East and is reflected in multiple states actively pouring billions of petrodollars into the new space economy, whilst it simultaneously transitions its Earth-based economies into service and knowledge-based economies, building its stake in the future of the human race.

As we have witnessed over the past ten years, the space industry has become especially more commercialized, with greater investment by the private sector (e.g. Elon Musk of Space Exploration Technologies (SpaceX), Richard Branson with Virgin Galactic). Both firms have investors from the Middle East, and Virgin Galactic will utilize a spaceport in Abu Dhabi. These new space entrepreneurs are focused on costs, and this has helped bring downward pressure on launch prices, which together with cost-saving advances in satellite technology, have combined to open the door for small and midsize space companies to enter the market, providing new niche services and solutions.

These companies, many of whom are basing themselves in the Middle East thanks to proactive local government support, are well-positioned to serve the increasing demand for bandwidth and services across regions that expect to see large population growth, such as Asia, Africa and the Middle East. You can read more about these firms opening up the ease of access to Space in later chapters of this book.

To really drive the new space economy forwards we must first reduce the cost of getting useful 'stuff' into space from the Earth's surface. Re-usable rockets like those of SpaceX, which land themselves after launch and can be repeatedly reused reduce the cost. Once we can produce rocket fuel in space and not have to launch it with any rocket or vessel, this can dramatically reduce the weight and cost of launch yet further.

In space there are many asteroids and mining opportunities for resources to build new, larger space ships and space stations, and potential to lower costs by extracting water from the Moon and turning it into rocket fuel. Nevertheless, the initial machinery and people required to make that happen will have to come from the Earth's surface.

The commercial space sector is driving the reduction in space launch costs, and in fact most of the approximately 5 percent per annum growth in the space economy is coming from the commercial space sector. Commercial products, services, infrastructure and support industries all add up to slightly more than three-quarters of the space economy (US$126 billion), with government spending constituting the remainder. In fact the US Government Space budget was only US$44 billion. To put this in perspective, the United Arab Emirates (UAE) Government budget is already US$5 billion. Given the relative sizes of the US and UAE economies, the Middle Eastern UAE is building a stronger budget for space exploitation.

Another trend to note is that the supply chains for spacecraft, launchers and parts are increasingly globalized. This is reducing the cost of building space craft and satellites, and also reducing the cost of launching them into orbit, with the current 1,000 operational satellites around Earth expected to double in five years.

The other big trend is 'nano-satellites'—small satellites using standard interchangeable parts at a cost of around US$1 million each instead of hundreds of millions of dollars. More and more information technology companies are becoming satellite operators; as a result there has been rapid growth in small satellite launches. This is just the start of good news for the private sector as other large companies have also experienced growth. This all translates into an increasingly commoditized space economy.

How Will the Deep Space Commodity Industry Develop?

Earth is probably the best life-supporting ecosystem ever created in space. Admittedly I have some human bias towards our home world, but on paper it has everything a human space colony needs. It has systems to clean the air, oxygen production systems, water production systems, fuel, food and energy, all wrapped up in a solar radiation protection system. It's also useful in helping us answer some questions regarding the future:

- How will the space economy develop?
- What commodities will be developed first?
- What will human colonies look to produce and purchase out in space?

We only have to look here on Planet Earth to find a lot of those answers. First, what do astronauts and humans in space NOT want to end up having? It's safe to say carbon dioxide in a spacecraft can be a killer, you only have to talk to the Apollo 13 astronauts to learn about that scary scenario as they had to improvise quickly to clean their air with an improvised carbon dioxide absorber or suffocate. Humans have to inhale oxygen in order to allow cells to release energy from carbohydrates and fats; the reaction also releases carbon dioxide as a waste product. In significant concentrations it is toxic, and in closed environments— most significantly in any air-tight environment, such as those experienced by divers, submariners and aboard space stations—carbon dioxide can very easily reach lethal concentrations without adequate means of removing it. The absence of any natural air flow on board a space station can also cause build-ups in unexpected ways, such as when sleeping astronauts discovered that going to sleep in an unventilated area could result in waking up gasping for air, choking on the CO_2 bubble formed from their own exhaled breath. So you don't want too much carbon dioxide in your space ship or space colony, you want a sustainable source of oxygen to breath, in addition to water and food.

To absorb carbon dioxide you can build high-tech CO_2 scrubbers and absorbers, which remove CO_2 from the air, or you can also grow crops in abundance as they absorb CO_2 and release oxygen—the space age office plant. Crops also provide food, another important ingredient to sustainable life in space and therefore a sustainable space economy.

Given all of these facts, perhaps the most valuable deep space commodity in the beginning of the new space economy could be water!

With water in space we have water to drink, water to help crops grow, and we have the component parts of water, oxygen and hydrogen, which we break down into oxygen for humans to breathe, whilst also retaining use as oxidizers and fuel to power our traditional rocket engines.

There are now other types of exciting propulsion systems which we will discuss in later chapters of this book.

So in terms of deep space commodity development, finding large concentrations of water on the Moon to extract could be the first big step in supporting human colonies in space, as to date all water, oxygen and rocket fuel in space was brought there by us. If we can have fuel, food, water and air waiting for us in space, scientists estimate we could see payloads of rockets launched from Earth reduced in weight by upwards of 70 percent. That is a big impact on reducing the cost of launching us or things in to space.

Shackleton Energy[5] and others are looking at creating orbiting refuelling stations, which once launched can serve as refuelling stations for space ships, using fuel made in space.

This highlights an important point. When we talk about asteroid mining or space commodities, the first reaction I get from most people I meet is they think about what the value would be if that was brought back here to Planet Earth. Most space commodities will never come back to Earth but be mined/generated in space for the new space economy, used to sustain life in space, build colonies and space ships in space. In a later chapter in this book you will read about the economic viability of colonizing Mars and how crops can grow well on Mars (much better than on the Moon).

Some rare Earth minerals and gases which are scarce commodities on Earth may well find their way back to mother Earth but otherwise a lot of these commodities in space will stay in space to fuel our species' advances to other planets, and ultimately to build new civilisations.

Deep Space Commodity Developments?

It does look like we can make a reasonable assumption that the foremost commodity which has value for us in space is water, or the component parts of it, oxygen and hydrogen. Human life also requires food, and certain key minerals and vitamins for our bodies to function, presenting more potential commodities. Other commodity developments could include earth to grow crops in, perhaps from Earth, or Martian soil, in addition to building materials to construct Moon bases with. It will be too expensive to bring all those materials repeatedly from Earth without some radical development in technology, so sourcing local metals for construction will be very important for the foreseeable future. Other commodities include metals for constructing next genera-

---

[5] The Shackleton Energy Company website for general reference, http://www.shackletonenergy.com/overview

tion space ships, space stations and permanent Moon bases for sustained astronaut life in space, and the occasional space tourist.

The most immediate valuable resource that people will pay a premium for in space will initially be water. Made up of hydrogen and oxygen, there is a lot of things you can do with it!

In fact, since 2013 reports confirm that NASA and universities around the world including scientists of Wageningen University and Research centre have been working on growing crops in Mars and Moon soil simulants.[6]

Just like the real Martian and Moon soil, these contain heavy metals in almost the same quantities. Four of the crops grown were tested for heavy metal content. No concentrations were detected that would be dangerous for human health. The four crops are therefore safe to eat and, for some heavy metals, the concentrations were even lower than in the crops grown in potting soil. In reality, the soil on Mars actually does have the nutrients plants would need to survive there.

Therefore, water could be the new gold currency in space!

Water as Fuel?

We can expect companies to launch satellites searching for rare gases and metals in asteroids within the next five years, with actual mining happening within eight. A single asteroid might contain 175 times more platinum than the entirety of Earth mines in a year, but it's not metal that is the most important commodity in the short term. It's water.

Before that we will see companies launch mini rovers to scour the surface of the Moon to find the main concentrations of potentially billions of tons of frozen water.

ispace Inc.[7] has turned its attention to the Moon. By taking advantage of lunar water resources, they plan to develop the space infrastructure needed to enrich our daily lives on Earth—as well as expand our living sphere into space. Also, by making the Earth and Moon one system, a new economy with space infrastructure at its core will support human life, making sustainability a reality. At the time of writing this chapter, they plan in late 2018 to be part of the Google Lunar XPRIZE journey to the Moon to land their group of Moon rovers, which will explore the lunar surface mapping water opportunities. If successful, they plan to start mining water on the Moon within the next five years, so circa 2023.

---

[6] Science News, "The Martian becomes reality: At least four crops grown on simulated Mars soil are edible", 26 June 2016, https://www.sciencedaily.com/releases/2016/06/160627095316.htm

[7] ispace announcement, "about us" 1 December 2017, https://ispace-inc.com

In the long term, most of the commodities mined in space will stay in space to power a low-orbit space economy built around satellites and space stations. In that scenario, water accumulated in space would become the most immediate valuable commodity, as it could be used for rocket fuel for interstellar voyages, and oxygen to keep astronauts and space colonies alive.

A major issue in making access to space cheaper is that every space mission must carry its own fuel for in-space operations, since in-space refuelling does not currently exist. Even if it did, that fuel would have to be lifted and stored in orbit in fuel depots at even higher prices. Currently it costs around US$8,000 per kilogram to US$12,000 per kilogram net cost to launch most payloads into low-Earth orbit (LEO).

New breakthroughs in technology must be realized to significantly reduce this high cost. We are starting to see some of those technologies now succeed. For example the SpaceX Falcon 9 rocket is truly re-usable and lands itself after a successful deployment of cargo into space. This type of technology combined with the large reduction in payload in fuel and supplies, when refuelling and resupplying in space is possible, will massively reduce payloads and costs even further. The corresponding cost and price benefit could give space corporations around a 30 percent discount over expendable rocket versions.

To avoid this high-cost barrier to real progress, a means to provide cheaper propellants in space has to be developed. One such firm, Shackleton Energy, mentioned earlier in this chapter, is working on the answer mining ice water on the Moon, but a key difference from ispace, which is looking for the water and to mine it, Shackleton Energy wants to turn that water into fuel and have already illustrated plans for their orbiting refuelling systems to enable you to refuel after launch from Earth.

Currently it seems that if we are to have successful large-scale missions to asteroids and other planets such as Mars, and build a large-scale space economy, a short stopover at the Moon base could be critical to refuel and refresh before launching off into deep space looking for those other commodities.

The Moon is just a few days journey away from Earth and offers a low-gravity launch pad where people can build larger space craft and use less fuel to get them out of the gravitational pull of the Moon and onwards to asteroids or other planets. Here on Earth, the strong gravity and the thick atmosphere allow us to live comfortably, but it also makes it difficult to leave the planet. Rockets have to exceed at least 25,000 mph to escape the Earth's gravity. That means spacecraft may end up using a substantial portion of their fuel before they even start heading to a far-out destination like Mars.

So if large-scale frozen water on the Moon can be located in quantities that can be mined over the next few years, then we can expect Moon base plans to evolve quickly, as NASA and others already have their eyes set on returning to the Moon with human astronauts. This was confirmed in December 2017, when President Donald Trump announced that the Moon would be the next destination for American astronauts. This marks a first step in returning American astronauts to the Moon for the first time since 1972 for long-term exploration and use. The intention is to use the Moon base as a foundation for an eventual mission to Mars.

Phillip Metzger a former research physicist at NASA's Kennedy Space Center co-authored a paper on how we could "bootstrap" across the solar system.[8]

In this paper, he gives an overview of how if we want to want to create a robust civilization in our solar system, more of the energy, raw materials and equipment that we use in space needs to come from space. Launching everything we need from Earth is just going to be too expensive and ultimately space corporations will need to evolve a complete supply chain in space, utilizing the energy and resources of space along the way.

The Moon looks like a good starting point for that Inter-Galactic supply chain, as aside from potential frozen water deposits under the lunar surface, scientists have also identified silicon, titanium, iron and oxygen in the lunar soil. All of these elements could be mined and turned into rockets and rocket fuel.

So any miners, riggers, supply chain experts or welders out there looking for an off-planet experience?

---

[8] Preprint of Journal of Aerospace Engineering, "Affordable, rapid bootstrapping of space industry and solar system civilization", 30 March 2012, http://www.philipmetzger.com/blog/wp-content/uploads/2014/09/Preprint_Affordable-bootstrapping-of-space-industry-and-solar-system-civilization.pdf

2

A New Space Race

Tim R. Bowler

The Russian space pioneer Konstantin Tsiolkovsky famously wrote in a letter in 1911 that "a planet is the cradle of mind (usually cited as 'humanity') but one cannot live in a cradle forever". A hundred years on, we are now witnessing dramatic advances in space. The sector, so long the preserve of governments and national agencies, is opening up to widespread competition.

The first decades of this century are witnessing a new space race, one that is being buoyed by technological revolutions both in orbit and down here on Earth—and this time it is being driven by commerce. It is businesses that are intent on developing practical and profitable applications that will benefit many of us here on Earth. The chapters in this book examine the opportunities and challenges we will face in developing a space-faring business sector as we look ahead to the rest of the twenty-first century.

Space Race

In the beginning, there seemed little room for business in space. During the Cold War, space was the pre-eminent theatre for the ideological struggle between the USSR and the US, with the USSR scoring a series of historic firsts.

T. R. Bowler (✉)
BBC News, London, UK
e-mail: tim.bowler@bbc.co.uk; https://www.linkedin.com/in/timbowlerbbc/

© The Author(s) 2018
T. James (ed.), *Deep Space Commodities*,
https://doi.org/10.1007/978-3-319-90303-3_2

The Space Age proper dates from 1957, the year the USSR launched the R-7, the intercontinental ballistic missile that would become the basis for a series of civilian rocket launchers still used today. It stunned the globe by putting the world's first satellite, Sputnik, into orbit that October and sent a dog, Laika, into space a month later. In 1961, Yuri Gagarin became the first man in space, while two years later Valentina Tereshkova became the first woman in orbit. In 1964, the USSR carried out the first multi-man spaceflight, while in 1965 Alexei Leonov pioneered spacewalking.

Yet by the time the Russians, again, beat NASA to put the Luna 10 spacecraft into orbit around the Moon in 1966, the baton in the race to be the first to land on the lunar surface had irrevocably passed to the US. With greater economic resources to pour into its Mercury, Gemini and Apollo programmes, it would be American astronauts Neil Armstrong and Buzz Aldrin who planted a flag on the Sea of Tranquillity in July 1969, rather than any Soviet cosmonauts.

As the US went on to develop the Space Shuttle, the USSR turned away from the Moon and towards long-term human spaceflights. The Soviet space programme was designed to work out how humans could live and work in orbit, and throughout the 1970s and 1980s its cosmonauts led the way in a series of Salyut, and later the Mir, space stations.

With the collapse of the Berlin Wall, the ending of the Cold War and the passing of the USSR itself, national space agencies moved to international collaboration as a way of pooling their resources and expertise—as well as sharing costs. The fruits of this can be seen to this day in the International Space Station (ISS); a collaboration between the United States, Russia, Europe, Japan, Canada and others.

Commercial Revolution

Throughout this tumultuous struggle for the 'high ground of space' business took a back seat, for it was governments that paid for and sustained the space effort. True, the world's first commercial satellite spacewalking Intelsat 1, or Early Bird—was launched in 1965, but until recently the commercial development of space was largely limited to big telecommunications satellites. Costing several hundred million dollars apiece and weighing several tonnes, these spacecraft are designed to last up to 15 years, so investors can recoup the expense of building them in the first place.

But a revolution has been taking place, overturning traditional models and methods of operating in space. A host of firms are now promising cheaper access to space, via cutting edge technology, renewable rockets and horizontal launch systems. At the same time, satellites are shrinking in size and becoming cheaper to build—CubeSats can be the size of a shoe box and weigh only a few kilograms.

A flood of data and imagery is flowing down from space and a host of new firms are processing, interpreting and marketing this information. And with access to orbit becoming cheaper, we are rethinking and revolutionizing the way we use space.

Investment is pouring into the sector, and the majority of big venture funds have all made investments in the space sector now, says Mark Boggett, the CEO of Seraphim Capital—one of the few venture capital funds to specialize in funding space start-ups.

In 2016, the global space economy totalled US$329 billion worldwide, up from US$323 billion in 2015.[1] Three-quarters of that is coming from commercial activity, according to the influential non-profit group, the Space Foundation. By 2040, the space industry will be worth more than US$1.1 trillion, estimates Morgan Stanley.[2]

Not surprisingly, the number of satellites is growing at an exponential rate. In mid-2017, there were 1,738 operational satellites orbiting the Earth, according to the United Nations Office for Outer Space Affairs (UNOOSA). The year 2017 also saw a record number of satellites being launched—about 50 percent more than any previous year. In the ten years to 2015, about 1,500 satellites were launched. In the ten years to 2025, we are likely to see about 9,000 satellites launched, estimates the analysts group, Euroconsult.[3]

Downstream Applications

While developments in rockets and satellites, the hardware of space, often grab the headlines, it is the downstream end—what we use space for here on Earth—that is seeing the biggest changes. Users of satellite images already include insurance companies, shipping firms, hedge funds, university researchers, farmers, oil and gas firms, and mining companies.

---

[1] Space Foundation, 3 August 2017, "Space Foundation Report Reveals Global Space Economy at US$329 Billion in 2016", https://www.spacefoundation.org/news/space-foundation-report-reveals-global-space-economy-329-billion-2016

[2] Morgan Stanley, 13 November 2017, "Space: Investing in the Final Frontier", https://www.morganstanley.com/ideas/investing-in-space/

[3] *Financial Times*, 4 May 2017, "A space engine that could make flying into orbit commonplace", https://www.ft.com/content/33f3cfe2-2ecd-11e7-9555-23ef563ecf9a

Space imagery can warn us about problems with soil conditions that could help governments prepare for poor harvests; microwave reflections from a forest can tell us if it is under stress, while monitoring ocean temperatures helps work out where fish shoals are likely to be.

With increasingly accurate resolutions, thanks to improved GPS such as Europe's Galileo satellite system, new possibilities for location-based technologies will open up. These will include autonomous cars, connected devices and smart city services. It will be possible to track individual trees as they are logged for timber—a check on deforestation—or to enable us to internally navigate our way around a building with our smart phones.

Much of this will come from mega constellations of small satellites from operators such as San Francisco's Planet Labs—and over the next few years, OneWeb and SpaceX. Putting these craft into low-Earth orbit (LEO) means they can use smaller cameras than satellites in higher orbits, and still get decent image resolutions—thus bringing the weight and cost down to a fraction of that of traditional Earth observation spacecraft.

Their small size and relatively low cost mean that new designs can quickly be tested and built. In 2017, for instance, Planet Labs sent 88 CubeSats into orbit on an Indian rocket—the largest number of satellites ever launched at once. With about 200 satellites in orbit, it means the company can now photograph every point on the planet every day.

While the resolution of cameras aboard commercial CubeSats is still at about 3–5 metres per pixel, this is improving; and some firms are now offering sub-pixel analysis, such as the UK's Terrabotics. Chief executive Gareth Morgan says: "There is rich information between pixels that is captured but that is not obvious".[4] The firm then processes this into commercially available 3D data sets. Alongside the CubeSat operators, there is US manufacturer DigitalGlobe whose two-tonne WorldView satellites offer resolutions of up to 25 centimetres. Until 2014, the US only allowed images this detailed to be sold to the American military, but since then it has allowed them be sold commercially.

Launcher Options

When it comes to challenging nationally-funded agencies and traditional manufacturers, entrepreneur-led start-ups have already carved out a sizeable niche in the launcher market. SpaceX is using its Falcon 9 rockets and Dragon

---

[4] BBC News, "The Disruptors – The new space race – BBC News", 13 September 2017, http://www.bbc.co.uk/news/resources/idt-sh/disruptors_the_new_space_race

capsules to supply the ISS, while Blue Origin is developing its family of sub-orbital and orbital New Shepard and New Glenn launchers. Both firms have demonstrated revolutionary first stages that can land vertically—a significant step in the drive for reusable rockets. Blue Origin is also working with the United Launch Alliance on an engine for the US's planned Vulcan heavy-payload launch vehicle, which is being funded through a public–private partnership with the US government.

Others like Virgin Galactic are working on air-launching satellites—alongside its proposals for sub-orbital tourist flights. In the UK, Reaction Engines is pushing ahead with its single stage to orbit (SSTO) Skylon spaceplane— SSTO being the 'Holy Grail' for rocketeers. At its heart is the hybrid air-breathing rocket engine, Sabre, which works using a revolutionary precooler that will take in air at 1,000 degrees Celsius— Skylon accelerates to Mach 5 climbing to orbit—and chill it to minus 150 Celsius in just a hundredth of a second for use in the engine. In 2017, the firm took a significant step nearer its goal by announcing it would build a ground test facility at Westcott, near London, the home of British rocket research since the end of the Second World War.

In New Zealand there is Rocket Lab, so far the only rocket firm in the world with its own privately owned launch complex; its Electron rocket is targeted at lofting CubeSats into LEO. The firm says once operational its launch costs will be around US$5 million and this will be as frequent as once a week. It is a bold claim, but Rocket Labs says that by 3D printing its engines, production and thus launch cycles can be dramatically speeded up.

At the moment, small satellite makers often hitch rides on existing launches that have a big satellite as main cargo but still have room enough to take smaller craft. The problem for owners of constellations of small satellites is that such launches are not frequent enough for them. It is this gap in the market that Rocket Lab is planning to fill.

Beyond Earth

Business is also driving innovations beyond Earth's orbit, spurred on by competitions such as the Ansari XPRIZE for a reusable crewed sub-orbital spacecraft, and now the US$20 million Google Lunar XPRIZE. This is for the first team to land a robot craft on the Moon, get it to travel 500 metres on the lunar surface and beam back images to Earth.

There are five teams: SpaceIL, from Israel; Moon Express, from the US; Synergy Moon, an international effort; TeamIndus, from India; and Hakuto, from Japan. While getting a rover to the Moon may not have an immediate commercial payoff, Rahul Narayan of Team Indus in Bangalore argues that if successful, it will be "a quantum step for every private space company to go out there and do more stuff in the future".

Another organization with its eye on the Moon is the US firm, Shackleton Energy Corporation, which aims to mine the lunar water and deliver it to a fuel station orbiting Earth. Shackleton says that working from the Moon, with its lighter gravity, it is possible to reduce the costs of getting materials to Earth orbit by a factor of 20 compared to bringing them up from Earth itself, where even getting payload to LEO means 85 percent of a rocket's mass is fuel.

Bringing lunar oxygen into LEO would be a major breakthrough—potentially allowing space missions on a much larger scale than we have seen so far. Cheap lunar rocket fuel would mean that missions to colonize Mars or to mine nearby asteroids would become far cheaper and more practicable.

Challenges

Yet this latest space race also presents its own practical, ethical and legal issues. The sheer volume of space imagery and data means that the current AI systems being used to automatically analyse it need to be speeded up if they are to cope in the long term.

More information may generally be a good thing, but because we are all now potentially being photographed from space, who should have access to this? As facial-recognition technology gets better and the speed of distributing images improves closer to real time, there's an increasing potential for invasive uses of satellite images. As private satellites proliferate and the big data revolution advances, critics argue we need to debate public and private roles in space. Regulation is currently nationally-based—but eventually we will need to set international standards on regulating who gets to buy high-resolution data.

Then there is space debris; it is a problem that can no longer be ignored as thousands of new satellites inevitably mean more space debris. In 2017, the European Space Agency's Earth observation satellite Sentinel-1A was hit by debris no more than a few millimetres in size. ESA estimates there are now 750,000 objects larger than 1 centimetre orbiting the Earth. Among the biggest of these is the imaging satellite Envisat, which stopped working in 2012 and is the size of a school bus. The Agency is now committed to leading European efforts to combat the dangers of space debris. The year 2018 sees the launch of Surrey Space Centre's RemoveDEBRIS mission, which is testing different methods of cleaning up space junk—but all space operators are going to have to grapple with this issue.

Mid-century and Beyond

Growing up in the Apollo era, it was impossible not to be swept up by the promethean promise of it all: humanity's future belonged in space and we would soon follow in the Moonwalkers' footsteps to Mars and beyond. The stars themselves would be humankind's destiny. Of course, the immediate post-Apollo period was somewhat different and quotidian; witness the fact that I am not writing this on some micro-g Lagrange space colony somewhere between the Earth and Moon.

It's always difficult to make predictions, as they say, especially about the future.

Yet as a business journalist for more than 30 years, I have been lucky to report on the real growth of the commercial space sector, a sector which is transforming all of our lives here on Earth. In his autobiography, Magnificent Desolation (2009) Apollo astronaut Buzz Aldrin wrote: "I believe that space travel will one day become as common as airline travel is today. I am convinced, however, that the true future of space travel does not lie with government agencies".[5] It is a statement that will resonate with many in the sector today. As the twenty-first century unfolds, it will be businesses that will be at the forefront of the human development of space.

---

[5] "Magnificent Desolation", Autobiography, Buzz Aldrin, Crown Archetype (23 June 2009) ISBN-10: 0307463451.

3

Launching from Earth: The Science Behind Space Law and Technological Developments

Tom James and Simon Roper

Given the ramping interest, burgeoning investment and exponential development of technologies associated with the commercialization of space, humankind's final frontier is about to be seriously breached, giving birth to a new era of space exploration, tourism and industrial development.

Whilst it may seem far-fetched at present, given the governments, corporate players and private investors rallying to the space crusade, space tourism, development and eventual colonization are a certainty. A reality that will come a lot quicker than we think—space is the next big thing and by definition alone its possibilities are limitless.

Romantic ideologists may dream of blasting off to a neighbouring planet, enjoying a holiday bounding around in an 'astro suit' amid alien terrain in a lower gravity atmosphere. Concurrently corporations and conservationists alike will likely covert the opportunity of the off-planet mining of essential minerals and metals, in a lucrative operation that also gives Mother Gaya a well-earned and necessary break.

T. James (✉)
NR Capital & Deep Space Technologies, Singapore, Singapore

S. Roper
Deep Space Technologies, London, UK

© The Author(s) 2018
T. James (ed.), *Deep Space Commodities*,
https://doi.org/10.1007/978-3-319-90303-3_3

Showcasing human fascination with space is American-born multi-millionaire Dennis Tito,[1] who in 2001 became the first 'space tourist'. He travelled past the exosphere, where the thinnest layer of our atmosphere shakes hands with space, to the International Space Station (ISS) via a stellar taxi ride in a Russian Soyuz capsule.

Tito's self-funded excursion, whilst not going down well with the National Aeronautics and Space Administration (NASA), at the time, showed there was money to be made and a palpable interest in space tourism. This escapade was just 40 years after Russian cosmonaut Yuri Gagarin became the first astronaut in space in a historic Soviet Government-funded mission.

And fuelled by ramping interest and the associated fast pace of space-related innovations, the privatization of space is developing way past joy flights. Privately-owned businesses and nations alike are investing billions in building satellites, space vehicles and creating networks, with an end goal of mining asteroids, moons and planets—eventually colonizing parts of our solar system. It's a science fiction dream that is now a plausible reality.

However, with space now destined to be the new playground and workplace for humankind, legitimate concerns are immerging regarding the governance of this unquantifiable area. Current laws for space-related operations were simply a legislative exercise and are not written for the current space climate given the new private and corporate activity with it.

The worry is that whilst the technology to achieve the aforementioned space operations has been, or is close to being, developed, space law is definitely not.

A legitimate system to apportion liabilities and obligations and regulate space organizations is necessary, as all participants from governments to privae participants require security associated with their plans, operations and ultimately investment. Space law needs significant modification to convey lawful assurances to all operating within it, be they private enterprises, commercial players or national operations, writing legislation and setting out guidelines to appease the security worries of all participants.

Space is currently governed by five arrangements, cumulatively referred to as the 'Five United Nations (UN) Treaties on Outer Space. These consist of the Outer Space Treaty (1967),[2] the Rescue Agreement (1968),[3] the Liability

---

[1] BBC News, "Profile: Tito the Spaceman", 28th April 2001, http://news.bbc.co.uk/2/hi/science/nature/1297924.stm

[2] United Nations Office for Outer Space Affairs (UNOOSA), "Treaty on Principles Governing the Activities of States in the Exploration and Use of Outer Space, including the Moon and Other Celestial Bodies", last updated 1966, http://www.unoosa.org/oosa/en/ourwork/spacelaw/treaties/introouterspacetreaty.html

[3] UNOOSA, "Resolution adopted by the General Assembly, Nov 1967, http://www.unoosa.org/oosa/en/ourwork/spacelaw/treaties/rescueagreement.html

Convention (1972),[4] the Registration Convention (1976)[5] and the Moon Agreement (1984).[6] The content of these reports indicates that they were drafted to address just member states.

Only participating states marked and endorsed the above UN legislation, private space organizations such as Virgin Galactic are not covered. Therefore, there are various inquiries that need to be conducted and additions made to address the relevance these agreements have for private space organizations.

For example, whilst the Rescue Agreement ensures the prompt protection of space explorers, do clients of private space flights qualify also? Encouragingly, the Outer Space Treaty supplies space travellers equally, viewing them as 'agents of humanity in space'. This status is given to them on the understanding that they enter space for the advantage of science.

The imminent flow of space vacationers also qualifies for this status for the purpose of individual recreation. But clients of private space flights will not be categorized as 'space explorers', which is significant.

This is because, for example, should a space tourist not be covered by the Rescue Agreement, since they are not classified as space explorers, then what— in the absence of the agreement—are they protected by?

Notwithstanding the Five UN Treaties on Outer Space, member states have authored their own national enactments to direct private space-related exercises, which may provide a few solutions to the grey areas that exist in space law. In the US, for example, the Commercial Space Launch Act (1984) and the subsequent Amendment Act (2004) were drafted in addition to the five acts within the UN treaties to address the existing patchy law.

These additional US directives stipulate that space flight members loading up private space vehicles in the US must conform to these laws over and above the UN's laws to show they have the capability to practically and safely enter space.

Yet the corpus of space law has yet to adequately define clear legislation for private, corporate and national operations in outer space. Space investigation is perilous—distinguishing what private space organizations and individuals are at risk is paramount in controlling their operations.

If this is not addressed it will trigger security worries for all those with something at stake. Case in point is the Cosmos 954 mishap. In 1978, a

---

[4] UNOOSA, "Convention on International Liability for Damage Caused by Space Objects", 1963–1970, http://www.unoosa.org/oosa/en/ourwork/spacelaw/treaties/liability-convention.html

[5] UNOOSA, "Convention on Registration of Objects Launched into Outer Space", 1975, http://www.unoosa.org/oosa/en/ourwork/spacelaw/treaties/introregistration-convention.html

[6] UNOOSA, "Agreement Governing the Activities of States on the Moon and Other Celestial Bodies", 1979, http://www.unoosa.org/oosa/en/ourwork/spacelaw/treaties/intromoon-agreement.html

Soviet atomic controlled reconnaissance satellite slammed into Canada, dispersing radioactive flotsam and jetsam more than 124,000 square kilometres from the crash site. This incited fears of an atomic blast that would be catastrophic for human wellbeing and the Earth. The 1972 Liability Convention empowered Canada to charge the Soviet Union over CAD$6 million for liability and damages.

Assume, in any case, that a private Russian organization claimed responsibility for the satellite. Who might be at risk here? The Liability Convention has no specific arrangements for private substances since it was not intended for them. Therefore, the liabilities of private space organizations manifest into the liabilities of the state from which these space vehicles originated. The effect of Article VI of the Outer Space Treaty renders states liable for both administrative and non-legislative space-related exercises.[7]

This new era of space exploration requires private space organizations to mandatorily purchase protection, an insurance vehicle based on the evaluation of any identified hazard, where the liable state becomes the guarantor for cited operations.

Whilst this may provide security for states in one area, it could come at the expense and security of others, as participating nations will likely compete, reducing the weight of risk from their country in a bid to attract more business from which they benefit financially.

Although compromising safety over profit is a serious allegation, business protocols suggest that privately-owned businesses will be attracted to governments whose legal frameworks are less stringent and make projects significantly more financially viable.

By smoothing the cost-base associated with any planned operation, with the passage of time these states would be able to aggregate the larger part of these organizations, this becoming the celestial equivalent for space operations to the Cayman Islands for tax on Earth.

As this practice grows, the space market will naturally adopt a competition model, with rival propellant states keeping costs down to attract business. Amid this rivalry, from a universal business law viewpoint, grave financial security worries for states at a worldwide level are bound to occur.

At present there is nothing stopping rival states from purposely making themselves more alluring to private space organizations in space law. But if countries are allowed to do this under international space law, the possibility of insufficient

---

[7] UNOOSA, "Treaty on Principles Governing the Activities of States in the Exploration and Use of Outer Space, including the Moon and Other Celestial Bodies", 1966, http://www.unoosa.org/oosa/en/our-work/spacelaw/treaties/outerspacetreaty.html

governance and required due diligence by a prospective privateer does raise concern that human security is being compromised by budgets and financial gain for both operator and facilitator. Worries genuinely exists at this stage of the new age new 'space race' that this is a conceivable situation. Space law needs to be bolstered, providing confidence amongst participants and potential third parties alike, guarding against the sufferance of collateral damage of both a physical and fiscal nature; not rendering it unverifiable and uncertain.

Perhaps space pioneers should take note of historical events that have many similarities to humankind's aspirations for space, such as the mantra eventually adopted during the construction of the Great Western Railway in the 1900s: "Wellbeing First". Because without security measures set up, much could be in question.

NASA's Collaboration: the SpaceX Commercial Crew Program

A Deal for Human Commercial Spaceflight

SpaceX, founded by Elon Musk, the South-African born organization's CEO and CTO of Teslar and PayPal fame, back in 2002 collaborated with NASA and the Boeing Space and Security division, joining forces to take over dispatches to the ISS from the Russian Soyuz capsule. Both entities envisaged initial plans for flights before the end of 2017 under the Commercial Crew Program (CCP).[8]

Sadly since its inception, the CCP was hampered by numerous setbacks. The programme, which tasks US private companies with building spacecraft that can transport NASA astronauts to and from the ISS, was originally supposed to get off the ground in 2017.

But SpaceX, armed with its collaboration with aviation colossus Boeing Aerospace's Space and Security division, currently tasked with the development of crewed spacecraft for NASA, has hit delays. They probably won't have their vehicles certified to carry astronauts until 2019, says the US Government Accountability Office (GAO), a federal agency that conducts audits for the US Congress.

Still the 2019 date conveniently coincides with the termination of the current deal NASA has in place with the Russians for shuttle services to the ISS

---

[8] NASA, "Commercial Crew Program", last updated Jan 11th 2018, https://www.nasa.gov/exploration/commercial/crew/index.html

via the programme, but it leaves no room for further delays. Currently the US space agency buys seats on the incumbent Soyuz capsule for its astronauts, tickets that cost about US$80 million per person. Not your average commute—but once the CPP is up and running, NASA astronauts will again be launched on American-made vehicles at a cheaper cost.

For its part in the programme, Boeing is developing a crew capsule called the CST-100 Starliner, which is meant to launch on top of the Atlas V rocket manufactured by the United Launch Alliance (ULA), a joint venture between Lockheed Martin Space Systems and the company's Space and Security subsidiary.

Meanwhile, SpaceX is adapting its Dragon cargo capsule, which is currently used to ship supplies to the station, so that it can carry humans to space. The so-called Crew Dragon is meant to piggyback on top of the established Falcon 9 rocket, much as the now redundant Space Shuttle initially did during testing with a modified 747 before solid fuel rockets launched it clear of Earth's gravity for actual missions.

The ultimate goal for the Atlas rocket is for it to assist in flying two paying private passengers on a trek around the Moon, Musk claimed in a statement on 27 February 2017.[9]

The two private subjects, who have not yet been named at the time of writing, approached SpaceX about travelling around the Moon and have officially "paid a noteworthy store" for the cost of the mission, roughly a week-long trip around the Moon, according to Musk, in its Dragon V2. So this could become a reality.

"This would be a long circle around the Moon," he said. "It would skim the surface of the Moon, going significantly further into profound space and afterward circle back to Earth."[10]

Musk also said that the Moon excursion will assist his company's definitive objective of setting up permanent Mars settlements, providing a kind of steppingstone for the process. The Moon Flight is scheduled to launch after SpaceX flies NASA space travellers to the ISS as a component of the CCP. Currently SpaceX wants to complete an un-crewed flight of the Dragon shuttle first and initial flights are proposed for mid-2018, according to Musk.

To make space explorers on Mars by circa 2030 a reality, NASA has enlisted six privately-owned businesses to outline and expand profound space territo-

---

[9] *The New York Times*, "SpaceX plans to send 2 tourists around Moon in 2018", Feb 27th 2017, https://www.nytimes.com/2017/02/27/science/spacex-moon-tourists.html

[10] ZeroGNews Publication, "SpaceX surprises with planned human lunar mission announcement", Feb 27th 2017, http://www.zerognews.com/2017/02/27/spacex-surprises-with-planned-human-lunar-mission-announcement/

ries under the second 'Next Space Technologies for Exploration Partnerships' (NextSTEP) 'Broad Agency Announcement'.

The selected companies, in no particular order, are:

- Bigelow Aerospace of Las Vegas
- Boeing of Pasadena, Texas
- Lockheed Martin of Denver
- Orbital ATK of Dulles, Virginia
- Sierra Nevada Corporation's Space Systems of Louisville, Colorado
- NanoRacks of Webster, Texas

SpaceX's, collaboration with Boeing had seen the development of both the Falcon 9 rockets and Crew Dragon shuttles vehicles to serve NASA's load requirements for the ISS. Musk has said that the Dragon could be prepared to dispatch space travellers inside three years of ratifying an agreement with NASA and conduct initial tests mid-2017. The organization had a US$1.6 billion contract to give 12 uncrewed load conveyances to the station. After delays past a planned 2016 launch, and following a further 24-hour delay on launch day, the vehicle successfully mated with the ISS in February of 2017.

The delays were mostly caused by technical problems pertaining to occasional cracking around the craft's propulsion units, an obvious risk described by NASA at the time as "unacceptable".

Concurrently the company is in the middle of upgrading its Falcon 9 rocket to a new version of the vehicle called the Block 5 rocket. The upgrade includes five major changes to the original design. The GAO reports that there may not be enough time for these changes to be implemented and reviewed by NASA before SpaceX begins uncrewed flight tests of the Crew Dragon. At the time of writing these had been scheduled for late 2017. It didn't happen.

Similarily, Boeing's Space and Security division had trouble gathering important information that NASA needs to certify the CST-100 Starliner. For instance, the Atlas V rocket that is supposed to carry the Starliner into space uses Russian-made rocket engines. But because of agreements between the USA and Russia, getting information related to the design of the engine has been difficult, making it hard for NASA to okay the engines for human spaceflight. Additionally, there are concerns as to whether Boeing will be able to get enough data about how the Starliner's parachutes work before humans fly in the craft.

Boeing got US$18 million from NASA for the preliminary development of the spacecraft and for a second phase US$93 million. The 12 August 2012 saw the company receive US$460 million to continue work under the Commercial Crew Integrated Capability Program (CCiCAP).

In September 2014, NASA selected the Starliner along with SpaceX's second version of the Dragon for the Commercial Crew Transportation Program, with the award of US$4.2 billion—as of mid-2017.

Boeing's Starliner crew transportation vehicle for NASA continued to meet its processing milestones at the US Kennedy Space Center and various test sites around the country. The ULA, the entity tasked with launching Starliner on its journey towards the ISS, has made the decision to swap the Atlas booster that will power Starliner's first flight in 2019. Meanwhile, the first crewed Starliner mission appears to be slipping to late 2018 with a test launch expected in August 2018.[11]

Notwithstanding the aforementioned problems and missed targets, private spaceflight is breaking new ground. And with NASA's space transports resigning, SpaceX and Boeing are the only two companies currently in the mix to dispatch freight and space travellers to the ISS anytime soon. Space is the next big thing, literally.

Generating competition, NASA has also commissioned another organization, an amalgamation in 1982 of Virginia-based Orbital Sciences, Orbital ATK and sections of Alliant Techsystems.

Orbital ATK's story differs from companies established by the likes of Branson, Musk and Bezos. It might seem like private space travel is the sole preserve of rich business visionaries. However, Orbital ATK has no such effectively definable figure and has the most reduced profile amongst its peers in spite of being the most seasoned by some way.

Ergo, flagged under the Orbital Science banner, in November 2017 this collaboration successfully launched a Cygnus resupply ship powered by an Antares rocket, also referred to as the Taurus vehicle, from NASA's Wallop launch facility in Virginia—destination the ISS.

The uncrewed resupply ship, Expedition 53, arrived at the ISS with almost 7,400 pounds of crew supplies, science experiments, spacewalk gear, station hardware and computer parts. Things are going well.

Regardless of its legacy, however, even Orbital isn't resistant from mishaps. NASA saw this firsthand in October 2014 when the organization's third freight mission finished with the Antares rocket detonating upon dispatch.

That was the third resupply mission to fall flat that year, joining another from SpaceX and the Russian vehicle Progress M-59. With something as complex as space travel, accidents happen, regardless of whether it's a privately-owned businesses or NASA itself.

---

[11] Business Standard publication, "Boeing, SpaceX progressing towards first crewed missions in 2018: NASA", Jan 5th 2018, http://www.business-standard.com/article/current-affairs/boeing-spacex-progressing-towards-first-crewed-missions-in-2018-nasa-118010500130_1.html

"Space is hard", as the old expression goes—similarly there's a lot of rivalry, guaranteeing that our best personalities In Space travel have additional motivation to split Space for the last time.

In addition to Boeing, SpaceX and Orbital, waiting in the wings are other corporate giants like Lockheed Martin and privately-owned companies born from the genius, and wallets, of infamous entrepreneurs such as Sir Richard Branson (Virgin Galactic), Jeff Bezos (renowned philanthropist and founder of Amazon) and Robert Bigelow (Bigelow Aerospace).

All of these companies are also competing for a slice of space in the race to construct shuttles to send humans into space with plans for regular joyrides around the Moon and the establishment of a Mars colony being muted by SpaceX's enthusiastic founder, Musk.

It's widely agreed amongst participants that reusable rockets are the best solution to penetrate into space, an objective that SpaceX is getting closer to accomplishing. Since 2006, the company has had an agreement from NASA to resupply payloads to the ISS. But so far, Musk is the only player with aspirations, fuelled by the experience and knowledge being gained on the ISS contract, to accelerate towards humankind's fantasy of establishing a Martian settlement.

Elsewhere, Bigelow Aerospace had a shaky start with its entrance to the space market after NASA initially licensed it back in 2000. It has been making ground-breaking progress with its Genesis programme detailing two smaller-than-usual space station models, called Genesis 1 and Genesis 2. The organization's bigger Sundancer and BA-330 vehicles are designed to fill in as space stations; furthermore, Bigelow has set his sights on building a private base on the Moon, utilizing the inflatable innovations also destined for installation on the ISS.

Bigelow, situated in North Las Vegas, Nevada in the USA, is building a model of an expandable living space called the Expandable Bigelow Advanced Station Enhancement (XBASE). The 330-cubic metre structure has already connected to the ISS in 2016, but the space pod company also wants to send an inflatable space hotel to orbit the Moon, with accommodations for astronauts and citizen space travellers alike.

Bigelow has announced that a bigger inflatable pod than that attached to the ISS, which it's calling the B330 lunar depot could be orbiting the Moon within five years. This is much more ambitious than the ISS add-on.

The B330 lunar depot is designed to stand alone and is about a third of the size of the ISS. The company suggests the pod could hold roughly six people—and is billing it as a hub for significant lunar business development.

Providing accommodations for future space travellers is a logical next step for the company's founder, Robert Bigelow, who owns the Budget Suites of America hotel chain and has been working on creating expandable space modules since 1999.

ULA, a joint venture between Boeing and Lockheed Martin, plans to partner with Bigelow to launch the habitat into space, then get it circling around the Moon.

And, of course, one can't talk about space tourism without mentioning Sir Richard Branson's Virgin Galactic enterprise, which was briefly touched upon at the beginning of this chapter. Established in 2004, it's has been a long time since Virgin Galactic's Space Ship Two's fatal crash in California's Mojave Desert a decade later.

Despite this setback, the notion of seeing our blue planet from space is proving popular with future travellers—some 500 potential customers have spent US$250,000 on reserving their spot on one of Virgin Galactic's trips.

After the crash, Branson said his dream of space travel might have ended. But Galactic under-boss and former NASA chief of staff George Whitesides regrouped, redoubled Galactic's focus on safety and appears to be making progress.

In August 2017 the company received its first operating licence from the US Federal Aviation Authority (FAA), subject to a series of conditions, including the regulator verifying test results before any passengers can board its main air-propelled vehicle Space Ship Two. The craft is designed to hold two pilots and six passengers, who will be carried by launch craft White Knight Two 62 miles into the sky to it.

Space Ship Two is still only a suborbital vehicle intended for space tourism. Galactic sets prices for these suborbital rides at about US$200,000 per person. In addition, Space Ship Two's ground to air transport, the enormous White Knight Two, could also be adapted to dispatch small rockets or satellites for NASA and other clients.

Staying with the entrepreneurs, Amazon founder, Jeff Bezos, who established Blue Origin in 2000, suggests that outer space is there for the taking.

Blue Origin, which had initially remained somewhat secretive about developments, announced in mid-2017 that it successfully tested its new engine the BE-4 at 50 percent power for three seconds.

This demonstration sent a clear signal that there is a new player in the industry preparing to compete both for national security and commercial launches. Some have derided Blue Origin for its original focus on New Shepard, a suborbital vehicle that the company plans to use for space tourism trips in a year or two. However, the brawny new engine supports the idea that Blue Origin is gearing up for orbital and deep space missions too.

Elsewhere, Sierra Nevada Corporation's plans for space included three to four rocket dispatches for a long-term living space that will be developed in space. Their model depends on the organization's Dream Chaser load module.

The outline incorporates an expansive inflatable texture condition module, an Environmental Control and Life Support System (ECLSS), and an impetus framework.

As for the Dream Chaser, originally configured to carry people, it lost out to both SpaceX and Boeing in 2014, during the last contract award of the CCP. Later, in 2016, NASA selected the Dream Chaser to fly six cargo missions to the ISS by 2024. The agency also selected SpaceX and Orbital ATK spacecraft at the same time.

California-based SpaceDev is an entirely possessed auxiliary of Sierra Nevada Corp, which procured it in 2008, that has been building the reusable Dream Chaser space plane to dispatch teams and freight into space on an Atlas 5 rocket.

Aviation giant Lockheed Martin also has great plans in the pipeline. NASA has given them the green light to refurbish an old ISS cargo container as a prototype for a deep space habitat. Lockheed Martin's goal is to help develop life-support systems that can protect astronauts as they travel beyond low-Earth orbit in alignment with NASA's NextSTEP programme, an initiative launched in 2016 in an effort to develop a suitable habitat for astronauts travelling farther than low-Earth orbit.

To this end Lockheed Martin is working to turn the old ISS cargo module into the prototype of a full-scale habitat at NASA's Kennedy Space Center. Work began in July 2017 and is part of a larger effort by Lockheed Martin to work with NASA on refining the design of the Deep Space Gateway, the agency's fabled key to sending future astronauts to Mars.

As the ISS won't be around forever, recycling could be the economical answer to its future and NextSTEP, if NASA entertain proposals from Lockheed Martin that essentially suggest cannibalizing the old parts of the ISS to turn into future spacecraft.

Mars Base Camp is Lockheed Martin's vision for sending humans to Mars in about a decade. The concept is simple: transport astronauts from Earth, via the Moon, to a Mars-orbiting science laboratory where they can perform real-time scientific exploration, analyse Martian rock and soil samples, and confirm the ideal place to land humans on the surface in the 2030s.

Finally we address the last, but not least, player involved in the exploration of outer space. Since 2009, Texas-based NanoRacks has been enabling space research and in-space services to customers globally from multiple platforms and launch vehicles.

The company reportedly offers low-cost, high-quality solutions for satellite deployment, basic and educational research both at home and in 30 nations worldwide for those new to the industry and aerospace veterans.

In July 2015, NanoRacks signed a teaming agreement with Blue Origin to offer integration services on their New Sheppard space vehicle. NanoRacks, along with partners at ULA and Space Systems Loral, was also selected by NASA to participate in the NextSTEP's Phase II programme, a step forward in developing commercial habitation systems in low-Earth orbit and beyond.

As of November 2017, over 600 payloads have been launched to the ISS that incorporated NanoRacks' services. The company is working with other organizations now familiar to us, not withstanding NASA and Blue Origin, including Virgin Galactic. Others include the European Space Agency (ESA) the German Space Agency (DLR), Planet Labs, Millennium Space Systems, Space Florida, NCESSE, pharmaceutical drug companies and organizations in Vietnam, the UK, Romania and Israel.

It's all go in space!

Increased interest from both national governments and the private sector present the opportunity for rapid growth in the commercialization of outer space. By 2030 the global market for space industries is expected to grow from £155 billion per annum to £400 billion per annum. Many of the companies mentioned in this section, like SpaceX and Blue Origin, will be at the forefront of pushing forward this new era of space exploration.

Launching from Earth: Technology Developments

Ready, steady—GO! A Whitehouse announcement last year underlined the rising interest in the space market, regarding its exploration, colonization, tourism and mining.

In one of his less-controversial statements, US President Donald Trump charged NASA to put humans back on the Moon and told the administration to also 'reach for Mars', in instructions warmly received by the space community on both national and private levels.

The news will re-seat America at the forefront of a new age space race for human space missions. It will likely trigger a fresh wave of collaborations with NASA and private entities, in addition to expanding current partnerships NASA has with contractors that include SpaceX and Boeing.

In late December, 2017, as introduced in the previous section, US-based company Blue Origin conducted the latest test flight of its New Sheppard rocket for over a year, according to media reports at the time from the FAA.[12]

Blue Origin didn't release any information immediately after the test, but Twitter speculation at the time reported that the flight was a success.

Much like Virgin Galactic's SpaceShip2, New Sheppard is designed to fly up to six passengers on brief jaunts to suborbital space. The booster comes back to Earth for a vertical touchdown via engine burns, in much the same way as the first stages of SpaceX's Falcon rockets will do in orbital flights. More about SpaceX and Galactic will follow.

The unpiloted New Sheppard capsule, meanwhile, lands softly under a parachute. The capsule features the biggest windows ever to fly in space, along with 530 cubic feet (15 cubic metres) of interior volume—enough for folks to turn somersaults inside, so Blue Origin representatives have said.

If the media was correct, this may well be a sign of some big things to come from Blue Origin in the near future. The company has said it plans to begin commercial flights of New Sheppard soon, perhaps in 2018, although they have not revealed how much a ticket will cost.

But not all the excitement was polarized towards the US in 2017. As the year came to a close, news from Asia broke that an uncrewed space vehicle developed by India will carry rovers and probes from the ex-British colony and other participating nations, touching down on the Moon (at time of writing) in 2018.

The mission had been delayed due to issues concerning a partnership with the Russian Federation Space Agency (Roscosmos), which was initially involved in the project until the partnership was dissolved in 2013 amid the failure of Roscomos' plans for Mars. These were detailed in the form of Russia's Fobos-Grunt spaceship, which shared technology with India's probe.

The Indian Space Research Organisation's (ISRO)[13] mission to our cosmic neighbour, the first since 2013 when China landed the Yutu rover there, is called Chandrayaan-2. The vehicle was developed from its earlier sibling, unsurprisingly named Chandrayaan-1, which made it into lunar orbit in 2008 and was able to detect 'magmatic water' within a crater on the Moon's surface.

Sadly, India's initial probe was ill-fated. NASA found it adrift in 2016, following news that the ISRO had lost contact with it ten months into a planned two-year mission. But the ISRO has other projects in the works as well. They

---

[12] Space.Com publication, "Blue Origin launches 1st new Shepard spaceship test flight in over a year", Dec 12th 2017, https://www.space.com/39070-blue-origin-new-shepard-test-flight-2017.html

[13] Indian Space Research Organisation (ISRO) website, last updated April 18th 2018, https://www.isro.gov.in

are working on Aditya, a mission that aims to study the Sun; and XpoSat, a five-year satellite programme that will improve working knowledge of cosmic radiation.

Aside from state enterprises, private companies are also moving forward, making significant advances in an already established market for what is commonly referred to as space tourism.

Humans in Space: The Companies Involved

Private spaceflight is breaking new ground with the likes of SpaceX, Virgin Galactic, Boeing and Bigelow Aerospace—just a few of the companies leading the current charge for outer space in the years to come.

As for the advancement of private enterprises with NASA, the association has partnered with SpaceX, Bigelow Aerospace and a number of other organizations to assist with cargo and crew flights to the ISS. Some privateers, including Virgin Galactic, are also in the space tourism business with aspirations to colonize the Moon and eventually Mars.

The Moon's colonization is on many participants' radars with a plethora of stellar announcements in late 2017, including one by Tokyo-based ispace. The company, founded in 2010, aims to be the first Japanese company to land on the Moon, joining the Former Soviet Union (FSU), China and the US as the only nations on Earth to successfully perform soft landings on the lunar surface.

ispace broke the fundraising record for commercial space exploration, far exceeding the previous achievement by SpaceX. The organization plans to land a rover on the Moon's surface by the end of 2020, having raised US$90.2 million in its latest round of funding, according to the company's press release. For context, the next highest amount raised was SpaceX with US$12.1 million.

ispace is responsible for the Hakuto team, which is competing for Google's US$30 million Lunar XPRIZE. The competition winner must land a commercial spacecraft on the Moon's surface that then travels a distance of 500 metres before beaming high-definition images and video footage back to Earth. It should be noted that no one managed to meet the timeline set for the Google XPRIZE (by early 2018) but ispace is expected to continue its mission to the Moon.

By 2040, ispace predicts that 1000 people will be living on the Moon, and that it will host 10,000 visitors each year.

"With the network and knowledge of our new shareholders, we will not only expand commercial space activities centred around lunar resources, but also create a sustainable living sphere beyond Earth", CEO Takeshi Hakamada said at the time.[14]

That announcement followed a landmark deal between Japanese Prime Minister Shinzo Abe and US President Donald Trump at their summit talks held in November 2017 to collaborate closely on a US-proposed project to build a space station in lunar orbit. It's expected to be completed in the late 2020s.

In Hawthorne, California, SpaceX had also been busy at NASA's Cape Canaveral launch pad. Following initial delays linked to the propellant craft's secondary booster systems, one of its Dragon spaceships blasted off from the Air Force station's Space Launch Complex 40 in Florida at the close of 2017—destination the ISS.

The mission was the company's thirteenth delivery flight to the ISS for NASA under its resupply contract with the agency. SpaceX's two-stage Falcon 9 rocket lifted off sending the company's robotic Dragon capsule to deliver nearly 4,800 pounds (2,177 kilogrammes) of food, supplies and science gear, plus some Christmas presents for the astronauts, given its mid-December schedule.

Never before had SpaceX launched a pre-flown spacecraft atop a pre-flown rocket—and this was the first time that a used rocket was employed on a cargo mission for NASA. The mission underlined SpaceX's belief that reusable rocket technology is the only sure-fire way to conquer space.

Whilst ISS missions are progressing after some teething problems, SpaceX founder Musk's plans for the Moon and Mars remain at the forefront of the entrepreneur's mind. He has announced his company's plans for an enormous new rocket that he says will go to Mars in 2022 and maybe eventually provide speedy trips around Earth.

The rocket, which Musk lovingly referred to as a BFR (the first and last letters stand for 'big' and 'rocket'), is smaller than the one he announced in 2016, carrying 150 tonnes compared to the previous design's 300. However, it's still more powerful than any of SpaceX's or NASA's other planned rockets.

Musk said that its successful development will see it supersede the current Falcon and Dragon spacecraft—at which point the company would use it for cargoes and crew missions to the ISS for NASA.

---

[14] Space.Com publication, "Japanese company raises record $90 million for Moon missions", Dec 12th 2017, https://www.space.com/39068-ispace-90-million-dollars-moon-missions.html

'All of our resources will then turn to the BFR, and we believe that we can do this with the revenue we see from launching satellites and from servicing the space station', he said at the time.

After that, SpaceX is widely expected to engage its lunar objectives, perhaps becoming neighbour with ispace's settlement. Back in 2017, Musk was adamant that humans need to be on Mars. President Trump was no doubt pleased.

Having always felt that the human race should have a lunar base, he feels that this achievement should be a steppingstone, with the next logical step being the establishment of a Martian settlement—thus making humanity a multi-planet species.

SpaceX's bold plans for 2022 are for a top stage rocket, big enough for 40 cabins, each of which could hold a maximum of six people, along with a solar storm shelter and entertainment area. Musk said that, about two years after the initial mission to Mars, four more BFRs would blast off for the far-away planet, two of which are set to be crewed. Musk's plan is to have the crew mine water and extract carbon dioxide from the atmosphere to make fuel for return missions.

Finally, once SpaceX has sent a BFR to Mars, Musk claims that the rockets might be used to travel between cities on Earth, shuttling passengers from New York City to Shanghai in 39 minutes, for example. Goodbye jet lag!

As we can deduce, lunar exploration continues to gain renewed attention. NASA is currently working on a Deep Space Gateway project with the Roscosmos, which could involve a site near the Moon that would serve as a 'pit-stop' for astronauts on long-term missions to Mars. NASA has stated that the site would have a "small habitat to extend crew time." In a statement sent to *Business Insider*, NASA confirmed that Bigelow is one of six companies the agency has selected to develop full-size prototypes for the habitat.

The US has pledged to send humans to Mars by 2033. Announcements surrounding Bigelow's B330 in 2016, along with the ULA, state that this habitat could house researchers on their way to the temping Red Planet itself.

In recent years, like the aforementioned companies and government agencies, billionaire entrepreneur and self-confessed philanthropist Sir Richard Branson (not content with trans-Atlantic aquatic crossings or hot-air balloon flights around the Earth, skirting the troposphere) is geared up and in motion for outer space.

As already discussed, his Virgin Galactic enterprise has conducted test flights, both successfully and unsuccessfully, but now Galactic looks set to breach the atmosphere by 2018 using its SpaceShipTwo vehicle christened VSS Unity.

Like fellow billionaires Elon Musk and Jeff Bezos, Branson has long been a fan of spaceflight. He was inspired by the Ansari X Prize competition that was the catalyst for the very first privately funded manned trip to space, flown in the reusable spacecraft called SpaceShipOne.

Branson founded Virgin Galactic in 2004, with the goal of selling flights on a space plane that travels to the border of outer space to briefly experience weightlessness and enjoy the view before returning home.

Over the course of a decade, Branson's space outfit built and tested VSS Enterprise, before the spacecraft exploded on 31 October 2014 during its fourth powered test flight ever, catastrophically killing its co-pilot and injuring the pilot.

Unity was launched after powered flight tests that superseded unpowered tests already conducted in 2017, which assessed the functionality of Unity's landing systems.

Unity won't orbit the Earth but will give passengers a 'taste of space', Branson said back in 2017. He predicts orbital flights followed by hotels in space, much like the ethos projected by Bigelow.

Galactic is close to its end goal and, despite being five years later than Virgin expected, this achievement is widely welcomed by all interested parties. Unity will be carrying the fortunate few who can afford up to US$1.2 million for about ten minutes in space, floating next to Sir Richard and his immediate family.

The world's most renowned British theoretical physicist, cosmologist and author, Stephen Hawking, who has been widely quoted on his hopes for mankind and space, was lined up for Galactic's first flight, sadly his death in March 2018 means he will not get to go on this trip. His death is a massive loss to humankind and the scientific community.

In an interview with the UK's *Independent* newspaper back in 2015, Hawking, who was a strong advocate of space travel believed human survival to be based on our ability to conquer this vast expanse. He suggested that "Human beings have no future if we don't go into space … I believe in the possibility of commercial space travel … for exploration and for the preservation of humanity".[15]

Space travel is exploding to the forefront of the agendas of privateers and companies, both national and international, not to mention government agencies from China, India, Japan, the UK, America and Russia.

---

[15] *Independent*, "Professor Stephen Hawking: Humanity will not survive another 1,000 years if we don't escape our planet", Nov 15th 2016, https://www.independent.co.uk/news/people/professor-stephen-hawking-humanity-wont-survive-1000-years-on-earth-a7417366.html

And the lure of our spiral galaxy has attracted a new generation of cosmic explorers, ready to put time, money and life on the line to venture out into our solar system and beyond. We are entering a new space age, one that could help humankind change the world for good.

Hawking believed that life on Earth is at an ever-increasing risk of being wiped out by a disaster such as a sudden nuclear war, a genetically engineered virus or other dangers. Hawking's claimed that the human race has no future if it doesn't go to space.

Space tourism, the colonization of moons, the colonization of Mars, deeper voyages into the solar system and beyond—these are no longer a fiction but an achievable reality.

Deep Space Industries and Asteroid Mining

Asteroid mining is an emerging industry that blends starry-eyed futurism with profit-driven capitalism. Thousands of near-Earth objects are chock full of rare metals including platinum, iridium and palladium, and are there for the taking if regulatory structures, legislation and fiscally viable technologies are present to harvest them. Anyone able to tap these outer space rocks could wind up controlling one of the most lucrative markets on Earth.

It is worth noting that to stand any chance of establishing long-term colonies as a precursor to permanent space settlements, we're going to need to mine asteroids for raw materials.

Alongside announcements, mostly in the last two decades, which catalogued a raft of developments and achievements from the private sector, pertaining to space tourism and ISS shuttle vehicles, came an announcement in December 2017 from metals.com. It stated that the company's private venture capital arm would fund the first asteroid mining operation by a non-government entity.[16]

The venture capital arm aims to invest in the private sector, with an end to enabling scientific teams to deploy asteroid mining probes to near-Earth orbit by 2026. Metals.com is a leading name in precious metals and now appears to be spearheading metal mining probes to near-Earth orbit asteroids. They are seeking to fund scientific teams to target M-Type (metallic) asteroids for their

---

[16] PR Newswire, "Metals.com announces world's first asteroid mining metals fund", Dec 12th 2017, https://www.prnewswire.com/news-releases/metalscom-announces-worlds-first-asteroid-mining-metals-fund-300569855.html

metals like iron, nickel, platinum and cobalt, which can be used to build structures in space with 3D printing.

Mining asteroids might sound like the premise of a science fiction movie, but thanks to private space billionaires like Elon Musk, Jeff Bezos and Sir Richard Branson, the cost of space travel is shrinking drastically. Space is becoming smaller, closer and cheaper according to both participants and industry commentators.

NASA scientists believe that Psyche, one of the largest objects in the asteroid belt, may contain enough nickel, iron and precious metals to fill the entire state of Massachusetts completely. Its value is said to be worth over US$10 quadrillion dollars and could supply the world production requirement for several million years.

To put this figure into perspective, US$10 quadrillion roughly translates into all of the money on the planet (from every country) that is currently in circulation, put together and multiplied by 111. A study at the Keck Institute for Space Studies at Caltech estimates that one full-cycle asteroid capture and return mission, moving an asteroid weighing 1.1 million pounds, would cost approximately US$2.6 billion.[17]

Doctor Lindy Elkins-Tanton, the mission's lead scientist and the director of Arizona State University's School of Earth and Space Exploration, confirmed the validity of the plans—going on record as saying it was a "very compelling target", because it would show scientists "a metal world for the very first time."[18]

Formed in January 2013, Deep Space Industries (DSI) is an asteroid mining company with aspirations to change the economics of the space industry. A company helping to manufacture dreams into reality.

Working in conjunction with existing participants in the space market, DSI aims to provide the technical resources, capabilities and cross-system integration required to prospect, recover, refine, produce and market in-space resources.

Basically the company presents itself as your 'go to guy', a one stop shop to aid in the harvesting of a multitude of mineral wealth tantalizingly close to our technological capabilities. These near-earth asteroids (NEAs) are expected to provide unlimited energy and supplies for a burgeoning space economy and hungry home marketplace.

The mining of resources contained in asteroids, for use as a propellant, for building materials or as a vital component in life support systems, has the

---

[17] Bank of America Merrill Lynch, "To infinity and beyond – global space primer", Oct 30th 2017, https://go.guidants.com/q/db/a2//1e1ffc185c1d44bd.pdf

[18] Medium Publishing, "Psyche Mission: Journey to a Metal World", Aug 3rd 2017, https://medium.com/the-lunarians/psyche-mission-journey-to-a-metal-world-b998432f4b6d

potential to revolutionize exploration of our solar system for humankind. But to make this dream a reality, we need to significantly increase our knowledge of the very diverse population of accessible NEAs.

Continuing on from early space initiative, which saw a primate in space and Russia and the US 'lock horns' in putting humans on the Moon, leading world asteroid scientists and asteroid mining entrepreneurs met in Riga, Luxembourg, in 2016, to form a definitive global think tank to further address all space matters.

The attendees mulled over key questions surrounding the mining of space and began to bridge the gaps, making advancements to current scientific knowledge that are paving the way for our future cosmic expansion.

Subsequently, Luxembourg was the stage for the introduction of ground-breaking legislation for space mining, as the country became the first European Union (EU) country to offer legal certainty that asteroid mining companies get to keep what they find in space.

Luxembourg seems an unlikely place to emerge at the forefront of future space activities and definitive mining laws, which until the turn of the century appeared firmly anchored in the USA and FSU. But when you think about it, it's not too surprising that a country like Luxemburg, a small but wealthy country with limited terrestrial resources, decided to take a gamble on space mining.

'It's a great law', Amara Graps, a planetary scientist, asteroid mining advocate and independent consultant for the Luxembourg Ministry of Economy based in Riga, Latvia, told reporters when the law was created in 2017. 'Space resources are capable of being appropriated.'[19]

The existing international space law standard, the Outer Space Treaty of 1967, as mentioned briefly earlier in this chapter and detailed later in the book, doesn't make it clear whether private companies active in space actually own the resources—that is, the minerals, water and other substances—they might discover. Indicating that they are the property of the sovereign state any company was based in and any mission was launched from.

Luxembourg's government announced plans to come up with its own legal framework for companies based in the county in 2016, releasing a draft law in the form of a White Paper a year later. Ministers claimed that the difference between existing space law, which originated in the US, and that penned in Luxembourg was that under US law a majority of a company's stakeholders must be resident in the US, whilst Luxembourg's law places no restrictions on stakeholder locations.

---

[19] Register Online publication, "Luxembourg passes first EU space mining law. One can possess the spice", July 14th 2017, https://www.theregister.co.uk/2017/07/14/luxembourg_passes_space_mining_law/

Asteroid mining is widely regarded as an incredible intersection of science, engineering, entrepreneurship and imagination by its participants, but it's a scientific field that still needs much significant development.

To that end, the 2016 conference in Luxembourg City detailed discussions pertaining to the specific properties of asteroids, kick-starting the process of developing the requisite engineering needed by space missions that target and utilize asteroids.

The resultant White Paper answered some of the questions surrounding the need for asteroid surveys in preparing for mining missions. Understanding the asteroid's surface and interior, implications for astrobiology and planetary protection, plus other issues relating to the policy and strategy to draw a definitive roadmap for in-space resource utilization.

A number of knowledge gaps were identified. Asteroid miners need a map of known NEAs with an orbit similar to the Earth so that they can fine-tune their selection of potential targets. Many objects are, as yet, undiscovered, or very little is known about them. Subsequently the need to develop and author a dedicated NEA discovery and follow-up programme emerged.

Space mining participants must be equipped with a database that catalogues mineral-rich targets and understands the composition of these celestial bodies so that more accurate simulant asteroid soils, or 'regoliths', can be created.

A Regolith is a layer of loose, heterogeneous superficial deposits covering solid rock. It includes dust, soil, broken rock, and other related materials and is present on Earth, the Moon, Mars, some asteroids, and other terrestrial planets and moons.

It's important to understand which asteroids hold which resources and also to aid in the preparation for the practical side of mining missions, such as landing and extraction of material.

According to Dr Amara Graps of the University of Latvia and the Planetary Science Institute, Tucson, Arizona: "Aside from samples returned from a handful of missions, the only way we can study the composition of asteroids is by analysing light reflected from their surfaces, or by examining fragments that have landed on Earth in the form of meteorites". She claims that "Both these techniques have limitations … spectral observations come from the 'top veneer' of the asteroid, which has been space weathered and subjected to other kinds of processing".[20]

Graps suggest that "Meteorites are crucial, but they also lack part of the story … fragile constituents of primitive material contained within asteroids

---

[20] Science Daily, "What do we need to know to mine an asteroid?", Sept 19th 2017, https://www.science-daily.com/releases/2017/09/170919092612.htm

may be lost during atmospheric entry". "At the moment, our mapping of types of meteorites back to the different classes of parent asteroid is not that robust", she adds.

Three quarters of known asteroids are classed as Carbonaceous or C-type, dark, carbon-rich objects. However, most NEAs are from the Siliceous S-type class of asteroids, which are reddish-coloured stony bodies that dominate the inner asteroid belt. For asteroid miners looking for water to use in rocket fuel or life support systems, being able to identify the class of asteroid is vital.

Carbonaceous chondrite meteorites have been found to contain clay minerals that appear to have been altered by water on their parent body. Whilst these meteorites are thought to be derived from sub-classes of C-type asteroids, there is not an exact match with any single spectral class.

A short-cut to understanding an NEA's composition could be to identify where in the solar system they formed and look at the characteristics of their 'orbital family'. Thus, another knowledge gap surfaces between the dynamical predictions of where an NEA originates and its actual physical characterizations.

"We will produce water, propellant, and building materials to serve growing space markets. From extending the profitability of commercial satellites to providing life support and power to new private-sector orbiting research stations", states DSI's website. "Deep Space Industries is industrializing the frontier."[21]

DSI could emerge as a key driver for the mining and exploration of space in coming years. It's in the business of identifying close-to-Earth space rocks that offer boundless vitality and supplies to a developing space economy, like that featured in metals.com's announcement regarding 'Psyche' Deep Space Industries is industrializing our dark wilderness, mentioned earlier in this chapter.

The American organization boasts a worldwide operation that is developing propulsion systems required for space rock mining and is presently offering satellites that utilize innovative lifting systems. The company plans to make in-space materials that are extracted from asteroids, which are projected to be economically viable by mid-2020.

Spacecraft such as NASA's OSIRIS-Rex, Dawn, the Japanese Aerospace Exploration Agency (JAXA)'s, Hayabusa and ESA's Rosetta have already visited resource-rich asteroids and comets. These missions have proved the concept and many of the technical capabilities required for asteroid mining.

---

[21] Deep Space Industries, general reference, website last updated Apr 18th 2018, http://deepspaceindustries.com/

However, these programmes were executed under large government cost structures and long timetables.

Dawn's mission is ground breaking. Prior to establishing its orbit around Ceres, it had circled the giant 'protoplanet' Vesta in 2011–2012, being successfully piloted from the Jet Propulsion Laboratory's (JPL) Institute of Technology base in California, US, and is mapping the rock.[22]

A protoplanet is defined as a large body of matter orbiting around a sun or a star that is thought to be developing into a planet.

Historically the probe became the first ever to visit a dwarf planet and the first to orbit two different bodies beyond the Earth-moon system. Now its mission, which has already been extended twice, is to continue operations around Ceres to measure and improve atomic composition measurements; and quantify cosmic rays at low altitude, which will aid the search for mineral wealth.

Largely, if not totally unnoticed by the terrestrial mining sector, NASA's other active probe, OSIRIS-Rex, is currently cruising through space enroute to a rendezvous with an NEA named Bennu (previously designated 1999 RQ36). Launched in September 2016, OSIRIS-REx (Origins Spectral Interpretation Resource Identification Security—Regolith Explorer) will rendezvous with Bennu in August 2018, subjecting it to a detailed survey involving mapping the chemistry and mineralogy of the asteroid, including the identification of sample collection sites.

This will take more than a year. Then the spacecraft will approach very close to Bennu, extend an articulated arm, and take a sample of the asteroid's loose surface material (regolith), including dust that covers solid rock. OSRIR-Rex will be able to do this three times (with the sampler arm touching the surface for about five seconds each time) and, hopefully, obtain samples totalling 60–2,000 grams.

The spacecraft is timetabled to break away from Bennu early in 2021, reaching Earth in 2023, where it will release its sample return capsule that will land in a test and training range in the US state of Utah. The length of the mission has been predicted by using calculations based on the Earth's gravitational field which was used to help propel it around its target.

OSRIS-Rex isn't the first asteroid sample return mission; that honour belongs to JAXA's, Hayabusa probe. However, the material retrieved by Hayabusa, returned to Earth in 2010 with particle samples that weighed only micrograms.

---

[22] JPL NASA, "Dawn's Split from Asteroid Vesta – Mission Insider Explains", Sept 5th 2012, https://www.jpl.nasa.gov/blog/2012/9/dawns-split-from-asteroid-vesta-mission-insider-explains

Spearheaded by the Hayabusa space vehicle (which means 'swooping bird' in Japanese), the agency, galvanized by the initial probe's relative success, is following up with Hayabusa2, which is designed to address shortcomings discovered during the initial stage of the programme.

In July 2009, at the twenty-seventh International Symposium on Space Technology and Science (ISTS) conference in Japan, Makoto Yoshikawa of JAXA, presented a proposal entitled the 'Hayabusa Follow-on Asteroid Sample Return Missions' ahead of the initial probe's return to Earth.

In August 2010, JAXA obtained approval from the Japanese government to begin development of Hayabusa2. The estimated cost of the project is 16.4 billion yen. The vehicle will feature ion engines, upgraded guidance and navigation technology, antennas and attitude control systems, speeding it towards the Ruyugu asteroid originally designated, less impressively, 162973.

Launched in 2014, the probe is expected back on Earth around 2020, with samples of the celestial body on board. Hayabus2 will have sampled the asteroid using explosive charges and other instruments developed by the German Aerospace Centre, who is developing MASCOT, or Mobile Asteroid Surface Scout, for the mission in cooperation with the French space agency, CNES (Centre national d'études spatiales—in English, National Centre for Space Studies).

Commentators like Wendy Zucherman, writing in the US publication *The New Scientist* in 2010, commented that Hayabusa will "search for the origins of life in space". No doubt fingers will likely be crossed that Hayabusa also brings back traces of mineral wealth too.

In Europe, the region's space agency, ESA, launched Rosetta in March 2004, propelled from Earth's atmosphere atop of the ESA's Arianne 5 rocket. Along with Philae, its lander module, Rosetta performed a detailed study of comet 67P/Churyumov–Gerasimenko (67P). During its journey to the comet, the spacecraft performed a fly-by of the Red Planet Mars, plus asteroids Lutetia and Šteins.[23]

It was launched as the third cornerstone mission of the ESA's 'Horizon programme'. In August 2015 the spacecraft reached the comet and performed a series of manoeuvres to eventually orbit the comet and successfully land its Philae lander module, which performed the first successful landing on any comet.

Battery power ran out two days later and after communications were briefly re-established mid-June/July 2015, due to diminishing solar power, Rosetta's

[23] Wikipedia, "67P/Churyumov–Gerasimenko", last updated Apr 4th 2018, https://en.wikipedia.org/wiki/67P/Churyumov%E2%80%93Gerasimenko

communications and lander module were switched off and latterly she hard-landed on the comet September 2016.

From DSI's perspective, the advancement of the space probes and the Nano-satellite industry showcased by NASA, JAXA and the ESA, is enabling it to develop smaller, cheaper components that makes commercial asteroid mining economically feasible for the first time in history.

It also maintains that the aforementioned projects, whilst proving that many of the technical capabilities required for asteroid mining were programmes, executed under large government cost structures featuring long timetables.

DSI's innovations are reportedly changing the way these types of missions are performed. It says it is building on existing space-related technologies' infrastructures by developing specific technologies that will drastically increase the functionality of off-the-shelf satellite structures. DSI claims its spacecraft components are to transform existing micro-satellite platforms into lean, agile and robust robots, ready for advanced space missions.

So to Prospector-X, a mission that is the product of a partnership with DSI and the Luxembourg Government, which are working together to develop the technology needed to mine asteroids and build a substantial supply chain of valuable resources in space amid a lenient space law. The collaborators' current plan is to mine water when near-Earth missions are successfully completed.

When this point is reached the partnership will have taken a significant step closer to liberating water supplies in space. Luxembourg is already home to several vibrant satellite operators, and its national space programme has researched futuristic, deep space propulsion technologies like solar sails.

Of course, Luxembourg isn't the only country interested in opening up the outer space commodities market. Superceeded by Trump, the forty-fourth president of the US, Barack Obama, signed the US Commercial Space Launch Competitiveness Act, making asteroid mining fully legal in the US.

So, although no company can claim ownership over a near-Earth object under international law, there is now a legal framework in place allowing American companies to keep any minerals they manage to extract in space. To some extent this is repolarizing 'matters space' to the country and those American-based companies working towards reconnaissance, mining and even the tourist market. Bigelow, SpaceX and Virgin Galactic all fall within this category.

The experimental Prospector-X mission is a low-Earth orbit technological mission designed to test the company's existing innovative deep space technology. The key-enabling technologies on test will be instrumental to the success of the company's first deep space resource exploration missions in the near future.

The spacecraft will be built at DSI's European headquarters, in Luxembourg, in conjunction with the company's international and US partners, including the Interdisciplinary Centre for Security, Reliability and Trust (SnT) at the University of Luxembourg.

"Water is an incredible wellspring of fuel (particularly as fluid hydrogen and fluid oxygen, or when consolidated with carbon dioxide to frame methalox)", according to Daniel Faber, CEO of the Silicon Valley-and Luxembourg-based organization. "Be that as it may", he continues, "water is likewise imperative for human residence, for drinking-water and oxygen to inhale, and to use as radiation protecting or for developing yields."

DSI has speculated that a refuelling 'station' in Earth circle would decrease the measure of fuel requirement for human treks to far-off planets like Mars, complementing plans already tabled by NASA, SpaceX and Bigelow. What's more it would likewise decrease the estimated US$10,000 per pound cost to shoot fuel cells into Earth orbit.

Making a step forward, Faber says the company's Prospector-1 vehicle will probably dispatch in or around 2020. Billed as a world first in commercial interplanetary mining, the craft will fly and rendezvous with a near-Earth asteroid to determine its value as a source of space resources.

Faber also thinks the success of the X and 1 missions could be a platform to provide an alternative shuttle option to those already on offer. The destination asteroid will be chosen from a group of top candidates selected by the world-renowned team of asteroid experts at DSI.

Once the spacecraft arrives at the asteroid it will map the surface and sub-surface, taking visual and infrared imagery and mapping overall water content. With the initial science campaign complete, Prospector-1 will use its water thrusters to gently touch down on the asteroid, measuring the target's geophysical characteristics.

Prospector-1 is a small spacecraft that strikes the ideal balance between cost and performance. In addition to radiation-tolerant payloads and avionics, all DSI spacecraft notably use the Comet line of water propulsion systems, which are being designed to expel superheated water vapour to generate thrust. Water will be the first asteroid mining product, so using water as a propellant will provide future DSI spacecraft with the ability to refuel in space.

The company expects journey time to prospective objectives to be about 12 years. The objectives are C-sort space rocks, the most widely recognized in the expanse, which have an effortlessly open and high wealth of water, says DSI. Regardless of whether it's water as ice as suspected on the Moon, or water caught in mud minerals or hydrated salts, the organization says it can be mined by basically collecting the 'space shake' and exposing it to the Sun for warmth.

DSI says that by the late 2020s space markets for water, metal and minerals be worth up to over US$1.5 billion. But space rock mining is a definitive, high-hazard, high-compensate business. Whilst there are without doubt billions, even some contended trillions, of US dollars of important minerals and metals in NEA space rocks, a large group of skeptics resonate about the feasibility of collecting them.

What amount of innovation is required to distinguish space rocks and concentrate the materials? How troublesome will it be to return them to Earth or other coveted goals? Furthermore, what will the forthright expenses be?

Notwithstanding these doubts, other organizations in addition to DSI—for example, another American company with a long-term goal of mining asteroids, Planetary Resources—believe this type of stellar activity is economically and practically viable.

Planetary Resources, formerly known as Arkyd Astronautics, was formed on 1 January 2009, being reorganized and renamed in 2012. Its stated goal is to "expand Earth's natural resource base" by developing and deploying the technologies for asteroid mining.

The company boldly, yet encouragingly, shouts of 16,000 NEAs rich in resources! Two trillion tones of water resources for life support and fuel being available in space! A perceived 95 percent reduction in space exploration costs utilizing asteroid mining techniques! Sounds good.

Like DSI, Planetary Resources is embarking on a ground-breaking commercial deep-space exploration programme. The purpose is to identify and unlock the critical water resources necessary for human expansion into space.

Sourcing water is the first step to creating such a civilization. Again, like DSI, Planetary Resources believes that space-harvested water must be utilized for life support functions and can also be refined into rocket propellant. The initial mission will identify the asteroids that contain the best source of water, and will simultaneously provide the vital information needed to build a commercial mine that will harvest water for use in space.

The programme is an extensive data-gathering series of missions in deep space that will visit multiple NEAs. The goal is to answer the question: where will we establish the first mine in space?

In 2020, Planetary Resources plans to deploy multiple spacecraft via a single rocket launch. The rocket will carry the exploration spacecraft just beyond the influence of Earth's gravity where they will continue their journey using low-thrust ion propulsion systems. Each spacecraft will visit a pre-determined target asteroid to collect data and test material samples.

Current plans indicate that data collection will include global hydration mapping and subsurface extraction demonstrations to determine the quantity of water and the value of the resources available. The information gathered could put Planetary Resources at the pinnacle of contemporary space mining, becoming the first successfully to design, construct and deploy the first commercial mine in space.

With the same mindset, DSI says it will build a water-powered spacecraft to search for resources. According to Rick Tumlinson, administrator of the board and fellow benefactor of DSI: "Expanding on our Prospector-X mission, Prospector-1 will be the subsequent stage on our approach to collecting space rock assets".

"We can state with certainty that we have the correct innovation, the correct group, and the correct arrangement to execute this notable mission", says Tumlinson.[24]

The organization says a small shuttle will utilize a water-based drive that removes superheated water vapour to produce thrust. Such a system was picked because the primary item mining organizations will try to remove from space rocks is water. They would like to re-pitch this water to NASA or other entities geared towards deep space investigation, as it can be separated into fluid hydrogen and oxygen, both of which are effective rocket fuels.

Utilizing water-based drive systems will likewise allow the organization's prospecting shuttle to refuel whilst working. Such a mindset is a piece of the new space vision to "live off the land" as people and machines expand into space.

At the time of writing, it's unclear as to whether DSI will prevail with the Prospector programme, or even figure out how to profit from space. In any case, it believes the pursuit for "previously unheard of wealth" will result in reduction of costs associated with accessing space, making its exploration and colonization a reality.

With its goal of handling and producing metals from space rocks, DSI developed a 3D printer from the Microgravity Foundry. The initial MGF-3 has been designed to make high-thickness, high-quality metal parts even in zero gravity. Its successor, the MGF-4, is a significantly bigger module for deployment in space as an outside module rack connection.

Both the MGF-3 and 4, together with mechanical arms, are intended for space mining, thus converting asteroids into valuable metals. The company estimates that one tonne of asteroid material would be worth US$1 million.

---

[24] DSI website http://deepspaceindustries.com/first-commercial-interplanetary-mission/

These printers can take their own parts, grind them up, and recycle them into new parts, Stephen Covey, a cofounder of DSI and inventor of the process claims. The devices can print heavy, massive tools in space, which can then be used in the manufacturing of space habitats, platforms and satellites.

"Using resources harvested in space is the only way to afford permanent space development", said former CEO and DSI cofounder, David Gump. "More than 900 new asteroids that pass near Earth are discovered every year … they can be like the Iron Range of Minnesota was for the Detroit car industry last century. …"[25]

A key resource located near where it was needed. In this case, metals and fuel from asteroids can expand the in-space industries of this century."[26]

Innovative Solutions in Space (ISISpace), a recognized leader in the worldwide 'nanosat' market, is also in collaboration with DSI, having announced a partnership that will deliver significant benefits to customers, at highly competitive prices. DSI will utilize ISISpace's flight proven hardware and avionics, in addition to their own proprietary technologies, to provide high-quality, low-cost, agile nanosat platforms in the US market.

"Deep Space Industries is extremely excited to be able to offer ISISpace's professional quality Cubesat-compatible flight systems to our American customers", said Faber. "This new partnership will enable U.S. customers to benefit from the finest quality European parts backed by years of success. …

Coupled with DSI's innovative new technologies and our integration and engineering expertise, this partnership will allow us to provide the highest quality nanosat platforms to our customers at competitive prices."

Jeroen Rotteveel, CEO of ISISpace, confirmed this, saying that both companies were "looking forward to the partnership" as they unite, pooling their teams, skills and capabilities to better serve customers.[27]

The companies will also partner on integration and manufacturing, allowing customers from both regions to benefit from additional manufacturing capacity and faster delivery. Additionally, ISISpace will now be the primary European distributor of DSI patented technologies in propulsion, Attitude Determination and Control Systems (ADCS) and Guidance Navigation and Control (GNC), providing a more diverse product offering in their existing market.

DSI's customizable agile nanosat platform provides significant benefits to customers with the perfect combination of cutting-edge capabilities and proven, reliable hardware. Competitive pricing allows customers access to the

---

[25] Space.com, mike wall, 22nd January 2013, https://www.space.com/19368-asteroid-mining-deep-spaceindustries.html

[26] http://www.businessinsider.com/deep-space-industry-asteroid-mining-plan-2013-2/?IR=T

[27] http://deepspaceindustries.com/dsi-isis-partnership/

best quality equipment, whilst end-to-end engineering and design services provide full customization to ensure that the customers' business and science goals are met or exceeded.

By 2020, the company hopes to get into commercial operation and begin producing materials to be used first in space. For example, as already mentioned, water harvested from asteroids can be broken down to make rocket fuel, which can power communication satellites. Low-cost asteroid-derived fuel will extend the working lifetime of these technologies. For each satellite, one extra month is apparently worth US$5–8 million.

So the feasibility of mining deep-space asteroids grows in stature amid the operations of NASA, JAXA, the ESA and DSI. Participants are mulling over the prime issues surrounding the launch of these mining vehicles out of Earth's atmosphere.

"The material sciences are attainable … financial aspects are an alternate story", according to Andrew Cheng, an advocate of space mining at the Applied Physics Laboratory of Johns Hopkins University in the US. Cheng said he's "cheerful" that endeavours such as those by the likes of DSI can prevail, made viable by completion and innovation spawned by an increase in new ventures in space and the diversification of existing companies into the sector.[28]

"In the event that somebody recognizes an approach to accomplish something out there that profits, and there's a great deal of movement and a greater market, at that point the cost will descend", said Cheng. "It's somewhat of a chicken and egg issue."

Be that as it may, DSI's Tumlinson, a long-term supporter of private space endeavours, states that the organization considers itself to be the twenty-first-century rendition of the "pilgrims and retailers" who took after the 'Lewis and Clark' campaign into the American West.[29]

"One organization might be a fluke. Two organizations showing up … that is the start of an industry", Tumlinson observed. "Space is huge … there's space for everyone."

Of the 9,500 or so NEAs currently known, approximately 850 are greater than 1 kilometre, and around 1,700 are easier to get to than the Moon. They have an extremely assorted scope of arrangements.

"Utilizing assets reaped in space is the best way to bear the cost of changeless space improvement", said Gump. "More than 900 new asteroids that pass near Earth are discovered every year."

---

[28] John Hopkins university, Geoff brown, 3rd July 2017, https://hub.jhu.edu/2017/07/03/nasa-asteroiddeflection-mission/

[29] National Park Service, USA, "Lewis and Clark Timeline 1806 – National Park Service", last updated Mar 30th 2018, https://www.nps.gov/jeff/learn/historyculture/lewis-and-clark-timeline-1806.htm

DSI gauges that for all intents and purposes all recuperated mass from space rocks will be of use. A huge market for DSI will be creating fuel for satellites that will broaden their working lifetimes, as already discussed.

"Digging space rocks for uncommon metals alone isn't prudent, however It makes sense on the off chance that you are preparing them for volatiles and mass metals for in-space utilisation", said Mark Sonter, an individual from the DSI Board of Directors.

"Transforming space rocks into force and building materials harms no ecospheres", said Tumlinson. "We might be guests in space until the point that we figure out how to live off the land there …

This is the Deep Space mission … to discover, gather and process the assets of space to help spare our progress and bolster the development of mankind past the Earth.'

Amid increasing, palpable interest in space, Deep Space Technologies (DST),[30] a space business ecosystem, space mineral trading company and wealth development vehicle for space mining (linked to a unique Crypto Coin), confirms humankind's future will see the advent of deep-space asteroid mining. It predicts many significant players will compete and unite to provide cost effective propulsion systems, self-sustaining mining operations and habitable space environments.

Future pioneering endeavours could see a raft of supplies harvested from mineral wealth contained off-planet, in the Milky Way and beyond, as the planned colonization of distant planets could provide convenient 'staging points' to reach out even further.

Other Useful Sources of Information

http://foreignaffairsreview.co.uk/2016/10/the-privatisation-of-space-tourism/

https://www.theguardian.com/science/2015/nov/20/nasa-signs-contracts-spacex-manned-commercial-spaceflight

http://www.space.com/35844-elon-musk-spacex-announcement-today.html

http://www.space.com/8541-6-private-companies-launch-humans-space.html

http://www.space.com/34357-private-deep-space-habitat-concepts-for-nasa.html

http://www.alphr.com/space/1003058/who-s-who-in-private-space-travel

---

[30] See http://www.deepspacetech.io

4

Humans Versus Machine: Who Will Mine Space?

Tom James and Simon Roper

Humans versus machine? A question humankind has posed to itself since Charles Babbage invented the mechanical computer, The Babbage Engine. Since World Chess Champion Gary Kasporov played a computer named Deep Blue in 1997 and famously lost.[1]

Since their inception, the paradox that something humankind has created for his own convenience would make him obsolete has existed. Which is faster? Which is more accurate? Stronger? More durable? And now, which should mine space?

Currently, we have synthetic technologies, ramping achievements in the field of artificial intelligence (AI), all of which are creating an exponential curve in the field's further development. In basic forms, AI has already helped us out, thanks to Google's 'Home' and Amazon's 'Alexa', happily assisting millions in their homes.

So just who, what or whom, should harvest the dark, cold, atmosphere-less expanse that is space? A place humans cannot travel to, or through, without the help of this technological achievement. Human or machine or a synergy of both?

---

[1] *Time Magazine*, "Did Deep Blue Beat Kasparov Because of a System Glitch?", 17 February 2015, http://time.com/3705316/deep-blue-kasparov/

T. James (✉)
NR Capital & Deep Space Technologies, Singapore, Singapore

S. Roper
Deep Space Technologies, London, UK

© The Author(s) 2018
T. James (ed.), *Deep Space Commodities*,
https://doi.org/10.1007/978-3-319-90303-3_4

History has proved that machines tend to do a better job all round, being devoid of emotion and any of the essential things humans need to function, such as oxygen, warmth, light, sleep, sustenance; they don't need oxygen, are mostly impenetrable to cold, don't need sleep and with a sustainable energy supply and some occasional maintenance, will last indefinitely.

Battery included and a software update when it's released. Job done? Well, the jury still remains out. Whilst appearing the obvious choice for space's exploration, colonization and production of mineable resources, can they really be programmed to make that all-important judgement call? Currently, as the definition of 'robot' stands, they are slaves to humanity and under our control.

And if not to be relied upon for cognitive thinking, can we develop a communications system fast enough to instruct from Earth? Is there a future where we have robots under local control of AI computer systems, or will humans also want to be, and need to be, around? Currently, our communications to probes and satellites are limited to radio waves. Future developments could see them impressively conducted at the speed of light using lasers. But will that be fast enough, the further they go?

In 1977, possibly one of the most audacious missions, the Voyager and its sibling Voyager 2 programmes proved that we would be in contact with two probes who slung-shot off in two different paths to "boldly go where no man has gone before" (quote: Gene Rodenberry's *Star Trek* franchise), and is not likely to go for some time. Maybe developments from NASA's Deep Space Network (DSN) team will answer this.[2]

DSN is a worldwide network of spacecraft communications facilities located in California in the US, Madrid in Spain and Canberra, Australia which support NASA's interplanetary spacecraft mission. It also performs radio and radar astronomy observations for the exploration of the system and supports selected Earth-orbiting mining missions. DSN is part of NASA's Jet Propulsion Lab (JPL). Similar networks are run by Europe, Russia, China, India and Japan.

Tracking vehicles in deep space is quite different from tracking missions in low-Earth orbit (LEO). Deep-space missions are visible for long periods of time from a large portion of the Earth's surface, and so require few stations (the DSN has only three main sites). These few stations, however, require huge antennas, ultra-sensitive receivers and powerful transmitters in order to transmit and receive over the vast distances involved.

---

[2] NASA, Jet Propulsion Lab, "Voyager Mission Overview", accessed 19 April 2018, https://voyager.jpl.nasa.gov/mission/

How to get further, faster then?

A spacecraft destined to explore a unique asteroid and also test new communication hardware that uses lasers instead of radio waves is the probe for NASA's 'Psyche Missions'. The Deep Space Optical Communications (DSOC) package on board utilizes photons (the fundamental particle of visible light) to transmit more data in a given amount of time.

The DSOC's goal is to increase spacecraft communications performance and efficiency by 10–100 times over conventional means, all without increasing the mission burden in mass, volume, power and/or spectrum. Using the advantages offered by laser communications is expected to revolutionize future space endeavours, a major objective of NASA's Space Technology Mission Directorate (STMD).

The DSOC project is developing key technologies that are being integrated into a deep-space worthy Flight Laser Transceiver (FLT), high-tech work that will advance this mode of communications to Technology Readiness Level (TRL) 6. Reaching a TRL 6 level equates to having technology that is a fully functional prototype or representational model.

"Things are shaping up reasonably and we have a considerable amount of test activity going on", says Abhijit Biswas, DSOC Project Technologist in Flight Communications Systems at JPL. "Delivery of DSOC for integration within the Psyche mission is expected in 2021 with the spacecraft launch to occur in 2022", he has explained in an article published by NASA.[3]

You can think of the DSOC flight laser transceiver on board Psyche as a telescope which is able to receive and transmit laser light in precisely timed photon bursts.

DSOC architecture is based on transmitting a laser beacon from Earth to assist line-of-sight stabilization to make possible the pointing back of a downlink laser beam. The laser on board the Psyche spacecraft, Biswas says, is based on a master-oscillator power amplifier that uses optical fibres.

The laser beacon to DSOC will be transmitted from JPL's Table Mountain Facility located near the town of Wrightwood, California in the Angeles National Forest. DSOC's beaming of data from space will be received at a large aperture ground telescope at Palomar Mountain Observatory in California.

Biswas anticipates operating DSOC perhaps 60 days after launch, given checkout of the Psyche spacecraft post-lift-off. The test-runs of the laser equipment will occur over distances of 0.1–2.5 astronomical units (AU) on the

---

[3] NASA, Jet Propulsion Lab, "Deep Space Communications via Faraway Photons", 18 October 2018, https://www.jpl.nasa.gov/news/news.php?feature=6967

outward-bound probe. One AU is approximately 150 million kilometres, or the distance between the Earth and Sun.

At present, back on Earth, more conventional mining ventures have progressively utilized 'robotization' to increase and in part supplant people for cost and durability issues. Robots that require human connection are also used on our battlefields, in surgical settings, in heavy industry and in in-atmosphere flights.

As for the roads, while appearing to be a long way from regular day-to-day existence, Google's declaration to introduce marketable, driverless autos to consumers in the near future; and the race to create in-home robots, will make the human-computerization allotment issue omnipresent.

The dominating designing principle is to computerize as much as possible and limit the measure of human collaboration. This trend is based on the fact that developing technologies make robots more capable, removing any human complications. It's true to say that many engineers see the human as an aggravation in systems that can and ought to be eliminated.

There is a multitude of Earth inhabitants, 7.6 billion and swelling, including a booming world-wide white collar class, according to international population statistics.[4] We are going to require an increasing number of off-Earth assets if the development of humanity is to proceed. They're not all going to be available on the planet.

Innovation will help alleviate these inescapable asset crunches. However, unless we find new wellsprings of materials to use, humanity's advancement is bound to be choked if not prevented.

A standout among the most goal-oriented of these corporate elements brings us back to Planetary Resources. This Redmond, Washington-based organization expects to prospect and loot space rocks for crude materials to power future space attempts. So, amidst successful missions into space and announcements from governments and privateers to conquer it, the once mooted idea of a stellar-fuelled existence is creeping from sci-fi to science reality.

Planetary Resources was helped to establish itself by XPRIZE master Peter Diamandis, and incorporates Larry Page, Eric Schmidt and Galactic's Sir Richard Branson amongst its initial financial specialists. The primary objective of Planetary Resources is to ensure you have the things that you require when you get into space. Amongst plans from other participants like DSI, one of the essential assets Planetary Resources would like to mine from space is

---

[4] Worldometers, "current world population", accessed on 19 April 2018, http://www.worldometers.info/world-population/

water, initial prospecting of which suggests it to be in plentiful supply among the space rocks and comets zooming around us; and within perceivable reach from advancing technologies in development right now.

Water will be a critical in space for key reasons:

1. We obviously need to drink it to live.
2. Water particles can be gathered for oxygen to harvest for sustainable inhalation.
3. Water is comprised of hydrogen and oxygen iotas, which are the substance-building pieces expected to make rocket fuel to power space trips.
4. Water can be utilized as a shield against lethal astronomical radiation that pervades extraterrestrial situations.

Asteroids and other planetary entities are brimming with crude development materials such as iron, nickel and cobalt. That's why we need to get to space. So we need to stay positive.

In the Stanley Kubrick exemplary film *2001: A Space Odyssey*, a character is delineated taking a Pan Am space flight in transit to a goliath space station. That is the sort of delightful space positive thinking that gatherings of people had in 1968 when the film was first released.

Obviously, things didn't generally play out as expected when we reached the first year of the new millennium, 2001. There were no private space ships, space visitors or vast cosmopolitan urban areas in the sky. However, for reasons unknown, Kubrick's forecasts weren't really wrong—just off by a couple of decades. A visionary.

Fast forward from Kubrick's world to 2016 and we see that humankind is close to building the space environment that sci-fi has been predicting and guaranteeing for some time—and may be delivered just in the nick of time.

Robots are vital to our future. Robby the Robot could make anything, from jewels to dresses, all for people living in a different universe. Yet, he lived on the fictional Altair IV in the anecdotal film *Forbidden Planet*. Currently here on Earth, while we have made astounding achievements, launching several probes into our universe, humans to the Moon and a rover to Mars, here on Earth robots fill in as voice assistants, toys or vacuum cleaners in human family units.

Despite the fact that today's robots do not have Robby's refinement, they could be destined for greater things and will no doubt become very capable as human intermediaries for space investigation. Truth be told, robots and space go together, so well that should we question whether to question or closely monitor their involvement in space? They are simply a less expensive, more durable and less needy mechanical substitution for flesh and blood.

Ronald Arkin, chief of the Mobile Robot Laboratory at Georgia Institute of Technology, revealed to Space.com that researchers can simply repackage a robot to make it smaller and more impervious to its environs, yet they can't repackage people by any means.[5]

Robots are great adventurers since you don't need to manage emotionally supportive networks that people would require, plus they are less demanding to deal with and substantially more versatile for antagonistic situations than individuals.

Have Robots, Will Travel

The most recent focus for space robots has been Mars, where the ESA's Mars Express, the first planetary mission attempted by the agency, touched down in December 2003. The mission detailed high-resolution imaging and mineralogical mapping of the surface, radar sounding of the subsurface structure down to the permafrost, precise determination of the atmospheric circulation and composition, and study of the interaction of the atmosphere with the interplanetary medium.

Due to the valuable science return and the highly flexible mission profile, the Mars Express was granted six mission extensions, the latest lasting until the end of 2016. It concluded 14 years and six months after launch date, spending 14 years on and around the planet.

NASA's Mars Exploration Rover (MER) mission, a robotic space mission involving two Mars rovers, Spirit 1 and Opportunity, explored the red planet too. It all began in 2003 with the launch of the two rovers to map and explore the Martian surface and geology.

Both landed on Mars at separate locations in January 2004. Both rovers far outlived their planned missions of 90 Martian solar days. MER Spirit 1 was active until 2010, while MER Opportunity was still active in 2017 and holds the record for the longest distance driven by any off-Earth wheeled vehicle.

The mission's scientific objective was to search for and characterize a wide range of rocks and soils that hold clues to past water activity on Mars. The mission is part of NASA's Mars Exploration Program, which includes three

---

[5] Ronald Arkin, "Regents' Professor, Director of Mobile Robot Laboratory School of Interactive Computing, College of Computing, Georgia Tech", accessed on 19 April 2018, https://www.cc.gatech.edu/aimosaic/faculty/arkin/

previous successful landers: the two Viking programme landers in 1976 and the Mars Pathfinder probe in 1997.

Nozomi—Japanese for 'wish' or 'hope'—'was another planned Mars orbiting probe. It did not reach Mars orbit due to electrical failures. The mission was terminated on 31 December 2003.

NASA sends robots into space where space explorers can't yet go.[6] Their last robot to the Red Planet was the Pathfinder's minimized, sun-powered, remote-controlled Sojourner unit, which arrived on 4 July 1997. The space office's first Mars robots were the two Viking landers, launched in the mid-1970s. They contained a suite of logic instruments including a mechanical arm to gather Martian soil tests.[7]

Smaller, smarter, cheaper.

"Sojourner flew with what the general population would liken to the main PC", said Paul Schenker, executive of JPL's Applied Autonomy Research Center, which importantly and significantly utilized PC processors to deal with problems such as space radiation.[8]

Publically available PCs and cameras were key to allowing the MERs to distinguish and evade hindrances without waiting for instructions from Earth.

Astro-Helpers and Robonauts

Confidence is palpable among the science fraternity that advanced robots may go with planet-hopping space travellers to Mars or elsewhere, collaborators to us humans for base development and a range of different errands. The idea is you could send robots as a forerunner to set up residence and science bases before people arrive. When space explorers arrive, the robots can be utilized as colleagues and helpers.

NASA has officially made some progress with its Robonaut machine for the International Space Station (ISS). Space explorer Nancy Currie effectively gathered a metal truss with the assistance of two Robonauts—able robots that could play a part in future ISS development.

Machines are advancing towards becoming humankind's future symbiont. This was showcased by the deployment of robots to assess and clean up the

---

[6] NASA Science, "Why do we send robots to space?", last updated 26 September 2017, https://space-place.nasa.gov/space-robots/en/

[7] NASA Mars Exploration, Mars Pathfinder, Mission Rover Sojourner, accessed on 19 April 2018, https://mars.nasa.gov/programmissions/missions/past/pathfinder/

[8] Dr Dobbs the world of software development, "A Conversation with Glenn Reeves", by Jack J. Woehr, 1 November 1999, http://www.drdobbs.com/a-conversation-with-glenn-reeves/184411097

nuclear disaster that befell Fukushima, Japan, where 'Scorpion' robots were used to try to assess the damage. Following a major earthquake, a 15-metre tsunami disabled the power supply and cooling of three Fukushima Daiichi reactors, causing the accident on 11 March 2011. All three cores largely melted in the first three days. Having been blocked by debris and their own limitations, aquatic 'Mini Sunfish' robots were utilized, piloted 300 kilometres away at tech-giant Toshiba's Yokohama Research Center. The Mini Sunfish were successful in identifying hazardous materials from the disaster.

Still, this shows to some extent the limitations we still have with our ground-based robots. So, in the interim, we mostly use 'unintelligent' robots to assemble the likes of cars, PC chips and other industry items that are generally repetitive in construction nature; and are relatively simple, featuring pre-determined parameters that rarely change.

But these automatons are advancing. The Roomba vacuum cleaner by iRobot, a global consumer company, will clean your floors for you in the event that you have US$200 to spare, while consumer tech-giant Sony offers the robot canine Aibo, a convenient robotic alternative to canine company. Another industrial Japanese heavyweight Honda has developed Asimo, a robot that has mastered the craft of balance, mobilizing like a biped, and speculations suggests one day it may be tasked as an assistant for disabled people.

All these devices get on with life and learn their environment, even user's facial expressions, to trigger their artificially generated responses. However, we still have many obstacles to overcome in the fields of self-governance and counterfeit consciousness.

And this is happening. World companies are spending billions to develop their robots, working towards to a fully working machine with AI, which governs itself accordingly and makes autonomous decisions. Could we eventually see American author Isaac Asimov's application of his 'Three Laws of Robotics' in his *I, Robot* short story collection, defined so as to protect humans from a renegade intelligent robot uprising.[9]

Moral issues brought up in Asimov's story are quite recently starting to be under consideration by the likes of NASA—an indicator that AI will rival humankind in terms of its consciousness, and be smarter, with an in-exhaustive capacity to learn and retain knowledge. NASA analysts are attempting to ascertain how much insight and autonomy their space robots ought to have. The trouble lies in figuring out how to evaluate precisely what mechanical

---

[9] Auburn University Alabama, "Isaac Asimov's 'Three Laws of Robotics'", last updated 2001, accessed on 19 April 2018, https://www.auburn.edu/~vestmon/robotics.html

processes are needed to do; and build AI systems that would permit correlation of knowledge over various stages.

Meanwhile, whilst the Russians and Americans may have concluded competition past Earth for now, another challenge for longevity of space stays has materialized, as this will be key to long-distance space travel. It's one that pits science and brains against circuits and chips.

To date robots have a great track record of achievements in deep space, in comparison to their somewhat more fragile creator's achievements (even thought they were incredible). As of yet, sci-fi fantasies such as cryogenic suspension, FTL (Faster Than Light) travel, warp drive or 'space-folding', which make life easier for 'biologicals' to travel in deep space, may stay on the cinema screen or pages of well-thumbed paperback books.

Robots have delved in the soil on Mars, flown in the air of Jupiter, cruised by the moons of Neptune, sling-shooting towards successful landings. The Voyager siblings are exploring on the boundaries of the close planetary system.

People, however, have been consigned generally to going round in circles over the surface of the planet. Other than the short Apollo mission triumphs on the Moon, around 250,000 miles away, people have never strayed more distant than 400 miles from the planet, not as much as a day's drive.

People Stay Close to Home for a Few Reasons

People stay close to home for a few reasons. Logistics; limitations of technology and propulsions systems; gravity; the need for supplies. All which culminate toward one simple factor: Cost.

NASA appears to have a difficult job on its hands according to the journal *Scientific American*. That job is convincing US taxpayers that space science is worth billions of US dollars each year. To achieve this goal, the agency conducts an extensive public relations effort that is similar to the marketing campaigns of America's biggest corporations.

NASA has learned a valuable lesson about marketing in the twenty-first century: To promote its programmes, it must provide entertaining visuals and stories with compelling human characters. For this reason, NASA issues a steady stream of press releases and images from its human spaceflight programme.

Every launch of the now-retired Space Shuttle was a media event. NASA presents its astronauts as ready-made heroes, even when their accomplishments in space are no longer ground-breaking. Perhaps the best example of

NASA's public relations prowess was the participation of John Glenn, the first American to orbit Earth, in the 1998 Space Shuttle mission 'STS-95'.

Glenn's return to space at the age of 77 made STS-95 the most avidly followed mission since the Apollo Moon landings. NASA claimed that Glenn went up for science. He served as a guinea pig in various medical experiments, but it was clear that the main benefit of Glenn's Space Shuttle ride was publicity, not scientific discovery, as the press reported.

The same miserable economics hold for the ISS, since during its development history the station underwent five major redesigns and fell 11 years behind schedule. NASA has spent over three times the US$8 billion that the original project was supposed to cost in its entirety. NASA had hoped that space-based manufacturing on the station would offset some of this expense. In theory, the microgravity environment could allow the production of certain pharmaceuticals and semiconductors that would have advantages over similar products made on Earth. But the high price of sending anything to the station has dissuaded most companies from even exploring the idea at this juncture.

No one throws a ticker-tape parade for a telescope. Human spaceflight provides the stories that NASA uses to sell its programmes to the public. And that's the main reason NASA was spending nearly a quarter of its budget to launch the space shuttle about 12 times every year.

Aside from generating less enthusiasm towards the mining and colonization of space, the fact remains that sending a human into space is extremely expensive. A single flight of the space shuttle cost about US$450 million in money-of-the-day. Robots and probes are vastly cheaper, despite being devoid of palpable personalities at present.

NASA is still conducting grade-A science in space, but it is being carried out by uncrewed probes rather than astronauts. In recent years, the 'Pathfinder' rover has scoured the surface of Mars, and the 'Galileo' spacecraft has surveyed Jupiter and its moons. The Hubble Space Telescope and other orbital observatories are bringing back pictures of the early moments of creation. But robots aren't heroes.

Generalizing, the cost of an orbital carry mission, for instance, varies between US$400 million and US$500 million. A satellite can achieve a circle around Earth for US$20 million. Uncrewed landers have touched down on Mars for a meagre US$250 million, although the more recent Mars Rover mission did hit US$2.5 billion. Yet, the evaluated sticker price for a human excursion to the Red Planet runs somewhere in the range of US$50–500 billion.

Also with an immense contribution to the success of humans in space are those issues of protection and safety. Sudden blasts of sunlight-based radiation can kill an unprotected spacewalker. Impacts with even the minutest of objects that litter the space surrounding our planets can puncture a ship. What's more, as the 1986 Challenger and the 2003 Columbia space shuttle accidents agonizingly show, dispatch and landing glitches can have fatal consequences.

And given that there is no gravity or resistance in space, Earth's sentient species has to address the issue of weightlessness, which over protracted months can truly debilitate human bones, muscles and vestibular systems. A roundtrip to Mars utilizing current rocket technology is tabled at present to take between six and eight months one-way. That's longer than astronauts currently stay on the ISS. Until we develop artificial gravity for long space journeys, at the moment if we ventured out to Mars we would potentially be partially blind and too weak to walk by the time we got there. These are all things NASA is researching on board the ISS.

So given the risk, the expense and the misfortunes, why send people into space?

Considering the known perils, justifying the billions of dollars spent on sending a couple of people into space as a beneficial venture to the billions of individuals on the ground takes some doing. Be it for research, science, survival of our species, even to develop a lucrative tourist market, which could lead to colonies, space is ultra-provocative for its mineral wealth.

So as scientists and analysts wrestle with a myriad of issues surrounding prolonged human activity in space, or even just getting them there, amid the developing role of crewed or uncrewed vehicles the present school of thought is as follows.

Asteroid Mining 101

As we are deducing, minerals can be mined from an asteroid or spent comet then used in space for construction materials or taken back to our planet. Most likely gases such as oxygen, water and hydrogen will be the first commodities we search for to support off-planet human colonies. But other rare earth or precious materials here on Earth can also be found off-planet in higher concentrations according to early deep-space surveys.

These deep-space commodities include gold, iridium, silver, osmium, palladium, platinum, rhenium, rhodium, ruthenium and tungsten, and useful back to Earth could be iron, cobalt, magnesium, molybdenum, nickel, aluminium and titanium for construction purposes.

Due to the high launch and transportation costs of spaceflight, inaccurate identification of asteroids suitable for mining, and in-situ ore extraction challenges, terrestrial mining remains the only tangible means of raw mineral acquisition today. However, because of the constantly decreasing cost of launching rockets from Earth (thanks to reusable rocket technologies perfected by SpaceX), it is quickly becoming a commercial reality and something Planetary Resources and Deep Space Resources companies are working hard to bring to a reality.

Some years ago the school of thought on mining and establishing colonies sided with machines first, then humans second, if at all, as it appears to be mining robots on larger planets (much impetuousness is present behind the development of these vehicles), which will be carried by the rockets planned by national institutions like NASA and privateers such as SpaceX.

Supporting Humans in Space

A little while back, plans surrounding the liberation of space decided that the least efficient way to get air, water and fuel into space is the way that we currently do it, as reported by the IEEE Spectrum portal in 2004. Packing as much of it as we can into rockets on Earth, and then firing them off into orbit to get supplies to the Moon, or Mars, is going to be ludicrously expensive and time-consuming. A much better solution is to extract everything that we need from wherever we are.

The process of robotic mining itself is well established on Earth, and NASA holds an annual Robotic Mining Competition (RMC) to help drive university-level research and innovation with robots competing to mine simulated Martian soil.

The most recent RMC competition, its Eighth Annual RMC awards ceremony in May 2017, held at the Kennedy Space Center Visitor Complex in Florida, saw teams compete to produce a winning solution to planet mining.

The 'Joe Kosmo Award for Excellence' saw a team from Alabama clinched first place. The whole initiative is designed to foster technology that can be used for NASA's trip to Mars. Joe Kosmo himself, a retired NASA engineer, has a background in robotic mining. "Before we go to Mars, we need to learn about it. We need to pre-stage supplies and equipment", said Kennedy Center Director Bob Cabana at the time of event. "There's a lot we can accomplish using robots".[10]

---

[10] NASA's John F. Kennedy Space Center, By Linda Herridge, "Robotic Miners Traverse the Martian Dirt for NASA's Robotic Mining Competition", 9 June 2017, https://www.nasa.gov/feature/robotic-miners-traverse-the-martian-dirt-for-nasas-robotic-mining-competition

In order to figure out the best way to mine, NASA has reportedly taken inspiration from some of the finest natural engineers on Earth that aren't beavers. Or termites. Our out-of-this-world mining hopes rest on the engineering prowess of the humble ant.

NASA's Swarmies robots, if they come to volition are designed and programmed to forage like ants. Each individual robot has basic hardware and follows a simple set of rules, so when it finds something interesting, the unit then communicates with other units to help exploit its find.[11] The current incarnation of this system only uses four robots, but it's been designed with scalability in mind, and it'll work for all different kinds of hardware. These small, relatively cheap robots can work together to efficiently perform much of the work that would take one big, expensive robot a very long time to execute.

Next, NASA will add some robots to the mix that actually do know how to get some work done. The plan is to incorporate 'RASSOR', "a concept robotic vehicle evaluating designs for a future craft that could work on another world", according to the space agency.

So in the near future of asteroid and planet mining, we can look to robotics as a solution to our needs. Advancing AI coupled with increasing speeds of Earth-to-robot communications should enable our creations to keep going to the places we haven't been before—this time not for exploration but for excavation.

Against all the benefits of machines going into space instead of humans, the question remains, would unmanned robotic missions be able to detect weird microscopic life-forms they are not programmed to recognize that might be lurking below the surface of Mars, or beneath the murky seas of Jupiter's jumbo moon, Europa? If you are just mining or doing specific tasks, then machines seem to be the better answer. See Table 4.1 for a comparison of attributes between machine robots and humans. For example, NASA currently operates more than 50 robotic spacecraft that are studying Earth and reaching throughout the solar system, from Mercury to Pluto and beyond. Another 40 unmanned NASA missions are in development, and space agencies in Europe, Russia, Japan, India and China are running or building their own robotic craft.[12]

What is not commonly known however is that many of NASA's leading scientists also champion human exploration as a worthy goal in its own right

---

[11] NASA Kennedy Space Center, by Steven Siceloff, 18 August 2014, "Meet The 'Swarmies' – Robotics Answer to Bugs", https://www.nasa.gov/content/meet-the-swarmies-robotics-answer-to-bugs

[12] NASA Goddard Space Center, Last updated 3 January 2018, "Goddard Missions – Present", https://www.nasa.gov/content/goddard-missions-present

Table 4.1 Comparison of attributes between machine robots and humans

Attribute	Machine	Human
Speed	Superior	Comparatively slow
Power output	Superior in level of consistency	Comparatively weak
Consistency	Ideal for consistent, repetitive action	Unreliable learning and fatigue are factors
Information capacity	Multichannel	Primarily single channel
Memory	Ideal for literal reproduction	Better for principles and strategies
Reasoning computation	Deductive, tedious to programme, fast	Inductive, easier to program, slow, accurate
Sensing	Good at quantitative assessment	Wide ranges, multifunction, judgement
Perceiving	Copes with variation poorly	Copes with variation better, susceptible to noise

Source: Tom James

and as a critically important part of space science in the twenty-first century. In *Scientific American*, Jim Bell, a stargazer and planetary researcher at Cornell University and creator of 'Postcards from Mars', notes that "you may believe that analysts like me who are included in mechanical space investigation would expel space explorer missions as expensive and pointless".[13] In spite of the fact that space human explorer missions are significantly more costly and dangerous than automated ones, they are fundamental to the accomplishment of NASA investigation programmes.

The heart of the open deliberation is this: automated machines will just do what they are modified to do; they are not customized to recognize unusual quality: the impossible, the obscure, the abnormal non-carbon life that we may have experienced on Mars; for instance with the two Viking vehicles, in 1976. Each conveyed hardware for inspecting the Martian soil and smaller than usual science research centres to test the specimens for indications of life. The results that these robotized labs radioed back to Earth were cryptic: the substance responses from the Martian soil were weird, not at all like anything seen on Earth. Be that as it may, they were likewise not at all like any responses that living life forms would create.

What are we searching for, precisely, when we scan for outsider life? That is the enormous question considered in another report from the National Research Council, 'The Limits of Organic Life in Planetary Systems'. For over

---

[13] Scientific American Magazine, Book Review, accessed 19 April 2018, "The Interstellar Age: Inside the Forty-Year Voyager Mission by Jim Bell", https://www.scientificamerican.com/article/book-review-the-interstellar-age/

five years, a board of trustees of researchers attempted to envision what life-as-we-don't-have any acquaintance with it may resemble. Their decision: Life may exist in non-carbon shapes totally unlike anything we see on Earth.

So for exploration at least, it seems humans may still have a job!

5

Scouting for Resources

Tom James

Harvesting minerals from asteroids and planets is still a decade away from becoming a reality, so Planetary Resources has discovered. Eighteen years on and with a preliminary Earth-satellite mineral scout system named Ceres now abandoned, the company is focusing on deep space.

Ceres was a US$21.1 million spend for the company in 2016, to equip ten Arkyd satellites with sensors to observe the Earth's surface. The company hoped to use the network to monitor water quality, locate new mineral sources or find other uses that weren't easily served by existing satellite services.

Whilst Ceres is shelved, the Arkyd satellites are still vital to the company and will continue to be deployed as part of its asteroid mining plan, utilizing and testing systems that will be on-board its tabled deep-space probes that include infrared imaging systems.

The company has been working on its Arkyd programme for years, the latest of which, Arkyd-6, began its journey to a launch pad in India at the close of 2017. The space vehicle is considered a technological trailblazer for the asteroid-observing probes that Planetary Resources plans to build at its headquarters in Redmond, Washington, US.

Infrared imaging will be useful for observing near-Earth asteroids (NEAs) to determine which could be the richest potential targets for robotic mining operations. Water ice is the primary target, at least for the early stages, as water

T. James (✉)
NR Capital & Deep Space Technologies, Singapore, Singapore

© The Author(s) 2018
T. James (ed.), *Deep Space Commodities*,
https://doi.org/10.1007/978-3-319-90303-3_5

can be turned into hydrogen rocket fuel as well as breathable oxygen and drinkable water for space travellers.

In 2017 Planetary Resources said the first steps in the company's asteroid prospecting campaign could be taken in 2020. Arkyd-6 represents "one small step", according to President and CEO Chris Lewicki, towards this goal.[1] How small? Roughly four by eight by 12 inches, in accordance with what is known as the 6U CubeSat standard.

The plan is for the Mars-bound rockets to carry five times more cargo than what is thought possible today—however, Planetary Resources is not planning to simply scale up current technology. Lewicki believes that rockets can free up some extra space by refuelling in space, rather than taking it up all at once from the ground. The key is to use the water extracted from asteroids or the Moon.

With its Arkyd-6 Nanosatellite in Earth orbit, Planetary Resources will use this vehicle to serve as a platform to try out different ideas, particularly ideas that could reduce the cost of asteroid exploration by a factor of 20.

Goldman Sachs is now taking an interest in space, and they released a report in 2017 looking in to the opportunities for commercial space business. This report really compared these projects in space as being, at this point in time, not much different than large projects on Earth. In short, Goldman Sachs basically compared the finances and the risk as the same, and the technology as equally accessible, so onwards we march into the new territory of space, identified, defined and legislated. Infrared systems, hardware and software aboard previous probes featured in this book to date have catalogued the wealth of resources waiting on our celestial doorstep, technology willing.

NASA's journey to put its boots on Mars, a 'three-line whip' laid down by President Donald Trump in 2017, is anticipated in the 2030s, reinforced by progress with multifunction Mars orbiters and the ideal approaches to utilize the Red Planet's assets to support both our robot and human space pioneers.

NASA has proclaimed that it will likely prospect almost 50 areas on Mars as conceivable spots for future human arrivals. Those arrival zone locales contain 'areas of intrigue' that could materialize as human touchdown spots, the agency said.

Suitable touchdown locales will enable groups to arrive securely and conduct operations in regions that are expected to contain an abundance of intriguing science exercises; and provide assets that the space travellers could

---

[1] Alan Boyle, 13 November 2017, "Planetary Resources' Arkyd-6 prototype imaging satellite has left the building", GeekWire, https://www.geekwire.com/2017/planetary-resources-arkyd-6-prototype-imaging-satellite-left-building/

utilize. For instance, any favoured investigation zones ought to enable expeditionary groups to take advantage of no less than 100 metric tonnes (110 US tonnes) of water, NASA authorities have said.

Landing Sites: 'To Do' List

With its suite of instruments and cameras, especially the sharp-shooting High Resolution Imaging Science Experiment (HiRISE), NASA's Mars Reconnaissance Orbiter (MRO) is being put through a demanding procedure called HiWish to catch new pictures of landing-zone candidates.

Launched on 12 August 2005, the MRO is searching for evidence that water persisted on the surface of Mars for a protracted period of time. While other Mars missions have shown that water flowed across the surface in the planet's history, it remains a mystery whether water was ever around long enough to provide a habitat for life.

NASA's Human Exploration and Operations Directorate has started to consider where human adventurers ought to go on Mars, and what conditions and assets, and in addition what science targets, might be available.

This is an indication that they are really considering sending individuals to Mars. In Chapter 12 you can read all about an economic viability plan for colonization of Mars right down to the detail of what equipment to take so we could grow food and a sustainable crop cycle.

In November 2006, after five months of deceleration, the MRO entered its final science orbit and began its primary science phase. It joined five other active spacecraft that were either in orbit or on the planet's surface: Mars Global Surveyor, Mars Express, 2001 Mars Odyssey and Mars Spirit and Opportunity rovers. This set a record for the most operational spacecraft in the immediate vicinity of Mars. Mars Global Surveyor and the Spirit rover have since ceased to function, with the others remaining operational as of September 2016.

The orbiters' telecommunications systems also have become established as a crucial service for future spacecraft, representing the first link in a communications bridge back to Earth. A so-called 'interplanetary Internet', which can be used by numerous international spacecraft in coming years. Telecommunications that feature a lower power drain were also on board and successful according to NASA reports. The orbiter also carried an experimental navigation camera. Similar cameras could be placed on orbiters of the future that would be able to serve as high-precision interplanetary 'eyes' to guide incoming landers to precise landings on Mars, opening up exciting, but otherwise dangerous, areas of the planet to explore. The mission concluded on 31 December 2010.

New Hardware to Observe Mars

In the near future, adding to the interest cultivated by the Red Planet, numerous specialists inside and outside of NASA might want the agency to dispatch a new, multifunctional, cutting-edge Mars orbiter. The potential advantage of this new hardware was laid out in a report by the Science Analysis Group of the Mars Exploration Program Analysis Group.

This Mars orbiter could utilize a Sun-oriented electric drive, broadcast communications apparatus and utilize radar to investigate and better group Martian assets for human landing parties. In the event that this project is given a green light, the rocket could be Mars bound by 2022, NASA authorities have said.

NASA has assigned assets to provide early performance indicators, a precursor to another Mars orbiter, according to Steve Jurczyk, chairman of the Space Technology Mission Directorate at NASA's base camp in Washington, DC. The mission is not confirmed for 2022, however a Mars media communications orbiter is under consideration, given the age of some of NASA's present orbiters. Mars Odyssey launched in 2001, for instance, and MRO lifted off in 2005.[2]

The harvesting and containment of water from planets and asteroids has already been identified. In Situ Resource Utilization, or ISRU as it is commonly referred to as, is a key process to successful deep-space missions. ISRU is defined as "the collection, processing, storing and use of materials encountered in the course of human or robotic space exploration that replace materials that would otherwise be brought from Earth", according to NASA. ISRU is the practice of leveraging resources found or manufactured on other astronomical objects like the Moon, Mars, asteroids and so on, to fulfil or enhance the requirements and capabilities of a space mission.

ISRU can provide materials for life support, propellant fuel sources, construction materials and energy to a spacecraft payloads or space exploration crews. It is common for spacecraft and robotic planetary surface missions to harness the solar radiation found in-situ in the form of solar panels. The use of ISRU for material production has not yet been implemented in a space mission.

NASA will be launching two IRSU projects in the near future but at the time of writing no dates had been fixed. The first is dubbed 'Resource

---

[2] NASA, edited by Loura Hall, last updated 7 August 2017, "Interview with Steve Jurczyk: Guiding NASA's Technology Future", https://www.nasa.gov/feature/interview-with-steve-jurczyk-guiding-nasa-s-technology-future

Prospector', where a rover will be sent to the Moon equipped with tools to look for hydrogen and scan for water vapor. The mission is set for some time in 2018, and researchers hope that their work will secure water so that the vital and heavy liquid doesn't have to be carried along the entire trajectory of a mission. This could offer a massive cost saving for missions but also ensure sustainability of long-term missions.

The second IRSU will hitch a ride on NASA's next planned rover to Mars in 2020. The technology has yet to be confirmed, but it will be responsible for grabbing oxygen from the atmosphere, screening out dust and preparing for the necessary steps to convert the gas into oxygen. If both of these small-scale demonstrations are successful, NASA hopes to progress towards larger operations that will eventually make way for a crewed mission to Mars.

Water on Mars is transformative and not only for drinking water. It can be used for farming, it can produce breathable oxygen and even fuel for Mars vehicles, in addition to other byproducts that could help human activities on the Red Planet.

Past projects have floated the idea of sending bacteria to the Red Planet to construct biobricks out of the planet's dusty terrain and set the path towards the potential terraforming of Mars to support human life As Nasa continues to make strides towards altering the landscape and atmosphere, it could be possible that these breakthroughs will someday see the human race establish its first interplanetary colony. In fact, with current technology it is widely believe we could terraform Mars in a period of 90 years or so. And that is with current known technologies and approaches.

Martian Water? From the Rocks, not from the Atmosphere

One asset discounted is the extraction of water from the thin Martian climate. The mass, power, volume and mechanical intricacy of the framework required for this are a long way from what is technically achievable at present.

However, water-rich minerals on Mars look significantly all the more encouraging, as they require a great deal less energy to free up the water atoms. Most achievable using current technology appears to be an approach whereby a gap is dropped down through the Martian soil, vaporizing subsurface ice and then bringing it up topside as a gas and then gathering that gas into fluid. Once a semi-lasting base on Mars is built up, teams could set up ISRU hardware, ensure any glitches in the apparatus are smoothed out and after that begin reaping assets. ISRU equipment would likewise work in self-governing mode when there were no people at the base.

It's evident that there aren't sufficient resources on Earth to go around amid our burgeoning population. We're always battling over everything. Turf wars for land, water and airspace; positioning for our home planet's precious stones, hydrocarbons and food resources. Sustainable or not. Over recent years it has emerged that we could tackle these human quarrels by mining deep space since all that we hold of significant worth on this planet, metals, minerals, land, vitality sources, fuel—the things we battle wars over—are available in large amounts in the nearby planets and asteroids. Naveen Jain,[3] of Moon Express, an entity formed by Silicon Valley and Space entrepreneurs, states that we need to do on the Moon what Planetary Resources plans to do with space rocks. Before beginning Moon Express, Naveen Jain was a senior official at Microsoft and afterward CEO of his own start-up, InfoSpace. Elon Musk[4] established PayPal and now has a private space organization, SpaceX, presently under contract with NASA to start conveying space travellers to the ISS, as we know.

Fundamentally, Naveen Jain and Peter Diamandis of Planetary Resources[5] preach that once you take a mentality of shortage and supplant it with an attitude of plenitude, astounding things can occur here on Planet Earth.

This sort of enthusiasm is not just confined to the current field of companies and countries lining up for deep space and Jain and Diamandis are certainly not the only vocal ones. Neil deGrasse Tyson,[6] a prominent member of the American space fraternity and regular face for news organizations, likewise voiced his fervour about the capability of space mining.

In the event that you pull a space rock the size of a house to Earth, it could have more platinum on it than has at any point been mined ever", said deGrasse.[7]

"More gold than has at any point been mined ever [and] at the point when that happens the shortage that has prompted human-to-human viciousness, there's a possibility it could all leave.

In the short term though it is much more probable that any commodities found in space will be put to use in space to begin with, not pulled back to Earth. Yet deGrasse's remarks encompass the space mining phenomena. It's unquestionable that space is brimming with resources given the knowledge base built to date.

---

[3] Moon Express, General Corporate Website, accessed on 19 April 2018, http://www.moonexpress.com/
[4] SpaceX, General Corporate Website, accessed on 19 April 2018, http://www.spacex.com/
[5] Planetary Resources, General Corporate Website, accessed on 19 April 2018, https://www.planetaryresources.com/
[6] Wikipedia Foundation, last updated 5 April 2018, "Neil deGrasse Tyson", https://en.wikipedia.org/wiki/Neil_deGrasse_Tyson
[7] Inc., by Graham Winfrey, 9 February 2016, "The Trillion-Dollar Industry in Search of Ambitious Entrepreneurs", https://www.inc.com/graham-winfrey/the-best-industry-for-becoming-a-trillionaire.html

Billions of years earlier, amid the development of the close planetary system, science tells us that gravity pulled the overwhelming materials on would-be planets toward their centres, compelling the lighter, yet robust material out to the surface.

At the point when those planets separated, they formed the basis of the asteroids everybody in the space mining industry is aiming for. Some are made of rough surface sections; some are made of 'nucleus' materials such as platinum, gold, silver and palladium, which are uncommon and valuable on Earth. What is exciting about the Asteroid mining is that quite literally nature has pre-filtered the elements for us. You find an asteroid space rock produced from the center of a planet that never survived, and there you have pure minerals in the palm of your hand.

There are quite simply riches (by Earth standards) beyond anything you could ever imagine, and in quantities never mined before on Earth in all of human history. And they are ready and waiting—you simply need to arrive first and lay your claim. Claiming rights in Space is another issue, and this is dealt with in two interesting chapters (Chapters 8 and 9) contributed by academics and lawyers on space law later in this book.

As for arriving first and laying your claim, it's not going to be a walk in the park and won't be a basic, or modest, venture. The greater part of the space rocks in the nearby planetary group are in the asteroid belt amongst Mars and Jupiter. Yet the paths and trajectories of some NEAs see them pass within reachable distance of our planned planet-born extraction vehicles, proposed 3D printing arrays and mining teams—that is, about 30 million miles away.

There is awesome potential for asset extraction in space, however, these endeavours will convey extraordinary expenses and a lot of instability about whether they can be conducted as planned and on budget. Amid the surge of off-planet interest, numerous due dates and courses of events appraisals are quickly drawing nearer or have passed as of now.

Unlike mapping the surfaces of planets, charting the solar system is complicated by the fact that planets and asteroids are moving in three-dimensional orbits around the sun. Plotting a course to visit an object requires that we know not only where it is now but also its precise orbital parameters so that we can calculate where its trajectory will take it. The cosmic map's unique component will be the NEAs, whose orbits bring them close to Earth and make them strategically, scientifically and economically important for our species.

The notion of harvesting Asteroids in space is not unconceivable.

Moon Express, calls the Moon the eighth mainland". Its mandate is to mine the Moon for natural resources of economic value. The company has close ties with NASA, announcing in 2017 the rocket architecture it has developed for a journey to our Moon.

In that same year NASA decide to extend the Lunar Catalyst agreement with the company for a further two years. And although the requisite legal framework to enable mining of lunar resources is not fully in place, major world space agencies have put in place a coordination plan to encourage the type of commercial activity proposed by Moon Express.

NASA will be launching two ISRU projects in the near future. The first is dubbed 'Resource Prospector' where a rover will be sent to the Moon equipped with tools to look for hydrogen and scan for water vapour. The mission is set for 2020 and researchers hope that their work will secure water so that the vital and heavy liquid doesn't have to be carried along the entire trajectory of a mission.[8]

The second IRSU will follow on in 2020. The technology has yet to be selected, but it will be responsible for grabbing carbon dioxide from the atmosphere, screening out dust and preparing the steps to convert the gas into oxygen. If both of these small-scale demonstrations are successful, NASA hopes to progress towards larger operations that will eventually make way for a crewed mission to Mars.

As our Earth orbits around the Sun some 13,000 asteroids pass close by, in galactic terms. These space rocks are more than just a heavenly curiosity; they are treasures. The resources contained within them mean they have the potential to provide untold riches, not just precious metals but what could be described as the future oil fields of space—the future mines.

The question is, would it be worth it? Some might ask whether it's realistic to stage such a seemingly out-of-this-world plan. Those involved in the nascent asteroid mining industry, however, argue that there are a number of misconceptions about their efforts.

NASA states that, in the twenty-first century, space exploration will be reliant upon what we can mine in the cosmos: that is, the metals and minerals found on asteroids will provide the raw materials for space structures.

One asteroid rock Planetary Resources has been following passes close to the Earth and is a 0.5 kilometre by 1 kilometre in size. A shuttle could reach it in around eight months, the company forecasts. Peter Diamandis of Planetary Resources gauges its aggregate worth at between US$300 billion and US$5 trillion. If it were mined there would be huge financial consequences, as it would drive down the worldwide cost of metals like platinum should the shuttle's return payload be successfully landed on Planet Earth.

---

[8] NASA, Advanced Exploration Systems, Edited by Erin Mahoney, last updated 4 August 2017, "Resource Prospector", https://www.nasa.gov/resource-prospector

The Frontier

On the precious metals theme, references to the Wild West are prevalent in much of the writing of space-mining organizations. The Moon Express website discusses "overcome pioneers" who investigated new domains with the sponsorship of a ruler or a state." For businesses like Moon Express, space is not an inaccessible vacancy as they imagine it to be a tangible business.

In fact, except for a Cold War-era scenario restricting national allocation of the Moon, there are no laws present about proprietorship in space. Its wealth is ready and waiting, similar to gold chunks in a California stream. At the American Museum of Natural History, the former Space Foundation CEO Elliot Pulham[9] said, prior to his very sudden untimely death in October 2017, that space asteroid rocks are unmistakably for the taking. The foundation is a Colorado-based non-profit organization that advocates for all sectors of the global space industry.[10]

The most far-out proposition in space mining is to divert an NEA toward Earth and into lunar circle. There, the space rock could orbit securely around the Moon, becoming available to our planet as a resource. A 2012 California Technical College, Pasadena, US (Cal Tech) paper confirmed that this strategy would be plausible, as well as "basic" for long-haul human space investigation. As indicated by the review, it will soon be feasible for an uncrewed shuttle to recognize an objective space rock, one around seven metres across and 500,000 kilograms in mass.

Cal Tech suggested that once the space rock and shuttle is associated, a Sun-based fuelled drive framework could fly the space rock back to our moon and store it in lunar circle. Contingent upon the mass of the asteroid, this recovery flight would last in the vicinity of six to ten years.

The gatherings of organizations established with the aim of mining space are upheld to a great extent by speculators who made their names and fortunes in tech. Peter Diamandis is the organizer of the X PRIZE Foundation and Silicon Valley's Singularity University, which he helped to establish with futurist Ray Kurzweil. Eric Schmidt is one of Planetary Resources' significant financial specialists. *The New Yorker*'s George Packer distinguishes the "clashing weights of Silicon Valley as "hard working attitude, status cognizance, optimism, and covetousness." All these 'heavy weights' involved in the space-mining race could turn out to be incomprehensibly well off.[11]

---

[9] Space Foundation, "Remembering Elliot Pulham", 1 November 2017, https://www.spacefoundation.org/news/remembering-elliot-pulham

[10] Space Foundation, "Who we are", accessed on 19 April 2018, https://www.spacefoundation.org/who-we-are

[11] The New Yorker, George packer, staff writer, may 25th 2013, https://www.newyorker.com/news/georgepacker/a-reply-from-silicon-valley

True, entering another, high-risk, cutting-edge field of business ought to accompany the likelihood for phenomenal rewards. Diamandis has kidded that his organization's financing arrangement is to purchase 'puts' (a derivative stock market instrument giving the participant the right to put, but not sell a given commodity and so on into a market) in the platinum market; and after that declare their arrangement to bring a platinum space rock home. Jain of Moon Express envisions returning from outings to the moon with payloads worth billions of dollars.

It's thrilling that technological advances could end mineral wealth and precious metal shortages on Earth, consigning wars to the pages of Earth's history. Surely no one is going to go to lead a conflict in space over them?

Well, that's open to debate. One would hope would-be space-mining organizations, and the countries behind them, do not become warring factions even though they have been frequently called 'insane', their aspirations portrayed as 'wild plans' in popular press.

Actually, these organizations are not insane by any means. As Jain, of Moon Express, has said, "it is not only a fun extend ... [It] is additionally an extraordinary business."[12]

Financial specialists associated with deep space mining are thinking differently in their approach to the vast expanse. That may clarify why, as the New York-based *The Wall Street Journal* revealed, "Planetary Resources has moved its investment concern's concentration from valuable metals to a more everyday space asset." And that asset is water, which as we now know could be prepared into fuel to develop the helpful existences of maturing business satellites and space missions.[13]

Granted, water has been a piece of Planetary Resources' marketable strategy for quite a long time. As John Logsdon of the George Washington Institute of Space Policy[14] said 'it's not as hot as platinum but rather, I think, the most significant asset in space [water].'[15]

There are perceived to be inexhaustible assets on our Moon, on Mars and throughout our nearby planetary group, yet we have to challenge and move

---

[12] *The Guardian* Newspaper International Edition, Moon Express raises US$20 m for 2017 voyage to the moon January 2017, accessed on 19 April 2018, https://www.theguardian.com/science/2017/jan/17/moon-express-raises-20m-for-2017-voyage-to-moon

[13] *The Wall Street Journal*, By Andy Pasztor, "What Happened to That Crazy Asteroid Mining Plan?", 7 May 2014, https://www.wsj.com/articles/space-miners-scale-back-their-mission-1399497240

[14] Planetary Society, "John M. Logsdon Board of Directors", accessed on 19 April 2018, http://www.planetary.org/about/board-of-directors/jon-logsdon.html

[15] The New Republic, By Rachel Riederer, 20 May 2014, "Silicon Valley Says Space Mining Is Awesome and Will Change Life on Earth. That's Only Half Right.", https://newrepublic.com/article/117815/space-mining-will-not-solve-earths-conflict-over-natural-resources

the up and coming era of space adventurers to make sense of how to get to those assets, gather them and, afterward, utilize them.

According to NASA, the space exploration of the twenty-first century will rely on what we can mine in the cosmos and that "The metals and minerals found on asteroids will provide the raw materials for space structures, and comets will become the watering holes and gas stations for interplanetary spacecraft."[16]

We now need to address the concepts under consideration for NEAs and deep-space mining.

Other Interesting Reading Resources

http://www.airspacemag.com/space/new-eyes-earth-180959777/

http://www.space.com/32882-nasa-crewed-mars-missions-resources-orbiter.html

https://newrepublic.com/article/117815/space-mining-will-not-solve-earths-conflict-over-natural-resources

https://www.nasa.gov/feature/tapping-resources-in-space-and-the-community

---

[16] Nasa Center for near earth object studies, website, last updated July 8th 2018. https://cneos.jpl.nasa.gov/about/nea_resource.html

6

Asteroid Mining Concepts

Tom James

Neil Armstrong, the very first human to step on the Moon, would never have predicted the advancements, ramping human interest, opportunities and sheer aspirations contained within the contemporary space community, accelerating space exploration at the technological pace it has since that landmark day for humanity in July 1969.

One such phenomena he wouldn't have likely considered is that of space asteroid mining, which details the extraction of raw materials from any given asteroid or moon identified as a viable target. Though this concept sounds new to many, it's been around for decades. These days, asteroid mining is no longer a mere dream.

Over a thousand million asteroids are present in space near the Earth. As we've established, these space rocks are also called near-Earth asteroids (NEAs), rich in mineral deposits and, with any luck, water. The relative proximity and abundance of these rocks makes asteroid mining a viable enterprise. That's the reason big corporates are getting drawn into a potentially risky but extremely lucrative industry. The funding for mining ventures has already begun and commercial prospecting missions are expected to begin as early as 2020.

Though it sounds like the type of science fiction resigned to a poster on a teenager's bedroom wall, asteroid mining is rapidly becoming a workable niche industry within the new space economy. This economy also features space tourism and colonization as vital components. Whilst the logistical

T. James (✉)
NR Capital & Deep Space Technologies, Singapore, Singapore

© The Author(s) 2018
T. James (ed.), *Deep Space Commodities*,
https://doi.org/10.1007/978-3-319-90303-3_6

challenges are substantial, early stage ventures are filtering down necessary technologies required for commercial positioning, so tangible operations, both economically and technologically, are not insurmountable.

Excavating an asteroid for resources would in theoretical concept function very much like terrestrial mining—except for lacking the environmental concerns integral to Earth-based practices. And an atmosphere; and gravity! But that's not putting companies and nations off. There are "lots and lots and lots" of US dollars out there according to a November 2017 report by web portal Visual Capitalist.

If humans were able to get their hands on just one asteroid, it would be a game changer. That's because the value of many asteroids is measured in quintillions of dollars, telephone numbers if you will, which makes the market for Earth's annual production of raw materials, at about US$660 billion per year, look paltry in comparison.

The reality is that the Earth's crust is saddled with uneconomic materials, whilst certain types of asteroids are almost pure metal. X-type asteroids, for example, are thought to be the remnants of large asteroids that were pulverized in collisions in which their dense, metallic cores got separated from the mantle, according to Virtual Capital.

And whilst asteroids are composed of a variety of compounds, there are a few that are of specific concern to prospectors, specifically hydrogen, water and platinum-group metals. The basic concept is to mine material from NEAs, those having orbits that come near the Earth, a set quite separate from the main belt asteroids that orbit between Mars and Jupiter.

Resources mined from the asteroids could be exploited in space to support space flight, space stations and potentially a lunar base. The most valuable material for these claims would likely be water, gases such as Methane or other compounds that could be either utilized as space rocket fuel or exploited to replace the consumable materials needed for sustenance and sustainable life. Some scientists have proposed that the metals in asteroids, such as iron and nickel, might also be extracted as raw materials for extracurricular space operations.

The other key purpose of mining asteroids would be to bring precious metals back to the Earth, which, as has been commented on previously, would have a drastic effect on commodity market prices. The most likely metals to extract would include the rare and expensive platinum and platinum-group precious metals as well as gold. Astronomers have confidence that an A-typical asteroid should have much higher quantity of these metals than usual rocks on Earth or even on the Moon.

In the past, asteroid-mining concepts required individuals to visit the asteroids and mine them, but now contemporary schools of thought have postulated innovative ideas that involve strictly robotic operations. One option would be simply to bring portions of the asteroid back to Earth and disassemble them in areas where a processing plant could be set up. Other ideas detail dropping segments of the asteroid on the Moon or treating materials in-situ, on the asteroid itself, perhaps bringing it into orbit around the Earth for this process.

The technology required to go to NEAs is to all intents and purposes established, bolstered by the fact that the amount of rocket power and fuel quantities required to go to a number of these astral bodies is less than it takes to travel to the Moon. And we've done that already.

In contrast, the technology necessary to mine them and generate usable materials has, as yet, not been developed. And it's not clear as to how tough and expensive this might be, neither is it apparent whether the task may well be conducted using robots or via systems requiring human remote oversight.

Back to the top and we see that articles regarding asteroid mining have appeared in magazines and the goliaths of business news television like Bloomberg, which has already interviewed astronomers and commodity specialists regarding the subject of space mining and its viability and development.

Originally, the concept of asteroid mining was primarily based on the history of the mining and oil industries. It had been assumed that investor-funded exploration of NEAs would begin first, followed by a small group of trained 'traveller–miners' being transported to and from the NEAs to partake in exploratory mining missions. Once the method for asteroid mining became standardized, then 'hyper-corporations' would send many trained traveller–miners deep in to the Asteroid Belt, where they would work and sleep for years before returning to Earth.

However, this concept of an asteroid-mining trade raised many queries, because, as has been discussed, humans are very delicate and their needs to function are immense in comparison to that of a 'well-oiled machine'. Why send many individuals to mine asteroids when robots can be designed to try to do it?

It is of notoriety that, whilst NASA and others are working on the problem, we still have unresolved issues regarding long-term zero gravity exposure for any human astronaut miners. Currently, Astronauts who stay for three months or longer on the International Space Station (ISS) report changes in their eyesight in zero gravity and also atrophy, where muscle-mass wastage sets in, causing limbs and muscles to degrade and weaken. Before humans can venture into deep-space operations with associated long-haul space flights and protracted periods of habitation, we first need to solve issues of zero gravity, perhaps developing our own artificial gravity to replicate conditions on Earth, such as rotating structures mimicking our Earth's spin of a scalable 1,000 miles per hour.

If the technological obstacles to actual asteroid mining are effectively overcome, that is, digging the stuff out, it could be supposed that an individual will be able to sit in front of a display and guide a robot in to deep space; trace and perform spectrum analysis of said asteroid; mine the asteroid for materials whilst the mining bot is tethered to a small spacecraft and pack the harvested materials into the spacecraft, before navigating the spacecraft to a crewed space station that serves as a collection point. From thereon in the materials would be processed whilst still in deep space.

To this end the agenda of so-called hyper-corporations would be to gather, sort and transport large quantities of asteroid constituents from the Asteroid Belt to the Earth or the Moon for onward sale and consumption.

Asteroid Composition

S-Type. These asteroids carry lesser quantity of water but appear more striking because they comprise various metals including nickel, cobalt and more valuable metals such as gold, platinum and rhodium. A minor 10-metre S-type asteroid contains about 650,000 kilograms (1,433,000 pounds) of metal with 50 kilograms (110 pounds) in the form of rare metals like platinum and gold.[1]

C-Type. These are the most common type of asteroids and comprise more than 75 percent of known asteroids. They also have a high abundance of water, which is not currently of use for mining but could be used in an exploration effort beyond the asteroid. Mission costs could be reduced by using the available water from the asteroid. C-type asteroids also have a lot of organic carbon, phosphorus and other key ingredients for fertilizer, which could be used to grow food.

M-Type. These asteroids comprise nickel and iron but are the least abundant. A very small percentage of asteroids fall in this category.

A burgeoning, sophisticated global society is stimulating an increasing demand for rare minerals and precious metals. However, there's a restricted

---

[1] Space.Com, By Charles Q. Choi, 20 September 2017, "Asteroids: Fun Facts and Information About Asteroids", https://www.space.com/51-asteroids-formation-discovery-and-exploration.html

quantity supplied of such materials buried within the Earth and acquiring them in even minute quantities is costly. If these materials can be nonheritable in giant quantities, then makers may lower the per-unit price of high tech product, thereby counterintuitively increasing profits by lowering net worth and increasing demand.

Mining and Processing

First, mining can be simply conducted by bringing the asteroid raw material back to the Earth.

Second, processing the raw material on site and bringing back only the processed material (and therefore also producing propellant for a return trip) has been established as a feasible scenario.

Processing in-situ with the aim of extracting high-value minerals can scale back the energy needs for transporting the materials, though the processing facilities should first be transported to the mining location.

Mining operations need special instrumentation to handle the extraction and process of mineral ores in space. The machinery can be anchored to the target, however, once on site, the ores would be expedited because of the shortage, or entire lack, of gravity, depending on the size of the rock or whether an asteroid of near-planetary proportion is being mined.

However, quite a lot of work still needs to be done to perfect techniques for refinement of ores in a zero gravity or low gravity environment. Tethering with an asteroid could be performed by employing a harpoon-like method, where a projectile would penetrate the surface to function an anchor; then a cable would winch the vehicle to the surface assuming the asteroid is both penetrable and rigid enough for a harpoon to be effective.

Due to the distance from Earth to a given asteroid identified for mining, the 'bounce-time' for communications will feature a significant delay, all be it a matter of minutes, it is still of great significance and a challenge when designing systems.

So, any mining paraphernalia will need to be highly automated or a human being is going to need to govern operations. Humans would also likely be useful for fault diagnosis, troubleshooting and maintaining the equipment. Still, 'multi-minute' communications delays haven't prevented the success of the robotic exploration of Mars, and automatic systems would be a lot less costly to create and deploy for muted mining missions.

Asteroid Extraction Techniques[2,3,4]

(a) Surface reclaim with 'snowblower':

Advantages—robust process; easy to handle loose soil; easy to monitor.

Disadvantages— problems with anchoring and containment; surface will be desiccated.

(b) Solar bubble vaporizer:

Advantages—simple, collects volatiles only.

Disadvantages—unacceptably high membrane tension; how to seal? How to anchor?

(c) In-situ volatilization:

Advantages—simple concept; asteroid body gives containment.

Disadvantages—needs low permeability; risks are loss of fluid; clogging; and blowout.

(d) Explosive disaggregation:

Advantages—very rapid release of mass, short timeline.

Disadvantages—capture of material is unsolved.

(e) Downhole jet monitoring:

Advantages—mechanically simple; separates mining from processing task.

Disadvantages—need gas to transport cuttings to processor; blowout risk high.

(f) Underground mining by mechanical 'mole':

Advantages—reduced anchoring and containment problems; physically robust.

Disadvantages—mechanically severe; hard to monitor; must move cuttings to surface plant.

Surface mining: on some forms of asteroids, materials could also be scraped off the surface by employing a scoop or auger, or for larger items, an 'active grab'. There's solid proof that several asteroids contain sizeable dust piles indicating this type of approach as being possible.

---

[2] University of Wisconsin, Madison, Department of GeoScience, accessed on 19 April 2018, "Extraction Techniques for Minerals in Space", http://www.geology.wisc.edu/~pbrown/spacemine/spacemine.html

[3] Department of Physical Geography and Ecosystem Science, Lund University, By Vide Hellgren, June 2016, "Asteroid Mining A Review of Methods and Aspects", https://lup.lub.lu.se/luur/download?func=downloadFile&recordOId=8882371&fileOId=8884121

[4] MIT, "Asteroid Mining", accessed on 19 April 2018, http://web.mit.edu/12.000/www/m2016/final-website/solutions/asteroids.html

Magnetic rakes: asteroids with a high metal content, also lined with loose grains and seams could be gathered by using a magnet.

Mond Process: The nickel and iron of an iron made asteroid can be extracted by the 'Mond Method'. The Mond Method, which is sometimes known as the 'Carbonyl Process', is a technique created by Ludwig Mond in 1890 to extract and purify nickel. The method was used commercially before the end of the nineteenth century on Earth. The process is repeated to get metal in a highly pure state. Nickel and iron may be retrieved from the gas once more at higher temperatures, much like a reverse refinery where cooling towers harvest liquids from a gaseous state here on Earth, then—in theory— when connected to a 3D printer you can manufacture items from the residue.

Shaft mining: a mine is conduit into the asteroid and materials are extracted through the shaft. This needs precise geological information to engineer the accuracy of the location beneath the surface and a facility to hold the retrieved ores for the process facility.

There also are some fascinating opportunities relating to the generation of electric power from space resources. The options here include the development of solar-power satellites in high orbits that will beam solar energy down to the surface via microwave energy.

The retrieval of helium from the surface of the Moon could also be economically engaging as a supply of fresh fuel for fusion power reactors on the Earth or for fusion on the Moon, with the ability to then transmit energy straight down to the planet. Similarly, solar collectors could also be designed on the Moon out of native materials to send their power back to the planet.

The construction of solar-power satellites, not to be mistaken with 'solar-powered satellites', could in theory take place in space itself, providing a progressive, less expensive build if the high-mass, low-tech elements of the power satellite are made-up off planet. This could be said of any space vehicle. Propelling mass over gravity and air resistance requires a huge explosion of energy, which is ultimately expensive to manufacture.

Looking further afield, the helium three and hydrogen atom contents of the large planets are so immense that schemes for extraction and retrieval of fusion fuel from their atmospheres, especially Uranus and Neptune given their geological makeup, have been suggested as being capable of powering the world till our Sun dies of maturity.

The most economical sources of space materials are those bodies that have the best richness of valued commodities that are most accessible from Earth.

Argon is particularly of current importance for the terrestrial metal industry, being used as an inert gas shield in arc welding and cutting. Other applications include non-reactive blankets in the manufacture of titanium and other reactive elements and as a protective atmosphere for growing silicon and germanium crystals. It is one of the noble gases, which are catalogued as Group 0 on the periodic table. Argon makes up about 0.9 percent of our air. The group consists of He—helium; Ne—neon; Ar—argon; and Kr—krypton.

Asteroid Mining System Program (AMSP) Risk Domains

Cost risk: the ability of the system to accomplish the programme's life-cycle value objectives. This includes the consequences of budget and affordability selections and also the effects of inherent errors within the value estimating technique(s) used, provided that the system needs were properly outlined.

Technology risk: the degree to which the technology planned for the system has been assessed as being capable of meeting all of the project's objectives.

Performance risk: the degree to which the projected system or method is capable of meeting the operational needs that embody responsibility, maintainability, reliability, accessibility and testability needs.

The most relevant consideration in quantifying performance of the asteroid mining mechanism is handling the asteroid's rotation. Scientists believe the answer to this downside is to connect rockets to the asteroid so as to counteract the direction of its spin. In other words, if the asteroid spins dextrorotary, the rockets can stabilize the asteroid by pushing it counter clockwise.

Mission assurance risk: the degree to which existing and potential deficiencies could pose a threat to system safety or jeopardize mission-critical components. Deficiencies embrace damage-causing hazards; mission-impacting failures; seepage from unaddressed requirements; ambiguous procedures; excessive environmental conditions; latent physical faults; inappropriate corrective actions; and operator errors.

Data access and protection risk: the degree to which essential knowledge—intellectual property—is protected from unauthorized access and guarded from loss, corruption or interruption. The operators of mining robots will

Table 6.1 Organizations involved in asteroid mining

Organization	Type
Deep Space Industries	Private company
Kepler Energy and Space Engineering	Private company
Planetary Resources	Private company

be required to be provided with secure, encrypted communication links to avoid, what is colloquially known as, 'hacking' for illegal agendas.

See Table 6.1 for a list of organizations that are involved in asteroid mining. Table 6.2 shows the Asterank database of potential targets as per most cost-effective asteroids.

Feasibility

There are six categories of cost considered for an asteroid mining venture:

- (i) R&D costs
- (ii) Exploration and prospecting costs
- (iii) Construction and infrastructure development costs
- (iv) Operational and engineering costs
- (v) Environmental costs
- (vi) Time cost

Ongoing missions include:

OSIRIS-REX— planned NASA asteroid sample return mission (launched in September 2016).

Hayabusa 2— ongoing JAXA asteroid sample return mission (arriving at the target in 2018).

Asteroid Redirect Mission— potential future space mission proposed by NASA (if funded, the mission would be launched in December 2020).

Fobos-Grunt 2— planned Roskosmos sample return mission to Phobos (launch in 2024).

Completed missions are shown in Table 6.3.

Table 6.2 Asterank Database: Potential Targets as per most cost-effective asteroids[a]

Name	Type	Value ($)	Est. profit ($)	Δv (km/s)	Group
Ryugu	Cg	82.76 billion	30.08 billion	4.663	APO (PHA)
1989 ML	X	13.94 billion	4.38 billion	4.889	AMO
Nereus	Xe	4.71 billion	1.39 billion	4.986	APO (PHA)
Bennu	B	9.05 billion	2.50 billion	5.096	APO (PHA)
Didymos	Xk	62.25 billion	16.39 billion	5.164	APO (PHA)
2011 UW158	Xc	6.69 billion	1.74 billion	5.189	APO (PHA)
Anteros	L	5.57 trillion	1.25 trillion	5.440	AMO
2001 CC21	L	147.04 billion	29.77 billion	5.636	APO
1992 TC	X	84.01 billion	16.78 billion	5.648	AMO
2001 SG10	X	3.05 billion	544.91 million	5.878	APO (PHA)
2002 DO3	X	334.44 million	59.00 million	5.897	APO (PHA)
2000 CE59	L	10.65 billion	1.80 billion	6.013	APO (PHA)
1995 BC2	X	78.87 billion	13.18 billion	6.016	AMO
1991 DB	C	168.20 billion	26.66 billion	6.148	AMO
2000 RW37	C	29.27 billion	4.53 billion	6.226	APO (PHA)
1998 UT18	C	644.70 billion	99.62 billion	6.221	APO (PHA)
Seleucus	K	33.52 trillion	5.02 trillion	6.287	AMO
1998 KU2	Cb	80.32 trillion	11.96 trillion	6.300	APO
1989 UQ	B	600.73 billion	87.58 billion	6.402	ATE (PHA)
1999 KV4	B	25.68 trillion	3.73 trillion	6.384	APO
1988 XB	B	217.07 billion	31.27 billion	6.415	APO (PHA)
1997 XF11	Xk	383.99 billion	52.97 billion	6.548	APO (PHA)
1997 RT	O	174.31 billion	24.21 billion	6.502	AMO
1996 FG3	C	1.33 trillion	181.33 billion	6.608	APO (PHA)
1992 QN	X	291.29 billion	39.63 billion	6.602	APO
1999 JV6	Xk	12.03 billion	1.59 billion	6.701	APO (PHA)
2001 TY44	X	3.50 billion	469.30 million	6.612	AMO
2002 EA	L	672.12 million	87.52 million	6.744	APO
2001 HK31	X	1.33 billion	172.74 million	6.723	AMO
2005 YU55	C	49.84 billion	6.23 billion	6.907	APO (PHA)
1992 BF	Xc	2.90 billion	357.72 million	6.982	ATE
2001 PD1	K	646.08 billion	80.62 billion	6.866	AMO
Lucianotesi	Xc	46.30 billion	5.66 billion	6.988	AMO
2002 CS11	X	766.16 million	94.49 million	6.918	AMO
1992 NA	C	3.96 trillion	476.47 billion	7.012	AMO
2002 BM26	X	77.75 billion	9.26 billion	7.073	AMO (PHA)
2002 AV	K	17.79 billion	2.12 billion	7.047	APO (PHA)
1999 NC43	Q	2.61 billion	307.48 million	7.126	APO (PHA)
2000 CO101	Xk	29.27 billion	3.39 billion	7.236	APO (PHA)
Dionysus	Cb	2.62 trillion	303.98 billion	7.182	APO (PHA)
1999 CF9	Q	152.75 million	17.53 million	7.247	APO (PHA)
2002 AH29	K	7.77 billion	892.45 million	7.212	AMO
1986 DA	M	4.25 trillion	484.67 billion	7.230	AMO
Davidharvey	C	53.90 trillion	6.14 trillion	7.237	AMO
1996 BZ3	X	73.17 billion	8.31 billion	7.254	AMO
2001 HA8	C	1.51 trillion	169.13 billion	7.319	AMO
Apollo	Q	805.03 million	88.33 million	7.486	APO (PHA)

(continued)

Table 6.2 (continued)

Name	Type	Value ($)	Est. profit ($)	Δv (km/s)	Group
2000 LC16	Xk	4.23 trillion	473.46 billion	7.325	AMO
2001 WH2	X	4.62 billion	497.01 million	7.547	AMO
2000 WC67	X	296.27 billion	32.12 billion	7.490	AMO
Atlantis	L	42.41 trillion	4.56 trillion	7.541	MCA
1998 HT31	C	10.42 billion	1.11 billion	7.590	APO (PHA)
2000 WJ10	Xk	3.50 billion	373.31 million	7.601	AMO
2001 HW15	X	3.50 billion	362.49 million	7.801	AMO
1999 VN6	C	62.78 billion	6.50 billion	7.787	AMO
2001 XS1	Cb	125.08 billion	13.15 billion	7.655	AMO
Eger	Xe	442.75 billion	44.75 billion	7.962	APO
Calingasta	Cb	18.08 trillion	1.87 trillion	7.764	MCA
Vishnu	O	242.46 billion	23.26 billion	8.356	APO (PHA)
2000 BG19	X	727.45 billion	74.70 billion	7.795	AMO
Zao	X	1.60 trillion	162.00 billion	7.885	AMO
1999 SE10	X	5.30 billion	547.05 million	7.750	AMO
1999 JM8	X	45.00 trillion	4.58 trillion	7.856	APO (PHA)
1994 AH2	O	21.02 trillion	2.11 trillion	7.952	APO
2000 WL10	Xc	80.47 billion	8.11 billion	7.907	APO
1997 SE5	T	66.28 million	6.74 million	7.826	AMO
2000 BM19	O	1.21 trillion	96.45 billion	9.949	ATE
1997 US9	Q	67.65 million	6.01 million	8.943	APO
2001 SJ262	C	30.61 billion	3.04 billion	7.984	AMO
Ra-Shalom	Xc	1.76 trillion	130.81 billion	10.649	ATE
1997 AQ18	C	286.95 billion	25.10 billion	9.072	APO
1999 HF1	X	9.21 trillion	556.48 billion	13.130	ATE
1999 YK5	X	7.66 trillion	475.70 billion	12.767	ATE
1999 JD6	K	4.77 trillion	254.78 billion	14.844	ATE (PHA)
2000 WO107	X	17.40 billion	726.21 million	18.990	ATE (PHA)
1997 AC11	Xc	2.92 billion	170.57 million	13.562	ATE
2000 EA107	Q	1.06 billion	61.22 million	13.755	ATE
2000 CK33	Xk	63.73 billion	4.55 billion	11.090	ATE
Poseidon	O	33.21 trillion	3.05 trillion	8.626	APO
2002 DH2	Ch	20.79 billion	1.96 billion	8.411	APO
Cruithne	Q	2.12 billion	117.66 million	14.240	ATE
1999 FB	Q	175.38 million	14.15 million	9.800	APO
2002 DY3	Xk	48.34 billion	4.31 billion	8.856	AMO
Izhdubar	Q	801.64 million	24.81 million	25.537	APO
2001 YK4	X	314.94 billion	29.45 billion	8.449	APO
2001 XS30	Xc	139.84 billion	7.00 billion	15.782	APO
2000 YH66	Xk	73.17 billion	4.62 billion	12.508	APO
David Hughes	Xe	12.14 trillion	1.11 trillion	8.634	MCA
Phaethon	B	> 100 trillion	5.30 trillion	15.344	APO (PHA)
Bede	Xc	11.47 trillion	1.04 trillion	8.661	AMO
Gressmann	B	81.81 trillion	7.76 trillion	8.314	MBA
2000 CN33	X	16.01 billion	1.51 billion	8.346	AMO
1995 BL2	L	261.02 billion	19.86 billion	10.364	APO

(continued)

Table 6.2 (continued)

Name	Type	Value ($)	Est. profit ($)	Δv (km/s)	Group
2000 BJ19	Q	2.42 billion	130.77 million	14.594	APO
2001 UY4	X	252.55 billion	18.59 billion	10.699	APO (PHA)
2000 WK10	X	48.34 billion	3.77 billion	10.096	APO (PHA)
2002 AU5	X	110.74 billion	9.60 billion	9.079	APO
Tantalus	Q	1.07 billion	35.86 million	23.458	APO (PHA)
Tapio	B	> 100 trillion	> 100 trillion	8.467	MBA
Heracles	O	> 100 trillion	30.31 trillion	9.641	APO

[a]Asterank, accessed on 19 April 2018, http://www.asterank.com/

Table 6.3 Completed missions

Nation	Flyby	Orbit	Landing	Sample return
USA	ICE (1985)	NEAR (1997)	NEAR (2001)	Stardust (2006)
Japan	Suisei (1986)	Hayabusa (2005)	Hayabusa (2005)	Hayabusa (2010)
EU	ICE (1985)	Rosetta (2014)	Rosetta (2014)	
USSR	Vega 1 (1986)			
China	Chang'e 2 (2012)			

Additional Information Resources

https://en.wikipedia.org/wiki/Asteroid_mining

https://techcrunch.com/2016/02/03/the-race-to-mine-asteroids-gains-international-support/

https://www.scientificamerican.com/article/ive-read-references-in-bo/

http://simanima.com/Papers/000001_Asteroid%20Mining%20Essay.pdf

7

Asteroid Impact and Deflection Assessment Mission (AIDA): Space Mining Concepts

Tom James

Introduction

Originated by NASA, the Asteroid Impact and Deflection Assessment (AIDA) mission concept has been tabled by an international collaboration between the US space agency, the ESA, Observatoire de la Cote d'Azur (OCA) and the John Hopkins University Applied Physics Laboratory (JHU/APL).[1]

It represents a world first and consists of a guided missile, which is aimed at a chosen asteroid with the agenda of quantifying and demonstrating the kinetic effects of an 'impactor' space vehicle into an asteroid moon, and to measure any resultant change in the regolith's trajectory. It is intended to assess whether or not such a mission might successfully deflect an asteroid away from, or onto, a direct course towards Earth.

This sounds like an alarming concept, however, the theory behind a pre-meditated effort to put an asteroid on a collision course with the Earth would be to bring it closer for mining operations, reducing technological necessities and the fiscal investment needed to mine NEAs that aren't that near Earth. Conversely it could be implemented to remove a potential hazardous space rock.

Any AIDA mission would likely be composed of two spacecrafts:

---

[1] NASA Planetary Defense, Edited by Tricia Talbert, Last updated 14 September 2017, "Asteroid Impact and Deflection Assessment (AIDA) Mission", https://www.nasa.gov/planetarydefense/aida

T. James (✉)
NR Capital & Deep Space Technologies, Singapore, Singapore

© The Author(s) 2018
T. James (ed.), *Deep Space Commodities*,
https://doi.org/10.1007/978-3-319-90303-3_7

- Asteroid Impact Mission, or 'AIM', which would orbit the asteroid.
- Double Action Redirection Test, or 'DART', which might impact its moon.

Besides the observation of the change to a chosen asteroid's orbital parameters, the observation of the plume, the crater and the freshly exposed material is expected to give decipherable and distinctive data for future asteroid deflections to the astrophysical, scientific and mining communities.

AIDA is, at its core, a science-driven test of developing Earth technologies for preventing the impact of hazardous asteroids. However, for mining purposes, controlling asteroids for easier resource mining is advantageous. AIDA's primary mission is to deflect the near-Earth binary asteroid 65,803 Didymos, which will be in unusually close proximity to Earth, relatively speaking, in October 2022.

The 300-kilogram DART space vehicle is designed to affect the Didymos at 7 kilometres per second and exhibit the ability to transform its course through momentum transfer, NASA states.

AIDA will be the primary demonstration of the kinetic impact technique to alter the motion of an asteroid in space. AIDA is a dual-mission conception, involving two freelance space vehicles: NASA's DART and ESA's AIM. The DART mission is in 'Formulation phase A', led by JHU/APL and managed by the Planetary Missions Program workplace at Marshall Space Flight Center for NASA's Planetary Defense Coordination workplace. AIM, managed by ESA's European Space Research and Technology Centre (ESTEC), is in 'Preliminary Definition phase B1'.

As of 2016, the missions were in formative planning stages, with a projected launch for AIM in October 2020, and for DART in July 2021. DART would commence operations to alter Didymos' trajectory around October 2022. As of December 2016, the AIM space vehicle component of AIDA had yet to be funded. Regardless, NASA plans to continue with its part of the programme.

Didymos consists of a primary body around 800 metres across and a secondary body, or 'moonlet', whose 150-metre size is typical of the dimensions of asteroids that would create a hazard to Earth.

The resultant effects of any kinetic impactor to an asteroid are poorly understood at present as to date only a few studies have been dedicated to the process. However, it is of great significance because:

1. It contributes to the understanding of the working environment for improved risk management of space rocks.

2. It provides crucial information for the ground-based observation of the impact outcome, which is planned for AIDA.
3. It contributes to the theoretical understanding of small binary formation mechanisms with a wealth of empirical data.
4. It can be used to estimate the momentum transferred to the impacted body.

Designing an Asteroid Mission

Didymos is a 'binary asteroid system' where one asteroid, in this case Didymos, is orbited by a smaller one. The first asteroid is approximated to be 800 metres (2,600 feet) in diameter; its tiny satellite is measured at 150 metres (490 feet) in diameter in an orbit of 1.1 kilometres from the primary asteroid. Didymos isn't an Earth-crossing asteroid, and there's no chance from preliminary calculations that the proposed deflection experiment would produce resultant danger to our Blue Planet. The assessment continues.

As already mentioned, under the current tabled proposal, AIM would launch in October 2020, and DART in July 2021. AIM would orbit the larger asteroid and study the composition of it and its moon. DART would then impact the laze in October 2022. AIM would study the result on the asteroid moon's orbit round the larger asteroid.

AIDA can give information on the asteroid's strength, surface physical properties and its internal structure. There's likely to be a wealth of information gleaned from the ensuing impact crater created by DART.

DART + AIM = A

Although DART and AIM are independent missions, together they will provide the first measurements of a planetary-scale impact experiment with controlled impact conditions on a well-researched and quantified target body.

DART

• NASA's DART mission[2] is currently a Phase A study. DART is a strategic technology demonstration that will launch in 2020 and impact the second-

---

[2] NASA, Edited by Tricia Talbert, Last updated 30 August 2017, "Double Asteroid Redirection Test (DART) Mission", https://www.nasa.gov/planetarydefense/dart/

ary rock of the Didymos binary system in 2022. DART will be a full-scale demonstration of asteroid deflection by kinetic impact.

- DART will develop our understanding of the impact effects at large scales, provide information of a given asteroid's properties and study long-term dynamics of impact ejecta.
- DART will use ground-based observations to measure the binary period change from kinetic impact with an accuracy of 10 percent.
- DART will return high-resolution images of the target prior to impact to determine the impact site and its geologic context.

AIDA: Critical Test of Asteroid Mitigation by Kinetic Impact

- The asteroid threat is simulated to be international, of global proportions. Initially following the discovery of a hazardous asteroid, its impact location is uncertain, spanning borders and continents. Eventually the predicted impact is to be pinpointed to a specific geographical and political point, but even then, its effects will likely be global. Prevention, preparation and recovery must be coordinated internationally to benefit from worldwide resources and expertise.
- Techniques for deflecting a hazardous asteroid require demonstration and validation prior to implementation against a real threat. Kinetic deflection facilitated by launching a rocket at an asteroid to move it off course has been identified as the most capable method of deflecting most asteroids, except for rare objects that may appear suddenly or are of an extremely large size.
- Sophisticated models exist for simulating kinetic deflection, but the predicted amount of deflection depends on physical properties that have never been measured on any asteroid, which is what the AIDA project is designed to measure.
- The scale of a kinetic deflection event is much larger than can be accessed in laboratory experiments, and occurs in a microgravity geology, so Earth-based experiments are helpful but insufficient.
- Until kinetic deflection models are benchmarked via data from actual asteroid/s, their predictions will have unknown uncertainties and the possibility of unexpected behaviour will persist.
- AIDA will characterize the physical properties and internal structure of the target asteroid prior to the kinetic impact, providing solid science for making quantitative predictions of deflection.

- AIDA will provide an end-to-end test of the integrated technology required to carry out an asteroid deflection mission.

DART Impact During Excellent Apparition

- Didymos at V~14–15 is very well placed for Chile and observable from other observatories.
- Didymos primary and secondary are separated by up to 0.02 arcseconds when 0.08 AU from Earth. Marginally resolvable with ALMA (sub-mm), Magellan adaptive optics.
- Post-impact brightening and ejecta stream as extended object (coma) may be observable from Earth.
- Debris cloud analogous to YORP-driven main belt comets (MBCs)?

A list of the investigation working groups is given in Table 7.1

Current Status

Together AIM and DART were given a green light for Phase A/B1 study in February of 2015 for a period of 15 months.

Baseline payloads for AIM include a navigation camera, a lander (based on DLR MASCOT heritage), a thermal infrared imager, a monostatic high frequency radar, a bistatic low frequency radar (on the orbiter and on the lander), and some opportunity payloads based on CubeSat standards. AIM is conceived as a small and simple platform with no mechanisms providing a flight opportunity to demonstrate technologies to advance future small and medium missions.

As such, AIM will also demonstrate for the first time the use of deep-space optical communication. It will allow for the first time accessing direct infor-

Table 7.1 AIDA investigation working groups

WG 1	Modelling and Simulation of Impact Outcomes	Angela Stickle, Paul Miller, Steven Schwartz
WG 2	Remote Sensing Observations	Andy Rivkin, Petr Pravec
WG 3	Dynamical and Physical Properties of Didymos	Derek Richardson, Kleomenis Tsiganis, Adriano Campo-Bagatin
WG 4	Science Proximity Operations	Stephan Ulamec, Olivier Barnouin

mation on the internal and subsurface structures of a small asteroid, and with DART, determining the influence of those internal properties on the impact outcome. The DART mission will use a single spacecraft to impact the smaller member of the binary near-Earth asteroid (NEA) Didymos in October 2022. DART uses a simple, high-technology-readiness and low-cost spacecraft to intercept Didymos. DART carries no scientific payload other than an imager for targeting and data acquisition. The impact of the >300-kilogram DART spacecraft at 6.1 kilometres per second will change the mutual orbit of these two objects. By targeting the smaller, 150-metre diameter member of a binary system, the DART mission produces an orbital deflection which is both larger and easier to measure than would be the case if DART targeted a typical, single NEA so as to change its heliocentric orbit. It is important to note that the target Didymos is not an Earth-crossing asteroid, and there is no possibility that the DART deflection experiment would create an impact hazard.

The DART asteroid deflection demonstration targets the binary asteroid Didymos in October 2022, during a close approach to Earth. The DART impact will be observable by ground-based radar and optical telescopes around the world, providing exciting opportunities for international participation in the mission, and generating tremendous international public interest, in the first asteroid deflection experiment.

Germany offered to cover 35 million of the 60 million required for the AIM portion to continue, but this wasn't enough to continue development. However, National Aeronautics and Space Administration will still continue with an alternative portion of the mission, DART, thus overall AIDA will continue in a way. The director has aforesaid that he may also be able to revive the AIM portion of the mission in future before the timeline for meeting the launch window passes. It's technically potential for the DART mission to continue, however, it's going to need a lot of support from the bottom, and therefore the AIDA programme overall would be empty information that AIM would supply.

The DART space vehicle can succeed the kinetic impact by deliberately colliding with the moonlet at roughly 6 kilometres per second, with the help of an aboard camera and an advanced autonomous navigation software package. The speed of the moonlet in its orbit around the main body will be altered by a fraction of 1 percent—large enough to be measured by exploitation telescopes on Earth. By targeting the little moonlet in an exceedingly binary numeration system, the AIDA mission set up makes these exact measurements achievable and makes sure that there's no probability of the impact unknowingly producing a hazard to Earth.

The DART space vehicle can utilize the National Aeronautics and Space Administration evolutionary Xenon Thruster—industrial and commercial

(NEXT-C) solar electrical propulsion system as its main in-space propulsion system. NEXT-C—developed at NASA's Glenn centre in Cleveland, Ohio—is the next generation system that has supported the Dawn space vehicle system. The use of electrical propulsion means that DART is ready to realize important flexibility to the mission timeline and expand their launch window.

The AIM space vehicle, with its in-depth collection of scientific instruments, should reach Didymos before DART's impact. It will then perform the first close-up study of a binary asteroid, supplying high-resolution images of the surfaces of the positional notation in addition to measurements of the densities, masses and shapes of its two bodies. AIM will be able to move to a secure distance from which to watch DART's impact and examine ejected material within the ensuing plume. AIM's instruments can observe the consequences of the collision and create precise conclusions of the momentum transferred to the moonlet.

AIM can investigate potential mass transfer between the two bodies, live crater formation and material distribution after the impact, and it can constrain the inner structure and make-up of this interesting binary asteroid. A surface package, MASCOT-2 (Mobile Asteroid Surface Scout), will be deployed by AIM to characterize the moonlet before, during and after the DART impact. AIM will be the primary space vehicle to demonstrate heavenly body visual communications.

This distinctive double mission situation incorporates the launch of ESA's AIM artificial satellite in October 2020. A meeting with the Didymos system will follow in 2022. The launch of NASA's DART artificial satellite will be in late 2020 and it will intercept Didymos' moonlet in early October 2022, when the Didymos system is less than 11 million kilometres from Earth. This will make facultative observations by ground-based telescopes and planetary radio detection and ranging possible.

Key benefits if AIDA data

AIDA can return fundamental new information on the mechanical response and impact cratering method at real asteroid scales, and consequently on the collisional evolution of asteroids with implications for planetary defence, human space travel and near-Earth object science and resource utilization. AIDA is able to return distinctive data on an asteroid's strength, surface physical properties and internal structure. Supporting numerical simulation studies and laboratory experiments are going to be required to understand the potential benefits of AIDA and these can be an integral a part of the mission.

Mining Concepts: Deflected or Not

Asteroid mining will shift from being relegated to the realms of enthusiastic sci-fi dreams to world-changing reality a lot quicker than one might think, as key participants in the push to mine all those regoliths, orbiting tantalizingly close to our technological capability, forge ahead with exploratory missions and flex their space muscles.

Whether we choose to deflect these space rocks a little closer for comfort or not, one company at the forefront of researching these asteroids is Planetary Resources. The company has deployed its first space vehicle from the International Space Station (ISS), the beginning of this Washington-based asteroid-mining concern's plans to launch a series of increasingly capable probes over the coming years.

Its goal is to find a rock containing sufficient water content to convert into a rocket propellant within a decade and eventually to reap valuable and helpful platinum-group metals from NEAs.

"We have every expectation that delivering water from asteroids and making an in-space fueling economy are a few things that we'll see within the next ten years … even within the half of the 2020s," Chris Lewicki, Planetary Resources President and Chief Engineer, claims.[3]

Talking about the timeline for going after asteroid metals, Lewicki commented: "After that, I believe it's progressing to be how the market develops".[4]

"If there is one factor that we have seen repeat throughout history, it's [that] you tend to over predict what'll happen within the next year, however you tend to immensely under predict what's going to happen within the next ten years", he added.[5]

Degrading and Exploiting the Resources of Space

Planetary Resources and Deep Space Industries (DSI) both aim to assist humanity in extending its stellar footprint out into the solar system by tapping asteroid resources.

---

[3] Space.Com, by Mike Wall, 11 August 2015, "Asteroid Mining May Be a Reality by 2025", https://www.space.com/30213-asteroid-mining-planetary-resources-2025.html

[4] Space.Com, by Mike Wall, 11 August 2015, "Asteroid Mining May Be a Reality by 2025", https://www.space.com/30213-asteroid-mining-planetary-resources-2025.html

[5] Space.Com, by Mike Wall, 11 August 2015, "Asteroid Mining May Be a Reality by 2025", https://www.space.com/30213-asteroid-mining-planetary-resources-2025.html

This whole concept relies upon harvesting water, which is in plentiful supply in a category of rock called carbonaceous chondrites. Asteroid-derived water may do much more than merely quench an astronaut's thirst, mining advocates say. It can be used to shield them from dangerous radiation and, once split into its constituent chemical element and oxygen, enable voyaging spaceships to replenish their fuel tanks whilst in transit.

The technology to locate and extract asteroid water isn't significantly difficult or overtly expensive to implement, so Planetary Resources has found out. Its exploratory scientific space vehicles have discovered this most precious liquid on celestial bodies—and obtaining this fluid from an asteroid may merely involve partitioning the strata of an asteroid containing water and exposing it to the heat of the Sun for collection.

Carbonaceous chondrites also usually contain metals such as iron, which is traditionally used in construction, so targeting these asteroids may permit miners to begin building off-Earth structures. That's the logical next step in the chain of opportunities derived from exploiting water.

The gold at the tip of the rainbow will be the extraction and exploitation of platinum-group metals that are rare here on Earth but extremely necessary to the manufacturing of differing sophisticated products.

Ultimately, what Planetary Resources wishes to try to do is produce a space-based business that is an economic engine that will actually reveal space to the remainder of the economy.

So far, every frontier that we've unfolded on our planet Earth has either been within the pursuit of resources, or we've been ready to keep in this frontier as a result of the native resources that were offered to us.

Why should space be any different?

Asteroid Mining Probes

As yet nobody is mining asteroids, however, companies like Planetary Resources and DSI do have some hardware in space. Planetary Resources Arkyd-3R CubeSat completed a 90-day mission to check astronautics, software and alternative key technology following its launch on 16 July 2015 from the ISS.

Planetary Resources is currently working on its next space vehicle, which may be a 6 U CubeSat known as Arkyd-6. One "U", or "unit", is the basic CubeSat building block, as was previously noted, a cube measuring 4 inches, or 10 centimetres, on its sides.

The Arkyd-6, was successfully launched into orbit from SpaceX's Falcon 9 rocket on 18 January 2018. It featured advanced astronautics and electronics, also acting as a colloquially-termed 'selfie cam' that was funded by a so-called Kickstarter Project years back. The CubeSat carried associated instruments designed to find water and water-bearing minerals for Planetary Resources.[6]

The data obtained from the Arkyd-6 will be valuable in the development of the Arkyd-301, the company's next spacecraft—marking the beginning of Planetary Resources' space resource exploration programme according to information provided by Brian L. Wang, MBA, a long-time futurist and lecturer at the Singularity University (and an author for internet portal Nextbigfuture.com).

In the process of engineering the Arkyd-6, the Planetary Resources' team was able to modify commercial hardware to be used in space, allowing for the possibility of deep-space missions at greatly reduced costs. This process also allows for control at every stage of development and production, resulting in a reliable and innovative product.

"The success of the Arykd-6 will validate and inform the design and engineering philosophies we have embraced since the beginning of this innovative project", said Lewicki.[7] "We will continue to employ these methods through the development of the Arkyd-301 and beyond as we progress toward our Space Resource Exploration Mission."

Out of 17 elements that will be tested during Arkyd-6's flight, one of the most crucial technologies is the on-board mid-wave infrared (MWIR) imager. The technical team qualified a commercial sensor to collect pixel-level data and integrated custom optics, creating the world's first commercial MWIR instrument to be used in space. Based on the findings from this initial flight, Planetary Resources will further develop this sensor technology into the most advanced water resource detection hardware available, which will be incorporated into Arkyd-301.

Chris Voorhees, Chief Engineer at Planetary Resources, said, "If all of the experimental systems operate successfully, Planetary Resources intends to use the Arkyd-6 satellite to capture MWIR images of targets on Earth's surface, including agricultural land, resource exploration regions, and infrastructure for mining and energy. In addition, we will also have the opportunity to perform specific celestial observations from our vantage point in low Earth orbit.

---

[6] Next Big Future, By Brian Wang, 12 January 2018, "Planetary Resources Arkyd-6 launched and deployed successfully", https://www.nextbigfuture.com/2018/01/planetary-resources-arkyd-6-launched-and-deployed-successfully.html

[7] Planetary Resources company site article 12th January 2018. https://www.planetaryresources.com/2018/01/planetary-resources-launches-latest-spacecraft-in-advance-of-space-resource-exploration-mission/

Lessons learned from Arkyd-6 will inform the company's approach as it builds on this technology to enable the scientific and economic evaluation of asteroids during its future Space Resource Exploration Mission."[8]

Arkyd-6 will be testing additional technologies such as power generation, attitude determination, instrument operation and two-way communication. Although the spacecraft is fully autonomous and able to execute all functions independently, it will continue to communicate with Mission Control through every critical check point.

Also in the mining mix, for its part, DSI is also building a space vehicle and aims to launch its initial resource-harvesting mission before 2020, company representatives have said.

The Competition to Mine Asteroids

It's still barely the beginning of the twenty-first century and already the personal space business is starting to take shape. Elon Musk's SpaceX has launched the world's first in private developed spacecraft, the Dragon, to dock with the ISS. Meanwhile, different private firms are developing space vehicles, and even toying with plans to send individuals to Mars. Several of those ideas are still barely past their origination, however, they are being taken seriously by the likes of NASA and Musk.

The two asteroid mining firms featured in this chapter, DSI and Planetary Resources, have an identical primary objective, however, their strategies are somewhat different. Planetary Resources is presently developing small, low-cost telescopes to survey asteroids from Earth orbit. They later plan to develop two larger styles of prospecting craft.

The aggressively named Interceptor can act as a prospector, with the ability to intercept any asteroids that come inside 10–30 times the Earth-moon orbit, a phenomenon which occurs quite frequently. Interceptor missions will allow Planetary Resources to quickly acquire data on several so-called NEAs.

Ultimately, the 'rendezvous prospector' spacecraft would be able to travel halfway across the inner system to assemble elaborate information regarding asteroids, in addition to cataloguing their size, shape, rotation and density. The company plans to develop craft to gather samples from and eventually mine whole asteroids, however, these plans have yet to reach the public arena.

---

[8] Planetary Resources website, Press release 12 January 2018, "Planetary Resources Launches Latest Spacecraft In Advance Of Space Resource Exploration Mission", https://www.planetaryresources.com/2018/01/planetary-resources-launches-latest-spacecraft-in-advance-of-space-resource-exploration-mission/

Conversely DSI is taking a more forthright approach. As already reported, it currently has two planned space vehicles. The first is the Firefly, which will prospect for appropriate asteroids to mine. Then its larger Dragonfly spacecraft comes in to play, designed to mine materials from the target asteroid.

The operations of private corporations such as SpaceX are funded by significant investment from NASA, unlike the billionaire backer behind Planetary Resources. It's notable, though, that several of the goals of the asteroid-mining corporations also are in line with NASA's existing science and exploration objectives. Rock samples taken from asteroids may prove very helpful in scientific research.

Where Might This All Lead?

Asteroid mining is already seen as becoming a necessity for the future of humankind, fuelled by advancing technologies that continue to facilitate the increasing consumption of Earth's resources. Asteroids are plentiful and jam-packed with usable metals and alternative resources, which means that any asteroid-mining venture stands to become terribly rich.

Couple this with the fact that proposed orbital fuel depots and off-planet construction facilities may considerably scale back the inherent problem of costs associated with space exploration, making things that bit easier. The net result could be that gathering resources from asteroids might not solely boost the economy here on Earth but become a key driver for the exploration of the solar system.

Reduced prices, the orbital production and accessibility of materials in space will likely facilitate the establishment of distant parts of the solar system and by the close of this century pundits suggest the space industry could see outposts, not that different in principle to the ISS, in remote parts of the solar system.

The end of this century might even see an 'asteroid rush' not dissimilar to the gold rushes of the nineteenth century in the Klondike, where an estimated 100,000 prospectors flocked to the region of the Yukon in north-western Canada between 1896 and 1899.

Yet the hard truth is that, whereas it has overwhelming potential, asteroid mining is fraught with difficulties and obstacles. To date, only one space probe has ever successfully retrieved and returned a sample of asteroid material; others have tried unsuccessfully. Much of the technology required by DSI and Planetary Resources does not exist, but there is an inevitability to it. Development continues regardless.

Add on Materials

Earth's resources are becoming more and more scarce. For example, the push for oil, gas and valuable minerals happening within the Arctic is the result of an amalgamation of world shortages, inflation and technical advances. Most commentators expect the Arctic to play a key role in meeting the world's energy needs throughout the twenty-first century.

The United States Geological Survey estimates that the Arctic holds 30 percent of the world's undiscovered gas and that 80 percent of that lies underneath the glaciers and waves offshore. On land, the areas exploited for minerals or hydrocarbons are likely to remain comparatively small.

So, it's high time to look off of our planet for essential resources, even deflecting the bounty towards us. There are still decades until the development of asteroid mining reaches a feasible and economically viable stage. Our scientific and technological developments will eventually see humankind expand, breaching the limits of our native star system.

Other Useful Information Resources
http://www.esa.int/Our_Activities/Space_Engineering_Technology/Asteroid_Impact_Mission/Asteroid_Impact_Deflection_Assessment_mission

https://hal-insu.archives-ouvertes.fr/insu-01282898

http://www.space.com/30213-asteroid-mining-planetary-resources-2025.html

https://www.seeker.com/asteroid-mining-booming-21st-century-gold-rush-1766444290.html

https://www.quora.com/Is-there-anything-of-worth-on-the-planets-in-our-solar-system-like-gold-or-something-like-helium-3

http://www.planet-science.com/categories/over-11s/space/2012/04/mining-in-space.aspx

https://astronaut.com/developing-an-off-planet-mining-industry/

8

A Briefing on the Legal and Geopolitical Facets of Space Resources

Michael J. Listner

Introduction

The issue of space resources is polarizing and fraught with misinformation and hyperbole. The purpose of this chapter is to dispose of the political narrative, posturing and hyperbole surrounding space resources and provide an objective analysis that briefly discusses the law surrounding the issue of space resources, a brief legislative history and a discussion of the legal theory, arguments and issues surrounding the model of space resources. Additionally, this briefing will discuss the potential geopolitical effects and consequences the paradigm of space resources could manifest as well as the pitfalls the concept might create internationally.

The Legal and Political Background of Space Resources

To understand the issue of space resources, it is helpful to preface the concept with a discussion of the international law of outer space and legislative history that surrounds the space resource debate before delving into the intricacies of the concept. A synopsis of the relevant space law and legislative history follows.

M. J. Listner (✉)
Space Law & Policy Solutions, Boston, MA, USA
e-mail: Michael@spacelawsolutions.com

© The Author(s) 2018
T. James (ed.), *Deep Space Commodities*,
https://doi.org/10.1007/978-3-319-90303-3_8

The Outer Space Treaty

The Treaty on Principles Governing the Activities of States in the Exploration and Use of Outer Space, Including the Moon and Other Celestial Bodies (Outer Space Treaty) represents the fundamentals of international space law both through principles and legal duties.[1] The Outer Space Treaty was suggested by President Eisenhower and was considered a non-armament treaty modelled on the Antarctic Treaty of 1959. The intent of the Outer Space Treaty, like the Antarctic Treaty, was to prevent so-called colonial competition, especially amongst the growing space powers of the time. The Outer Space Treaty was signed and ratified by the US and Soviet Union in 1967. As already noted, the Outer Space Treaty was modelled after the Antarctic Treaty and mirrors many of its provisions, including the concept of *res communis* or the province of all humankind.[2]

The concept of *res communis* is found in two places in the Outer Space Treaty. Article I, paragraph 1 articulates the "province of all mankind" language:

The exploration and use of outer space, including the moon and other celestial bodies, shall be carried out for the benefit and in the interests of all countries, irrespective of their degree of economic or scientific development, and shall be the province of all mankind.

Article II continues to articulate the *res communis* principle in that:

Outer space, including the moon and other celestial bodies,[3] is not subject to national appropriation by claim of sovereignty, by means of use or occupation, or by any other means.

---

[1] *See generally*, UN General Assembly Resolution 2222 (XXI). Treaty on Principles Governing the Activities of States in the Exploration and Use of Outer Space, including the Moon and Other Celestial Bodies available at http://www.unoosa.org/oosa/en/ourwork/spacelaw/treaties/outerspacetreaty.html

[2] *Res communis* is a concept derived from Roman property law that refers to the light and the air. *See* Merriam-Webster Dictionary at https://www.merriam-webster.com/dictionary/res%20communes. *See also*, BLACK's LAW DICTIONARY, Sixth Edition, *res communes*—"In the civil law, things common to all; that is, those things which are used and enjoyed by everyone, even in the single parts, but can never be exclusively acquired as a whole, e.g. light and air." The idea behind *res communis* in the reference to both the Antarctic Treaty and the Outer Space Treaty is that no sovereign can extend (state) ownership much in the same way no one can extend control over the air or the light. In other words, in the case of outer space and celestial bodies, they belong to no nation. It is notable in regards to usage and passage, the high seas are considered *res communis*.

[3] The Outer Space Treaty does not define the term 'celestial bodies', but it is accepted that celestial bodies are any natural body residing outside of the Earth's atmosphere. This includes everything from stars and planets to meteoroids that have not survived reentry to land on the surface of the Earth. One legal defini-

Proponents of property rights in celestial bodies and their resources note the exclusion of the express prohibition of private individuals, which leads to the reasoning private individuals are not prohibited from owning celestial bodies and the resources on or within. This has led to a multitude of 'private claims' including one individual who has claimed the Moon and is selling parcels of lunar real estate to include the mineral rights.[4] Others have claimed asteroids in their entirety to include mineral rights, and one challenge in particular made it to federal court where it was rejected.[5] Despite these attempts at asserting private property rights on celestial bodies, the general legal sense is that Article II does not create a loophole for private individuals.

The fundamental effect of Article I and Article II is that property rights, whether real or personal, are precluded by the *res communis* principle.[6] This means mining in the traditional legal sense, which recognizes natural resources within and affixed to the land as a real property interest, is precluded for both sovereign nations and its citizens. However, the inherent ambiguity of the Outer Space Treaty and Article II in particular has created a split with regards

---

tion that was proffered for celestial body is "natural objects in outer space ... which cannot be artificially moved from their natural orbits." *See*, M Smirnoff, 1966, "Introductory Report and Summary of Discussions – Draft Resolution on the Legal Status of Celestial Bodies", 9 PCLOS 8, quoting IISL Draft Resolution, principle 1. This definition opens the potential scenario where a celestial body such as an asteroid or comet could be moved by artificial means, which would no longer make it legally a celestial body, thus subjecting it to national appropriation.

[4] Dennis Hope is the creator of Lunar Embassy. He emphasizes the express lack of a prohibition for private individuals to own celestial bodies in the Outer Space Treaty to assert a claim to the Moon in its entirety. He has built a substantial business selling parcels of lunar real estate to private citizens. His claims also extend to other planets in the solar system using the same legal rationale. *See* Lunar Embassy at https://www.lunarembassy.com/. At this point, Mr Hope's claims have neither been challenged nor supported by the US government, but the government of China did move against an office Lunar Embassy opened in that company and shut down Mr Hope's activities in that country.

[5] Gregory W. Nemitz, the self-proclaimed owner of Asteroid 433, Eros, fined NASA US$20 for landing the NEAR/Shoemaker spacecraft on the surface of the asteroid on 12 February 2001. NASA refused to pay the fine and Nemitz subsequently filed a *pro se* lawsuit in the federal district court for the district of Nevada alleging a taking under the 5th Amendment of the US Constitution. NASA, through the Department of Justice, filed a motion to dismiss arguing Nemitz failed to establish a cognizable property interest in the Eros asteroid, which is required for there to be a taking. The Court agreed with NASA and dismissed Nemitz's lawsuit. Nemitz appealed to the 9th Circuit Court of Appeals (*Nemitz v. N.A.S.A.*, 126 Fed.Appx. 343 (Cir. 2005)), which upheld the district court's decision. Although Nemitz filed both his lawsuit and appeal *pro se*, he reportedly received assistance from a space law attorney who is a known advocate of space property rights. Information on Nemitz's website suggests he manufactured the dispute for the specific reason of proving the existence of private property rights in celestial bodies and the resources affixed and within. Nemitz maintains a website detailing his exchange with NASA and the Court at http://www.erosproject.com/

[6] One solution to alleviate the restrictions of the Outer Space Treaty with regards to private property ownership is to invoke Article XVI, which allows withdrawal from the Treaty. Withdrawal from the Outer Space Treaty would not leave a legal vacuum as many of the principles and legal obligations could continue as customary international law while eliminating the *res communis* principle. At this juncture, there is little political appetite to withdraw from the Treaty and may remain so for the foreseeable future.

to resources on or within celestial bodies as to whether their extraction is prohibited as well. The consensus position is that natural resources on or within celestial bodies are not subject to the prohibition because 'resources' are not explicitly mentioned in Article II. This distinction is critical to make the theory of space resources.[7]

Two other provisions of the Outer Space Treaty relevant to space resources are Article VI and Article VIII. Article VI creates a legal duty on a government to 'authorize' and 'supervise' the outer space activities of non-governmental entities, that is, private individuals.[8] Article VI in essence permits a government to create a private interest in outer space activities for its citizens but requires that government to authorize (license) and supervise those activities. Article VI privileges for private entities in the US was created by the Reagan Administration in National Security Decision Directive Number 42 (NSDD Number 42).[9] The directive in NSDD Number 42 was enacted legislatively on 30 October 1984 in the Commercial Space Launch Act of 1984 [Public Law 98–575].[10]

The final provision of the Outer Space Treaty pertinent to space resources is Article VIII. Article VIII states:

---

[7] There is no legal or historical rationale for excluding resources from the prohibition of ownership of 'celestial bodies' in Article II. Indeed, the only reason for supporting an interpretation that separates resources from the prohibition surrounding celestial bodies is to facilitate a geopolitical/industry end. In other words, proponents of space resources are taking advantage of allowance of broad interpretations of the Outer Space Treaty to make the Outer Space Treaty say what they want. On the other hand, even though a prohibition on resource extraction is not expressly prohibited in Article II of the Outer Space Treaty, a prohibition could be implied taking into consideration the context of its sibling the Antarctic Treaty and its 1992 Environmental Protocol, which specifically bans mineral exploitation. *See* Protocol on Environmental Protection to the Antarctic Treaty, art. 7, available at http://www.ats.aq/documents/ recatt/Att006_e.pdf. *But see*, Protocol on Environmental Protection to the Antarctic Treaty, art. 25(5)(a), which stipulates "the prohibition on Antarctic mineral resource activities contained therein shall continue *unless there is in force a binding legal regime on Antarctic mineral resource activities that includes an agreed means for determining whether, and, if so, under which conditions, any such activities would be acceptable.*" (Emphasis added.)

[8] During the negotiations for the Outer Space Treaty, the United States insisted on the recognition of the right for private entities to perform commercial activities in outer space. The USSR pushed back, insisting only government actors be allowed to perform outer space activities; however, a compromise prevailed where the view of the US was accepted by the USSR with the caveat outer space activities by private entities must be authorized and supervised.

[9] "The United States Government will provide a climate conducive to expanded private sector investment and involvement in civil space activities, with due regard to public safety and national security. Private sector space activities will be authorized and supervised or regulated by the government to the extent required by treaty and national security." National Security Decision Directive Number 42, paragraph III (B) available at http://marshall.wpengine.com/wp-content/uploads/2013/09/NSDD-42-National-Space-Policy-4-Jul-1982.pdf

[10] *See generally*, Commercial Space Launch Act [Public Law 98–575], available at http://uscode.house. gov/statutes/pl/98/575.pdf

A State Party to the Treaty on whose registry an object launched into outer space is carried shall retain jurisdiction and control over such object, and over any personnel thereof, while in outer space or on a celestial body. Ownership of objects launched into outer space, including objects landed or constructed on a celestial body, and of their component parts, is not affected by their presence in outer space or on a celestial body or by their return to the Earth. Such objects or component parts found beyond the limits of the State Party to the Treaty on whose registry they are carried shall be returned to that State Party, which shall, upon request, furnish identifying data prior to their return.

The effect of Article VIII is that any object launched into space continues to be the property of and under the jurisdiction of the nation that launched it. The legal effect of Article VIII cuts off a right to salvage or possession via the law of finds and pure salvage as recognized by maritime law.[11] The continuing jurisdiction of Article VIII also extends to objects launched by non-governmental entities, but more importantly the continuing jurisdiction of Article VIII extends to personnel. This means those personnel will be performing their space activities under the colour of their respective governments.

The Moon Agreement of 1979

Ancillary to the Outer Space Treaty is the Agreement Governing the Activities of States on the Moon and Other Celestial Bodies, otherwise known as the Moon Agreement of 1979.[12] The Moon Agreement was an effort to prevent a perceived threat to the exploitation of extraterrestrial resources and the resulting potential of conflict over those resources by the US and potentially the USSR.[13] The Moon Agreement espouses the principle of *res nullius* or the common heritage of humankind. In the context of the Moon Agreement, both *res nullius* and the common heritage of humankind means the exploration and use of outer space resources; non-appropriation of *in-place* resources relating specifically to outer-space mining activities; and the institution of an international regime to supervise commercial resource extraction on celestial

---

[11] In this way, Article VIII makes objects launched into space similar in principle to the legal status of federal warships, which are not subject to the law of finds or pure salvage unless they are expressly abandoned. *See R.M.S. Titanic, Inc. v. The Wrecked & Abandoned Vessel*, 742 F.Supp.2d 784, 793 (E.D.Va. 2010) available at http://law.justia.com/cases/federal/district-courts/FSupp2/323/724/2492882/

[12] *See generally*, UN Resolution 34/68. Agreement Governing the Activities of States on the Moon and Other Celestial Bodies, available at http://www.unoosa.org/oosa/en/ourwork/spacelaw/treaties/moon-agreement.html

[13] *See* Matthew Kleinman, Jennifer Lamie, and Maria Vittoria, *The Laws of Spaceflight*, p. 66.

bodies.[14] Notably, the *res nullius*/common heritage of humankind principle is also applied by the Law of the Sea Convention.[15]

The Moon Treaty creates a legal environment that envisions commercial resource exploitation of resources with the caveat that the extraction of the resources would be licensed by an international regime subject to royalties. While this regime is not defined in the Moon Agreement, it is likely similar in scope to the proposed 'Enterprise' in Article 170 of the UN Convention on the Law of the Sea.[16] It is because of this (and other reasons that go beyond the scope of this chapter) that the US, the Soviet Union and by extension the Russian Federation and the People's Republic of China refused to sign, ratify or otherwise become a party to the Moon Agreement.[17] Twenty-one nations are presently parties to the Moon Agreement with 17 either ratifying or acceding to it.[18] Contrast this with over 100 nations who have signed, ratified or acceded to the Outer Space Treaty.

Even though there are sufficient ratifications/accessions to the Moon Agreement to make it legally-binding international law, the Agreement is considered failed international law because of the refusal of the US, Russia and China (the Big Three) to become a party to it.[19] Despite the Moon Agreement's questionable legal standing, it does stand at loggerheads with the concept of space resources, which makes it relevant to the discussion.

---

[14] *See Common Heritage of Mankind Principle*, Encyclopedia.com available at http://www.encyclopedia.com/science/encyclopedias-almanacs-transcripts-and-maps/common-heritage-mankind-principle

[15] The Law of the Sea Convention and the Moon Agreement were created concurrently, which makes them sibling treaties. In fact, the Moon Agreement has more in common with the Law of the Sea than it does with the Outer Space Treaty.

[16] *See* United Nations Convention on the Law of the Sea (UNCLOS), art. 170, available at http://www.un.org/depts/los/convention_agreements/texts/unclos/unclos_e.pdf

[17] The Moon Agreement was open for signature and ratification at the end of the term of President Jimmy Carter, who supported ratification. Due in part to persistent lobbying by the L5 Society, the Senate Foreign Relations Committee refused to hold a session on ratification. When President Reagan took office, he considered both the Law of the Sea and the Moon Agreement and made the decision to continue negotiations to annex the Law of the Sea and put the Moon Agreement off to the side. *See generally*, UN Moon Treaty Falling to US Opposition Groups, L5 News, March 1982, available at http://www.nss.org/settlement/L5news/1982-opposition.htm, for a brief history of the Moon Treaty and the L5 Society's involvement.

[18] Those countries ratifying/acceding to the Moon Agreement are Australia (1986), Austria (1984), Belgium (2004), Chile (1981), Kazakhstan (1981), Kuwait (2014), Lebanon (2006), Mexico (1991), Morocco (1993), Netherlands (1983), Pakistan (1986), Peru (2005), Philippines (1981), Saudi Arabia (2004), Turkey (2012), Uruguay (1981) and Venezuela (2016). *See generally*, UN Treaty Collection at https://treaties.un.org/Pages/ViewDetails.aspx?src=TREATY&mtdsg_no=XXIV-2&chapter=24&clang=_en for the status of the Moon Treaty.

[19] One of the sticking points of the Moon Treaty with the Big Three is the inclusion of the common heritage of mankind language. Ironically, this same language appears in the UN Convention on the Law of the Sea to which both the Russian Federation and China have ratified; the US is a signatory. *See,* Thomas Gangale, Myths of the Moon Agreement, American Institute of Aeronautics and Astronautics, p. 8, available at https://ops-alaska.com/publications/2008/2008_AIAA-2008-7715.pdf

The Legislative History of Space Resources

The prohibition of private property rights via the *res communis* principle and the failure of the Moon Treaty to provide a solution has not deterred lawyers from finding a work-around to the Outer Space Treaty in the form of domestic legislation. Particularly, legislation in the US led to the concept of space resources, but it was not without failed attempts.

The first attempt at legislation occurred in 2013 with the introduction of H.R. 5063 on 10 July 2014 during the 113th Congress (2013–2014). H.R. 5063 was known as the American Space Technology for Exploring Resource Opportunities In Deep Space Act or the ASTEROIDS Act.[20] The ASTEROIDS Act intended to "promote the right of United States commercial entities to explore and utilize resources from asteroids in outer space, in accordance with the existing international obligations of the United States, free from harmful interference, and to transfer or sell such resources" and develop a legal framework to meet legal obligations under international law. H.R. 5063 went before the House Science, Space and Technology Committee and failed to emerge from Committee after a hearing on the bill.

The second attempt at legislation occurred less than a year later during the first session of the 114th Congress with the introduction of S. 976—Space Resource Exploration and Utilization Act of 2015—in the US Senate on 16 April 2015. The original draft of S. 976 was peculiar in that it expressly sought real property rights as required in traditional mining. However, a review of S. 976 by the Department of State identified that the Outer Space Treaty prohibited private property rights whether real or personal. This forced the industry drafters of S. 976 back to the drawing board, which led to the introduction of the theory of space resources in the place of real property rights. The refined language of S. 976 was then absorbed into H.R. 2262–US Space Launch Competitiveness Act of 2015.

The space resource provisions of H.R. 2262 commanded the attention of the Democrats—who were the minority party—in the House of Representatives. The Democrats on the House Science, Space and Technology Committee called for a hearing to explore the potential international implications of the space resource provisions. However, unlike H.R. 5063, the Republicans refused to grant a hearing over H.R. 2263 and its space resource

---

[20] The text of H.R. 5063 is available at https://www.congress.gov/113/bills/hr5063/BILLS-113hr5063ih.pdf

provisions.[21] The bill passed Committee without a hearing and was subsequently passed by the House of Representatives and the Senate and became Public Law No: 114-90[22] on 25 November 2015.[23]

Understanding the Legal Concept of Space Resources

The concept of space resources is in essence an end-run-around to the *res communis* principle in the Outer Space Treaty and its prohibition of private ownership of celestial bodies, including the resources upon and within. Fundamentally, a mining interest involves a real property interest in that resources within and affixed to the land are considered real property. The space resources law as codified in 51 U.S.C. § 51303 of the United States Code evades the real property nature of mining and converts the "mining" of space resources into an activity and does so by analogizing the harvesting of space resources as an activity similar to "harvesting fish from the sea."

Principally, the concept of space resources relies on a legal theory that real property rights are not necessary to acquire extraterrestrial resources. Rather the concept of 'use' articulated in Article I, paragraph 1 of the Outer Space Treaty[24] proposes to allow certain activities with regards to resources that do not involve a claim of real property.[25] The space resources model theorizes while the Outer Space Treaty forbids the claim of large tracts of real property, it does permit the activity of use[26] so long as its confined to the area and time

---

[21] The lack of a hearing over the space resource provisions of H.R. 2263 likely saved it from suffering the same fate as H.R. 5063 in the 113th Congress. After passing through Committee, H.R. 2263 and its space resource provisions went on to be passed by both the House of Representatives and the Senate. While space resource proponents laud this as a bipartisan victory, the reality is Democrats who voted for the final bill did so as a compromise to pass provisions of H.R. 2263 of interest to their constituency. The lack of a formal hearing does present a risk the law granting the 'right' to acquire space resources has very little legislative history behind it. Indeed, if the law was challenged in a federal court, the court would have to rely on the statute on its face to determine what it is and what it does.

[22] The text of Public Law 114-90 can be found at https://www.congress.gov/114/plaws/publ90/PLAW-114publ90.pdf

[23] The space resource provisions within H.R. 2263 became Title 51, Chapter 513 of the United States Code, availableathttp://uscode.house.gov/view.xhtml?path=/prelim@title51/subtitle5/chapter513&edition=prelim

[24] In particular the opening sentence of Article I, paragraph 1 is pertinent: "The exploration and *use* of outer space" (emphasis added).

[25] *See* Taylor R. Dalton, *Developing the Final Frontier: Defining Private Property Rights on Celestial Bodies for the Benefit of All Mankind*, Cornell Student Law Papers, August 16, 2010, pp. 15–16, available at http://scholarship.law.cornell.edu/cgi/viewcontent.cgi?article=1041&context=lps_papers

[26] The term of what constitutes use is much debated in the legal community and the concept of space resources has only increased the debate. Essentially, it is agreed that 'using' resources in situ is acceptable

of an on-going recovery operation.[27] This idea of use is further analogized by a theory advocated by John Locke, whereby resources are reduced to possession by the act of appropriation, which involves the mixing of labour with resources. Locke theorized in the case of the world's oceans, which are recognized as *res communis* in terms of free passage; the labour of removing fish (the resource) from the ocean reduces the resource to private ownership through the legal principle of appropriation, that is, use.[28]

Applying these concepts to resources affixed to and within celestial bodies, the idea of space resources theoretically slips around the property prohibition in Article II of the Outer Space Treaty by reducing recovered resources to personal possession through the labour of removing them (appropriation) and classifying the result of that labour as use as articulated in Article I, paragraph 1 of the Outer Space Treaty.[29] In essence, this is a legal two-step attempt to bypass the real property aspect of resources by converting mining from a property interest prohibited by Article I and Article II of the Outer Space Treaty to an activity that is permitted by the Outer Space Treaty through authorization and supervision in Article VI and the continuing jurisdiction under Article VIII, which leads to use as purportedly espoused by Article I.[30]

This theory of use is further elaborated in the Commentary to Luxembourg's draft space resource law whereby French and Belgian law is applied to justify space resources. Specifically, the Commentary to Article I of the Luxembourg law references French and Belgian law to highlight the activity of appropriation whereby unowned natural resources (in this case space resources) are reduced to ownership by the act of physically removing them from a celestial body.[31] The Commentary of the draft Luxembourg law in particular refer-

---

under the Outer Space Treaty. 'In situ' refers to the use of resources to build, maintain and support installations and activities on celestial bodies. In other words, using resources to live off the land is acceptable under the Outer Space Treaty.

[27] *See* Taylor R. Dalton, *Developing the Final Frontier: Defining Private Property Rights on Celestial Bodies for the Benefit of All Mankind*, Cornell Student Law Papers, 16 August 2010, p. 16, available at http://scholarship.law.cornell.edu/cgi/viewcontent.cgi?article=1041&context=lps_papers

[28] *See id.*

[29] 51 U.S.C. § 51303 specifically alludes to use in Article I, paragraph 1 in that "[a] United States citizen engaged in commercial recovery of an asteroid resource or a space resource under this chapter shall be entitled to any asteroid resource or space resource obtained, including to possess, own, transport, **use**, and sell the asteroid resource or space resource obtained in accordance with applicable law, including the international obligations of the United States." Significantly, the US law not only allows use of but also the sale of space resources. As noted in Footnote 21, in situ use of resources is accepted. It's the conversion of those resources for sale that is questionable.

[30] Notably, per Article VIII of the Outer Space Treaty, the personnel and/or spacecraft performing the activity remain under the continuing jurisdiction and color of law of the nation where they launched from, which would be the US in this case.

[31] Significantly, original appropriation also involves land and in fact the act of homesteading is in and of itself an act of appropriation.

ences nineteenth-century French Civil law related to mining and the writings of François Laurent who asserts that even though the high seas could not be appropriated (*res communis*), the fish and shellfish within could.[32]

The end result is that both the US law and the draft Luxembourg law perform an intricate tap dance that relies on the silence of the Outer Space Treaty with regards to mining resources and an allowance to broadly interpret that silence.[33] Critically, the theory of appropriation of space resources depends on an interpretation of Article II where the resources on or within a celestial body are not considered part of the celestial body. Otherwise, if the space resources are considered part of a celestial body, the real property nature of mining asserts itself and makes any law purporting to harvest space resources *void ab initio* (without legal effect or invalid from the outset). It's this distinction that has been the focus of political manoeuvring by proponents of asteroid mining and non-governmental organizations who support their efforts.[34]

The space resources theory and its harvesting fish from the ocean analogy present some problems. For example, given the *res communis* principle and the free access of outer space, how will a nation respond if the space resource operation of one of its citizens is challenged by the operation belonging to the citizen of another nation? As noted earlier, Article VIII of the Outer Space Treaty grants a nation continuing jurisdiction and control over objects and personnel launched into space. If a nation were to intervene to prevent citizens from another nation from interfering with a space resource operation of one of its citizens, an argument could be made that the intervening nation is exercising sovereignty over not only the space resources within a celestial body

---

[32] *See* Draft law on the exploration and use of space resources, Commentary to Article 1, pp. 3–6 available at http://www.gouvernement.lu/6481974/Draft-law-space_press.pdf

[33] Proponents of space resources point to the fact the Outer Space Treaty is silent on the topic of resources and uses that silence to claim mining is not forbidden to create the theory of appropriation of space resources. However, while the Treaty says nothing to forbid mining, they assume that silence permits them to fill in the blanks and that the supposition mining of resources must be allowed. Indeed, a strict reading of the Outer Space Treaty in the historical context of Antarctica, which has been analogized to the Outer Space Treaty by several authorities, including the federal district court in Washington, DC, would argue for an interpretation of Article I and Article II that mining would be prohibited. *See generally, Beattie v. United States*, 756 F.2d 91 (D.C. Cir. 1984) available at https://law.resource.org/pub/us/case/reporter/F2/756/756.F2d.91.84-5413.html (where the district court analogized the Outer Space Treaty to Antarctica when deciding whether it had jurisdiction to hear a claim that arose in Antarctica under the Federal Torts Claims Act).

[34] Less than a month after the Commercial Space Launch Competitiveness Act was signed into law, the Board of Directors for the International Institute of Space Law (ISSL) issued a consensus statement declaring that the concept of space resources does not violate the Outer Space Treaty. The tone of the public relations statement accompanying the statement gave the impression there was harmony amongst the Board members in coming to the consensus, but reportedly there was at least one member of the Board who did not immediately agree the US law harmonized with the Outer Space Treaty. The 25 December 2015 statement is available at http://www.iislweb.org/docs/SpaceResourceMining.pdf

but the celestial body itself or at the very least the tract of area being exploited.[35] Another issue arises with smaller celestial bodies such as asteroids and comets. If a private company is extracting space resources from a small asteroid rich in mineral resources, the physical dimensions of the asteroid could very well preclude the citizens of other nations from extracting resources from the same celestial body. In this case, there is an argument that the private company's operations fall outside of the theory of appropriation and represent a real property interest in the entire asteroid.[36]

There is also an argument that space resources will implicitly be appropriation by the nation under whose colour and jurisdiction private entities will be performing their extraction activities. Consider once space resources are given economic value through the activity of appropriation or use, those resources will contribute to the natural capital[37] of the nation under whose jurisdiction the operation is taking place per Article VIII of the Outer Space Treaty. The addition to a sovereign nation's natural capital via the activities of its private individuals could be considered "national appropriation by claim of sovereignty, by means of use or occupation, *or by any other means*", which is prohibited by Article II of the Outer Space Treaty. These are just a few of the potential issues surrounding the theory of space resources.

The bottom line is at this point the concept of space resources is both a legal and a political position, which the US is using to encourage a customary interpretation of Article I and Article II of the Outer Space Treaty.[38] Indeed, the concept of appropriation of space resources is a 'one foot in, one foot out' approach that has no solid legal delineation and in effect depends on the lack of legal demarcation to justify itself. Until a state practice is performed where a private entity extracts and possesses space resources to solidify this customary legal interpretation of Article I and Article II, the ambiguity and uncer-

---

[35] Proponents of space resources push back on this issue by asserting that mineral-rich asteroids are so prolific that private companies will not interfere with their respective operations.

[36] *See* Footnote 35.

[37] Natural capital is defined as indispensable resources and benefits, essential for human survival and economic activity, provided by the ecosystem. Natural capital is commonly divided into renewable resources (agricultural crops, vegetation and wildlife) and non-renewable resources (fossil fuels and mineral deposits). *See* http://www.businessdictionary.com/definition/natural-capital.html

[38] The concept of space resources and the supporting law is also intended to provide a 'legal' foundation to encourage financiers to invest the billions that will be needed to develop the technology and techniques required to extract space resources. This has created the desired effect as Luxembourg was not only motivated to create its own law but also decided to invest a substantial amount of money into the development of the industry, including direct investment in several asteroid-mining companies. It appears that Luxembourg has the goal through this initiative to become an economic hub to liquidate and/or become an economic exchange for space resources for the European Union, which would be consistent with its involvement with terrestrial mineral trading. *See generally*, SpaceResources.lu at http://www.spaceresources.public.lu/en/index.html

tainty will remain and the concept will not be accepted as a binding customary interpretation of the Outer Space Treaty.

It's noteworthy that, while many in the industry claim this is the end-all to create rights in space resources, the US law and subsequent laws adopted by other countries are not the end of the legal story.[39] More to the point, the lawyers who propagate the concept of space resources acknowledge this is not the end of the legal road but the first step. Notably, one impetus for creating the concept of space resources is to provoke an international discussion and a possible treaty. This end has been effective to the extent that a Space Resource Working Group[40] was established at the Hague to discuss the regulation of space resources and the matter included in the 56th Session of the Legal and Technical Subcommittee of the Committee on the Peaceful Use of Space (COPUOS).[41]

Despite this reality, many in the space mining industry have come out and compared the 'break-through' of space resources as a grant of property rights as opposed to the activity of use, and have even analogized space resources to the Homestead Act of 1862.[42] This and other hyperbole over space resources promulgated by the media and space advocates who do not understand the intricacies of the theory of space resources serves only to add confusion to the issue and fuel misconceptions, which makes it difficult to make a business case whether by creating a business model or investment.

---

[39] Aside from the US, the United Arab Emirates (UAE), Japan and China either have or reportedly are drafting domestic space laws that include space resource provisions. The UAE is likely positioning itself as a hub for the economic exchange of space resources in the Middle East in much the same way as Luxembourg is positioning itself in the European Union. The UAE's position runs contrary to its neighbours Kuwait and Saudi Arabia who have acceded to the Moon Agreement.

[40] The author was invited to be an Observer to the Working Group. Information regarding the Space Resources Working Group is available at http://law.leiden.edu/organisation/publiclaw/iiasl/working-group/the-hague-space-resources-governance-working-group.html

[41] This will be discussed in more detail in the next section.

[42] The Homestead Act of 1862 [Public Law 37-64, 05/20/1862] was a sovereign grant of territory by the federal government of the US that was formerly held by Native Americans. The Act allowed any adult citizen, or intended citizen, who had never borne arms against the US government to claim 160 acres of surveyed government land. Claimants were required to 'improve' the plot by building a dwelling and cultivating the land. After five years on the land, the original filer was entitled to the property, free and clear, except for a small registration fee. Title could also be acquired after only a six-month residency and trivial improvements, provided the claimant paid the government US$1.25 per acre. Notably, the grant of land did not include mineral rights, which the federal government retained. *See* Homestead Act 1862, www.ourdocuments.gov, available at https://www.ourdocuments.gov/doc.php?doc=31. While the Homestead Act was an example of original appropriation, the drawback to analogizing space resources with the Act is its proponents' risk analogizing space resources with a real property interest.

The Geopolitical Effects and Potential Consequences of Space Resources

The legal position taken by the US presents the potential for unintended consequences considering the ability of the US to create new international law and interpretation of current international law through custom.[43] In other words, the influence the US exerts in the international arena, including outer space activities, positions it to not only create new international law but also create interpretations of the Outer Space Treaty through the concept of space resources created by its domestic law.[44] However, beyond creating a customary interpretation of the Outer Space Treaty, Luxembourg's use of nineteenth-century civil law to justify the theory of space resources not only potentially helps to create a customary interpretation of Article I and Article II of the Outer Space Treaty, but also opens the door to an interpretive mechanism for future interpretations of the Outer Space Treaty.

That is to say, collaboratively, the US law and the Luxembourg law with its references to French Civil law open the door to potential anomalous interpretations of the Outer Space Treaty that could result in broader elucidations that might lead to theories that justify eventual territorial claims in outer space. This creates the potential that countries such as China might use this

---

[43] Customary international law is defined as international obligations arising from established state practice, as opposed to obligations arising from formal written international treaties. It consists of two components. First, there must be a general and consistent practice of states. This does not mean that the practice must be universally followed; rather, it should reflect wide acceptance among the states particularly involved in the relevant activity. Second, there must be a sense of legal obligation, or *opinio juris sive necessitatis*. In other words, a practice that is generally followed but which states feel legally free to disregard does not contribute to customary law; instead, there must be a sense of legal obligation to the international community. States must follow the practice because they believe it is required by international law, not merely because they think it is a good idea, or politically useful, or otherwise desirable. The definition of customary international law is nuanced because not all states are equal when considering whether a state's practice and *opinio juris sive necessitatis* reaches the level of customary international law. *See United States v. Bellaizac-Hurtado*, 700 F.3d 1245, 1252 (11th Cir. 2012) available at http://caselaw.findlaw.com/us-11th-circuit/1615347.html. In the case of space resources, the State practice and *opinio juris sive necessitatis* of the United States, which holds a special place and position of prestige in the field of outer space activities, will be given more weight than a state that has a fledgling space programme, and would be more likely considered to be customary international law than those of a state with a nascent space programme.

[44] The US space resource law, 51 U.S.C. § 51303, represents bottom-up rulemaking to create international law. Bottom-up rule-making involves lawmaking by private parties, but also has been defined to cover lawmaking made by domestic government actors and government agencies. Conversely, top-down international rulemaking typically centres on a state's treaty-based commitments or on an intergovernmental institution born from a treaty. The US space resource law represents a bottom-up approach to create a customary interpretation of the Outer Space Treaty. *See generally* Janet Koven Levit, *A Bottom-Up Approach to International Lawmaking: The Tale of Three Trade Finance Instruments*, The Yale Journal Of International Law, Vol. 30, p. 125, available at http://digitalcommons.law.utulsa.edu/cgi/viewcontent.cgi?article=1237&context=fac_pub

interpretive practice and colour Article II based on their domestic law, which has a longer history than French or English forms of property law. China could even take this practice a step further and apply historical claims to reinterpret Article I and Article II of the Outer Space Treaty much in the same way it used historical claims to reinterpret its legal obligations under UNCLOS to make territorial claims in the South China Sea.[45] The end result is that, in their enthusiasm to create a legal basis for space resources, both the US and Luxembourg may be inadvertently creating a customary interpretative mechanism that could lead to destabilizing interpretations of the Outer Space Treaty and completely unzip its non-sovereignty provisions.[46]

Beyond the potential interpretive issues surrounding space resources, the legal concept itself is meeting resistance in the international legal community. Space resources became an agenda item for the United Nations Legal and Technical Subcommittee for the COPUOS during its 56th Session (27 March–27 April).[47] A synopsis of the proceedings with regards to space resources is beyond the scope of this chapter; however, it can be said that the topic generated much discussion and met with significant scepticism not only over the theory of space resources itself but the rapid pace at which the issue is developing. Belgium's statement to the Subcommittee on space resources in particular addressed the issue of why celestial bodies are differentiated from their natural resources for the purpose of their regulation.[48] This comment references the interpretation of Article II of the Outer Space Treaty by space resource proponents that is key to the theory of space resources.

Additionally, those nations who are party to the Moon Agreement are not favourable to the idea of space resources nor are some nations who are not part of that Agreement. Indeed, the Russian Federation's opposition to space

---

[45] China is reportedly drafting its own domestic space law, which allows its private citizens to perform space activities and purportedly contains a provision to allow its citizens to extract space resources. A scenario exists where the Chinese government could use the activity of its private citizens gathering space resources to create a customary legal bridge that would unzip the non-sovereignty principle of the Outer Space Treaty and allow China to assert sovereign territorial claims in outer space.

[46] While the space resources law has created much rancor in the international community, including disapproval by Russia, China has been relatively quiet about the idea. Several of China's legal experts have examined the concept of space resources, tacitly accepted the theory and are participating in the development of an international regulatory regime. What is not publicized is China is allowing the US to mature the theory of space resources and do all the heavy lifting, taking all the political punches in the geopolitical arena and then reaping the benefits after the US has done all the work.

[47] See generally, Legal Subcommittee 2017, 56th Session, at http://www.unoosa.org/oosa/en/ourwork/copuos/lsc/2017/index.html for a listing of available documents relating to the 56th session.

[48] Contribution from Belgium to the discussion under UNCOPUOS Legal Subcommittee on item "General exchange of views on potential legal models for activities in exploration, exploitation and utilization of space resources", V.17-01885 (E), p.3/4 paragraph 4, available at http://www.unoosa.org/res/oosadoc/data/documents/2017/aac_105c_22017crp/aac_105c_22017crp_19_0_html/AC105_C2_2017_CRP19E.pdf

resources could potentially encourage them to at least sign the Moon Agreement, which would give that accord new life and legitimacy and could stymie the US effort to promote space resources.

The point of this discussion is summed up as follows: the promotion of space resources creates uncertainty not only in the international legal community but in the geopolitical realm itself. It not only brings into question the interpretation of current international space treaty law but the means by which the corpus of international law, including space law, will be interpreted in the future. That uncertainty can lead to unintended consequences beyond the issue of mining in outer space that could affect multiple aspects of international law.[49]

Conclusion

The issue of space resources is indicative of a larger issue where technology is quickly outpacing the current body of law. Certainly, the law needs to keep pace with technology and the ability to access outer space, but not at the expense of degrading the fidelity of the law. That said, the technical ability to exploit resources from celestial bodies is an eventuality, and whether the theory of space resources will be the legal means to facilitate that outcome remains to be seen.

Michael J. Listner is an attorney, the founder and principal of the legal and policy think-tank/consultation firm Space Law and Policy Solutions and the editor of the subscription space law and policy briefing-letter, The Précis. He can be reached via his website www.spacelawsolutions.com or via email at Michael@spacelawsolutions.com.

---

[49] Much concern has been expressed by the international community, including the US, over China's unilateral interpretation of UNCLOS to justify its claim of territorial sovereignty in the South China Sea and potentially other swaths of in international waters. Yet, the US through its attempt to create a customary interpretation of the Outer Space Treaty to justify space resources is arguably following the same practice.

9

The Problems with an International Legal Framework for Asteroid Mining

Kamil Muzyka

Introduction

Asteroid mining has been the topic of both future and legal studies for nearly half a century. It wasn't until recently, however, that a legislative action would take place. The US commercial Space Launch Competitiveness Act has accomplished a major breakthrough,[1] even though it was preceded by the unsuccessful ASTEROIDS Act.[2] It has been a beacon for other nations, such as Luxembourg or the United Arab Emirates (UAE) to create its own legislature regarding the ownership or extraction of extraterrestrial resources.[3] Even the EU Commission and European Space Agency (ESA) will address the idea of space mining, as the aftermath of the 2016 Citizens' Debate.[4]

---

[1] H.R.2262—US Commercial Space Launch Competitiveness Act, https://www.congress.gov/bill/114th-congress/house-bill/2262/text

[2] H.R.5063—ASTEROIDS Act, https://www.congress.gov/bill/113th-congress/house-bill/5063

[3] Oriane Kaesman "Luxembourg and the Space Mining Industry", https://www.oximity.com/article/Luxembourg-and-the-Space-Mining-Indust-1; Draft law on the exploration and use of space resources. https://www.gouvernement.lu/6481974/Draft-law-space_press.pdf

[4] Results of the ESA Citizens' Debate. http://www.citizensdebate.space/results

This chapter was originally published as an article, available at http://www.academia.edu/32453498/The_problems_with_an_international_legal_framework_for_asteroid_mining_by_Kamil_Muzykag

K. Muzyka (✉)
The Institute for Legal Studies of the Polish Academy of Sciences,
Warsaw, Poland

© The Author(s) 2018
T. James (ed.), *Deep Space Commodities*,
https://doi.org/10.1007/978-3-319-90303-3_9

Current State

As for the current state of existing asteroid-mining laws, the first and most important general law is the Outer Space Treaty of 1967.[5] Article I of this treaty states that outer space is to be recognized as the province of all humankind.[6] That, along with Article II's non-appropriation principle, makes a clear statement that the usual international law allowing sovereignty rights over un-owned lands does not apply to the ground on which every asteroid,[7] gas giant,[8] or moon miner is standing.[9] Non-appropriation means that state parties shall not claim sovereignty,[10] or land ownership,[11] over the respected parts of the Moon or other celestial bodies, by means of occupation,[12] or usage (neither military nor peaceful). In effect, building a station,[13] a tunnel,[14]

---

[5] Treaty on Principles Governing the Activities of States in the Exploration and Use of Outer Space, including the Moon and Other Celestial Bodies. http://www.unoosa.org/pdf/publications/ST_SPACE_061Rev01E.pdf

[6] Joanne Gabrynowicz "The 'Province' and 'Heritage' of Mankind Reconsidered: A New Beginning" in *Lunar Bases & Space Activities* 1988. http://www.nss.org/settlement/moon/library/LB2-805-ProvinceAndHeritage.pdf

[7] John S. Lewis *Mining the Sky: Untold Riches From The Asteroids, Comets, And Planets* London: Basic Books, 1997; John S. Lewis *Asteroid Mining 101: Wealth for the New Space Economy* Deep Space Industries, 2014; Dana G. Andrews et al. "Defining a successful commercial asteroid mining program".

[8] Jeffrey E. VanCleve, Carl Grillmair, Mark Hanna and Rich Reinert "Helium-3 Mining Aerostats in the Atmospheres of the Outer Planets" – NASA 2005. https://solarsystem.nasa.gov/docs/5.6_Reinert.pdf; Bryan Palaszewski "Atmospheric Mining in the Outer Solar System" NASA 2006. http://mdcampbell.com/TM-2006-214122AtmosphericMining.pdf

[9] Chamberlain, P. G., Taylor, L. A., Podnieks, E. R. and Miller, R. J. "A Review of Possible Mining Applications in Space", in *Resources of Near-Earth Space*. Edited by John S. Lewis, Mildred S. Matthews and Mary L. Guerrieri. Space Science Series. Tucson, London: The University of Arizona Press, 1993, p. 51. http://www.uapress.arizona.edu/onlinebks/ResourcesNearEarthSpace/resources03.pdf; L. S. Gertsch "Lunar mining: Knowns, Unknowns, Challenges, and Technologies" Lunar Reconnaissance Orbiter Science Targeting Meeting (2009). http://www.lpi.usra.edu/meetings/lro2009/pdf/6031.pdf; Ian A. Crawford "Lunar Resources: A Review" Progress in Physical Geography. https://arxiv.org/ftp/arxiv/papers/1410/1410.6865.pdf

[10] Kamil Muzyka "Questions of the space law: The Moon". SLR series part1. Space Law Resource, 22 January 2017. https://www.spacelawresource.com/single-post/2017/01/27/Questions-of-Space-Law-the-Moon---The-SLR-series-1

[11] Jacek Machowski *Paragrafy dla kosmosu*. Omega, 1965.

[12] Norry Harn "Commercial Mining of Celestial Bodies: A Legal Roadmap". https://gielr.files.wordpress.com/2015/12/harn.pdf

[13] Gennady M. Danilenko "Outer Space and the Multilateral Treaty-Making Process" *Berkeley Technology Law Journal* Vol. 4 Issue 2 Autumn 1989. http://scholarship.law.berkeley.edu/cgi/viewcontent.cgi?article=1076&context=btlj

[14] Greg Baiden, Louis Grenier and Brad Blair "Lunar Underground Mining and Construction: A Terrestrial Vision Enabling Space Exploration and Commerce". http://ssi.org/2010/SM14-proceedings/Lunar-Underground-Mining-and-Construction-A-Terrestrial-Vision-Enabling-Space-Exploration-and-Commerce-Baiden-Grenier-Blair.pdf

adaptation of a lava tube,[15] or a mining operation,[16] is viewed as an act of appropriation and exclusivity, although those actions still are permitted when authorized by proper national authorities, under Article VII of the Outer Space Treaty. The failed adoption of the 1979 Moon Agreement resulted in dropping the idea of an international space resource governing body,[17] as well as changing the status of outer space and celestial bodies, from "province of [hu]mankind" to "common heritage of mankind".[18] The latter distinction might deal a serious blow to any private or public–private space pioneer.

The common heritage principle is based on the post-colonial approach to international politics and governance. The point of this principle was to undo the years of exploitation for former colonies, which gave the former colonizers a leading edge over other states of the world, in the case of mineral exploitation technology, making them more accessible to those powers than the smaller developed or developing nations. However, one must clearly state that introducing *lex talionis* into international law, especially more than half a century after colonial exploitation has ended, isn't helpful. The international community should rather encourage developing countries in their participation in the exploration and utilization of outer space and its resources, not burden the space explorers with an actual colonial tax that would benefit the terrestrial community. The shadow of the space-based common heritage principle still looms in the UN Committee on the Peaceful Uses of Outer Space (UNCOPUOS) sessions, although with the current state of national laws made in Luxembourg and the US, such approaches might have little to no effect on future space resource governance.

States adopt their own national legislation, "filling the gaps" in international law,[19] in order to help increase and regulate the activity of their respective nationals. Those regulations have, however, little to no effect on foreign

[15] Andrew Daga "Lunar and Martian Lava Tube Exploration as Part of an Overall Scientific Survey" Planetary Sciences Decadal Survey 2013–2022. http://www.lpi.usra.edu/decadal/leag/AndrewWDaga FINAL.pdf

[16] Shane D. Ross "Near-Earth Asteroid Mining" Caltech 2001, Space Industry Report. http://www.nss. org/settlement/asteroids/NearEarthAsteroidMining(Ross2001).pdf

[17] http://www.unoosa.org/oosa/en/ourwork/spacelaw/treaties/intromoon-agreement.html

[18] Hamza Hameed and Dimitra Stefoudi "Report on the Symposium on Legal Aspects of Space Resource Utilisation" IIASL, Leiden University, 17 April 2016. https://www.universiteitleiden.nl/binaries/content/ assets/rechtsgeleerdheid/instituut-voor-publiekrecht/lucht--en-ruimterecht/symposium-on-legal-aspects-of-space-resource-utilisation/report-on-the-symposium-for-space-resources.pdf

[19] Kuan-wei Chen, Tanveer Ahmad "Promotion for development of national space legislation in developing states to ensure globar space governance" UNOOSA – 10th United Nations workshop on space law contribution of space law and policy to space governence and space security in the 21st century 5–8 September 2016. http://www.unoosa.org/pdf/SLW2016/Panel5/2._Chen_Ahmad_National_space_Legislation_Presentation_Chen.pdf

nationals residing outside of that country's space station or spacecraft. Yet, while most of the national legislature is focused on exploiting the principle of province of humankind, there is still a major problem to be addressed. As US asteroid-mining law is not binding to companies registered in Luxembourg, there is no procedure for even an unlikely encounter, such as two companies landing almost simultaneously on an asteroid.

Possible Solutions

Solutions Involving the UN

As the UN is regarded as the guardian of international law, including space law, many scholars today, such as Ricky J. Lee,[20] and Magdalena Polkowska,[21] still regard it as the best auditor of compliance and its agency as a governing body for space-mining activities. While Lee argues for establishing a common heritage-oriented regime, Polkowska sees the International Civil Aviation Organization (ICAO) as a model for governance of space activity.

This was also the intent of the Moon Agreement,[22] yet the vague terms that outlined this have resulted in the space-mining advocacy community's rejection of the said international treaty.[23] However, there may be several models where this would work and provide reasonable incentive for asteroid-mining companies.

Model A: The UN–Miner Contract Model

This model is based on the basic principle of contract. After establishing a UN space resource governance body, with the authority to order and supervise asteroid-mining operations, miners enter into a mining contract with said international body. In effect, miners are being paid their operational fees, but

[20] Ricky J. Lee *Law and Regulation of Commercial Mining of Minerals in Outer Space* London: Springer, 2012. http://www.springer.com/gp/book/9789400720381

[21] Małgorzata Polkowska *Prawo kosmiczne w obliczu nowych problemów współczesności*. Liber, 2012; Małgorzata Polkowska *Prawo kosmiczne w nowej erze działalności w kosmosie* Oficyna Allerhanda, 2015.

[22] Thomas Gangale "Common Heritage in Magnificent Desolation" 46th AIAA Aerospace Sciences Meeting and Exhibit 7–10 January 2008, Reno, Nevada. http://www.astrosociology.org/Library/PDF/ASM2008_MagnificentDesolation.pdf

[23] Keith Benson "Bulletin from the Moon Treaty Front" L5 News 1980. http://www.nss.org/settlement/L5news/1980-bulletin.html; Thomas Gangale "Myths of the Moon Agreement". https://ops-alaska.com/publications/2008/2008_AIAA-2008-7715.pdf

they do not receive a share of the resources. Those resources are being sold by the space resource governing body and profits are shared on the basis of equity among the nations of the UN, with the emphasis on helping the developing nations of Planet Earth. That model combines the alleged intent of the Moon Agreement with the subcontractor model for construction or mining operations. It gives mining companies the incentive and authorization by the UN space resource governance body, while at the same time forbidding any form of appropriation, hoarding or stockpiling of potential asteroid resources. Asteroid miners in this model are only the operators. The model, however, has its drawback; not in the sense of international law, but in the sense of possible politicization of such a body, where certain superpowers might manipulate the international space resource fund to reap profits rather than to equally or evenly distribute the benefits of asteroid mining. The UN has a record of failures and malpractices among its institutions,[24] or simply has a lack of means to fight such phenomenon as 'paper satellites'.[25]

Model B: Retrieving the Salvaged Common Heritage

This model also requires a UN-based or otherwise established international body, yet the main difference is the issue of initiative. Miners capturing and retrieving an asteroid to the proper extraction point, such as the Lunar L1 point, may file a salvage claim with the proper court, in the same way that maritime salvage is done.[26] Miners still don't own the asteroid, nor can they in any way claim right to its resources, yet they are entitled to the salvage reward, similar to Article 12 of the 1989 International Convention on Salvage,[27] upon successful salvage. The advantage this model has over the previous one is that

---

[24] Norah Niland "Inhumanity and Humanitarian Action Protection Failures in Sri Lanka" Feinstein International Center, September 2014. http://fic.tufts.edu/assets/Inhumanity-and-Humanitarian-Action_9-15-2014.pdf; *The Economist*, 9 August 2005 "Corruption at the heart of the United Nations". http://www.economist.com/node/4267109

[25] Aleksey Shtivelman "Solar power satellites: The right to a spot in the world's highest parking lot". https://www.bu.edu/jostl/files/2015/02/Shtivelman_web.pdf; Audrey L. Allison "The Current State of Virtual Satellites" in: *The ITU and Managing Satellite Orbital and Spectrum Resources in the 21st Century*, pp. 55–73, London: Springer, 2014; Regulation of Global Broadband Satellite Communications. ITU, April 2012.http://www.itu.int/ITU-D/treg/broadband/ITU-BB-Reports_RegulationBroadbandSatellite. pdf; Robert Jones "Scrambling for Space in Space – ITU Plenipotentiary to Tackle 'Paper Satellite' Problem" Geneva: ITU, 16 September 2002.

[26] F. Lansakara "Maritime Law of Salvage and Adequacy of Laws Protecting the Salvors' Interest" *International Journal on Marine Navigation and Safety of Sea Transportation* Vol. 6, Number 3, September 2012. http://www.transnav.eu/files/Maritime%20Law%20of%20Salvage%20and%20Adequacy%20 of%20Laws%20Protecting%20the%20Salvors%E2%80%99%20Interest,381.pdf

[27] 1989 International Convention on Salvage. https://cil.nus.edu.sg/rp/il/pdf/1989%20International%20 Convention%20on%20Salvage-pdf.pdf

reward is paid upon successful return of the salvaged heritage of humankind,[28] and thus one cannot extend the mission forever. Also, it would be the miners themselves initiating the process of homing in on and capturing an asteroid, not the governing body or agency assigning missions.

Model C: Agency Assigned Missions

The agency assigned mission model is based on a mechanism whereby certain companies enter tenders, set up by the proper governance body. The governing body is the one choosing which companies get contracts for mining asteroids, as well as setting the terms of such cooperation. Applying for several missions may allow companies to secure any future asteroid mission windows—additionally blocking others from such opportunity. This is a model based on the satellite orbit assigning that takes place under the International Telecommunication Union (ITU).[29] The ITU has the power and authority to assign or refuse assigning a particular orbital slot around Earth. While this was first considered to be a means to ensure safety and reduce the risk of collisions in outer space, such a mechanism would eventually lead to the creation of paper miners. A paper miner, or an astrotroll,[30] is a mining rights holding company, which does not exercise its rights by mining asteroids, but rather uses those rights on speculative markets, or to generate even more wealth by granting subcontracts to actual mining companies.

The aforementioned models have their pros and cons—that is, administrative indolence, corruptibility, lack of sufficient anti-abuse mechanisms, and favouring larger multinational entities over smaller asteroid miners.

To an extent, models A and B may seem reasonable approaches to the Moon Agreement's Article XI. Either way, a serious drawback to the UN treaty-based systems, especially those from the common heritage family, is that some states may choose not to adhere to them, by either not entering or not ratifying the treaty. This is the case for the US concerning the UN Convention on the Law of the Sea (UNCLOS),[31] and the Moon Agreement, as well as Israel in the case of the Non-Proliferation Treaty. States that are not

---

[28] M. A. Wilder "Application of salvage law and the law of finds to sunken shipwreck discoveries" *Defense Counsel Journal* 1 (2000).

[29] Art. 44 of the ITU Constitution. http://search.itu.int/history/HistoryDigitalCollectionDocLibrary/5.17.61.en.100.pdf

[30] Maayan Perel "From non-practicing entities (NPEs) to nonpracticed patents (NPPs): A proposal for a patent working requirement". http://www.clb.ac.il/images/files/From%20NPEs%20to%20NPPs%20pdf.pdf

[31] www.un.org/depts/los/convention_agreements/texts/unclos/unclos_e.pdf

party to the treaty might exercise their own national rules, which may either adopt the same principles or basically contradict the rules set in said treaty. This is a serious disadvantage for both the treaty system and the states who actually signed the treaty, as entities registered in non-party states—especially if they possess sufficient space launching capacity—would not be bound by any restrictions, such as equitable sharing, which are covered in the treaty's provisions.

Non-UN-Based Solutions: An Extra UN Governing Entity

Models involving an extra UN governing entity mostly revolve around the idea of an independent, intergovernmental organization. Basically, some may resemble models A and B, with miners contracting the authority either before or after retrieving asteroids or asteroid resources, yet others may pursue a more liberal or even libertarian approach.

An Intergovernmental Entity

Based on a similar idea to the ESA,[32] this governing body would be composed of representative space agencies of other nations. This entity would work as a collective body, supervising and commencing asteroid operations, using mechanisms explained in models A and B, as well as proposed mechanisms of staking claims on asteroids or being the arbitrator between disputing miners. There are several other intergovernmental organization (IGO) models, including the North Atlantic Treaty Organization (NATO),[33] and the Organization of the Petroleum Exporting Countries (OPEC),[34] which play a major role on the political and economic scene.

An Asteroid Prospecting and Utilization Organization would have allegedly been established, creating standards, rules and codes of conduct for member states. There have been instances where countries establishing an international endeavour in outer space have created an intergovernmental agreement (IGA), rather than an international treaty—that was the case with the International Space Station (ISS).[35] Rules being set by participating parties

---

[32] Convention for the establishment of a European Space Agency & ESA Council. http://www.kosmos.gov.pl/download/ESA_Convention.pdf

[33] The North Atlantic Treaty (1949) http://www.nato.int/nato_static/assets/pdf/stock_publications/20120822_nato_treaty_en_light_2009.pdf

[34] http://www.opec.org/opec_web/en/index.htm

[35] https://www.state.gov/documents/organization/107683.pdf

working as partners are easier to enforce than those based around international treaties. Despite this, altering an IGA to adapt it to the changing environments wouldn't require lengthy sessions of UNCOPUOS, but rather just General Council meetings. Also, in this manner, the non-involved parties would have no say in the terms and provisions of such an IGA or the politics of this IGO. It might raise questions about lack of inclusivity for states that are not active in asteroid mining; however, Article I of the 1967 Outer Space Treaty clearly states that outer-space exploration should be carried out "for the benefit and in the interests of all countries, irrespective of their degree of economic or scientific development"—I could not disagree more. Countries developing their own programmes may join the venture, and private entities may become its prime contractors, as is the case with the ISS or OPEC. The basic idea, however, boils down to the principle that the decisions on mining, prospecting and the distribution of wealth in the space-based economy remain in the hands of participating nations, and are not subjected to external pressure and political influence from non-participatory parties. This, however, does not prevent participating countries creating specialized international aid and development funds in order to raise the welfare of developing countries. As is the case for the ISS, developing countries can contribute to and benefit from its presence and equipment, despite not being signatories of the IGA. This also ties in with the second extra-UN model.

Extragovernmental Entity

This idea comes from an article titled "Celestial Anarchy: A Threat to Outer Space Commerce?",[36] by Alexander W. Salter and Peter T. Leeson, published by the CATO Institute. The authors argue that asteroid miners and spacefaring actors should be the ones deciding their internal regulations and affairs. In their work, Leeson and Salter propose the use of the law merchant analogy, where medieval merchants had their own laws and courts, governing and ruling in their respected internal affairs. Allowing space-venturing companies or public–private partnerships to form such an entity is both fascinating and risky. In my own work on legal aspects of asteroid mining,[37] I use the nineteenth-century whaling norms analogy as principles for unsolved

---

[36] A. W. Salter and P. T. Leeson "Celestial Anarchy: A Threat to Outer Space Commerce?" *Cato Journal* 34(3) 2014.

[37] K. Muzyka "Gdzie asteroidy kruszą, tam surowce lecą. Prawne aspekty wydobywania kopalin w przestrzeni kosmicznej", Technologiczno-społeczne oblicza XXI wieku, Wydwenictwo Libron 2016.

questions of priority,[38] as well as addressing the issues of non-practising entities. Although whaling norms had a purpose in eliminating false claims or foul play in the whaling trade, the drawback was that they were not recognized in admiralty courts as part of common law. A duck-hunting precedent was used by Thomas E. Simmons,[39] and Andrew Tingkang proposes creating a separate legal category for asteroids,[40] thus recognizing them as chattels rather than real property.

Miners creating their own rules and customs might be a more flexible solution to the problem of jurisdiction, judicial power and the rule of law. Yet that would be the case only in the aftermath of such programmes as CisLunar-1000.[41] In this case, courts and law enforcement must have the physical capacity to enforce the rule of law on self-sustaining human habitats,[42] while enforcing criminal law or forcing compliance with asteroid-mining law in an environment where all actors are based on Earth, irrelevant of one's citizenship, is simpler than in the case of space-based entities.[43] There were similar approaches made in the cases of Mars explorations,[44] where permanent settlers were supposed to be able to set up their legal authorities and enact their own codified law, while still being compliant with the UN charter or the Declaration of Human Rights.

One such model might be the International Chamber of Commerce (ICC).[45] The ICC serves as a dispute resolution organization, as well as setting standards for business practices and lobbying the EU and the UN. The main

---

[38] R. C. Deal "Fast-fish, loose-fish: how whalemen, lawyers, and judges created the British property law of whaling". Ecology Law Quarterly, 1. (2010); Wilson, B. J. et al. "The ecological and civil mainsprings of property: an experimental economic history of whalers' rules of capture". *Journal of Law, Economics and Organization*, 28. (2012).

[39] Thomas E. Simmons "When robots trespass". Space Review 16 January 2017. http://www.thespacereview.com/article/3146/1

[40] Tingkang, A. "These aren't the asteroids you are looking for: classifying asteroids in space as chattels, not land". Seattle University Law Review, 2/(2012).

[41] United Launch Alliance "Transportation Enabling a Robust Cislunar Space Economy". http://www.ulalaunch.com/uploads/docs/Published_Papers/Commercial_Space/2016_Cislunar.pdf

[42] Dana Andrews "Space colonization, a study of supply and demand". http://spacearchitect.org/pubs/IAC-11-E5.1.8.pdf; Sara Bruhns and Jacob Haqq-Misra "A Pragmatic Approach to Sovereignty on Mars". https://arxiv.org/ftp/arxiv/papers/1511/1511.05615.pdf; James Grimmelmann "Sealand, Havenco, and the rule of law". https://illinoislawreview.org/wp-content/ilr-content/articles/2012/2/Grimmelmann.pdf

[43] Jim Pass "The Astrosociology of Space Colonies: Or the Social Construction of Societies in Space". http://www.astrosociology.org/Library/PDF/submissions/STAIF_Astrosociology%20of%20Space%20ColoniesPDF.pdf

[44] Konrad Szocik et al. "Political and legal challenges in a Mars colony". http://www.sciencedirect.com/science/article/pii/S0265964616300200

[45] T. Taylor "Property rights in space". http://conversableeconomist.blogspot.com/2014/12/property-rights-in-space.html

principle for such an organization would be dispute resolution, for in an environment of free space enterprise and authorizations given *en masse* there will be tensions and disputes between miners. Furthermore, such a 'spaced-up' ICC model would provide not only arbitrations between asteroid miners themselves but also space settlers, who might also be interested in asteroid resources or hollowed out asteroids. This model provides far more space for ingenious frameworks such as claim staking or miners-keepers.[46]

Lack of Authority

This concept might seem similar to those presented in the section on extra-governmental entity, such as celestial anarchy, but this one actually focuses on lack of any authority. While models based on the ICC or merchant courts function without an administrative authority, the actual anarchistic model recognizes no authority of any kind.

Basically, due to investment security risks, neither nations of the world, nor asteroid-mining companies—even multibillion dollar corporations—would settle for a lack of any rules. While miners-keepers models, or those bearing more maritime analogies, tend to focus on securing the rights of the entity, which has performed sufficient action in order to obtain the resources,[47] each and every one of them needed to have a 'dispute resolution' body. This might be the case when there is no actual consensus between the nations of the world on establishing a new or amended international space law treaty, or creating a governing body; or as in the case of the UNCLOS, some states with space-mining capabilities would simply refuse to sign such a treaty or recognize the authority of such a body. In this case, where there's a collision of mining or transport spacecrafts, or other damage is inflicted on a mining operation, the Liability Convention should be viewed as a framework. Also, parties might pursue arbitration before the Permanent Court of Arbitration (PCA), on the basis of their internal agreement. Such agreement would even

---

[46] Craig Foster "Excuse me, you're mining my asteroid: space property rights and the u.s. space resource exploration and utilization act of 2015". http://illinoisjltp.com/journal/wp-content/uploads/2016/11/Foster.pdf; Kastalia Medrano "Luxembourg's New Space Mining Law Is Basically 'Finders, Keepers'" Inverse November 14, 2016. https://www.inverse.com/article/23694-luxembourg-space-asteroid-mining-law-rights-resources

[47] One should not forget the problems of patent trolling, market speculations and such. Abuse of free-market principles and toying with the market using speculations might lead to a situation where large mining companies achieve monopoly through sufficient output volume. Thus in this scenario, smaller companies can't create a sustainable business model.

resemble the ISS IGA,[48] where according to Articles 16, 17 and especially 22, partnering states retain their jurisdiction over their respective nationals and equipment, yet any dispute rising from a liability for damage can be settled before respective courts. This still requires countries and their agencies to conduct long negotiations and set those rules.

Additional Issues

When discussing issues of international law and the possible governing entity, or lack of it, space lawyers might forget about current shifts in our terrestrial environment. Although asteroid-mining techniques are meant to work in a vacuum, the asteroid-mining law itself won't.

The Benefits of Space Exploration

When thinking about benefits of space exploration and utilization in the context of space mining, one forgets that it's not only the benefit of pure resources. This however works mostly for asteroids and heavy materials. Most open market models work outside of the remaining questions, such as sustainability, manufacturing and habitation, and are focused only on asteroids—not say the Moon, Mars or Jupiter. From the perspective of humans living on Earth, any form of enforced sharing of benefits sounds very reasonable, both economically and geopolitically. We are the literal mouths to feed, and many lectures focus on 'what kind of materials our consumer commodities require'. We, the people of Earth want—or rather some of our representatives claim that we want—space miners to bring us the cornucopia. Space mining might have the power to make exploitation of developing countries disappear, to end wars and famine, to make even transhumanist or Kardaschev scale dreams come true. But following that path, we are not far from exploiting others. Space mining includes in-situ space resource utilization (ISRU), which doesn't actually involve introducing those resources to the terrestrial market. ISRU covers a broad range of applications, including refuelling space vehicles, construction, sustainable habitation, manufacturing of spare parts or exotic goods. Although the first entity to master and industrialize the process of refuelling space vehicles might claim itself to be the first space fuel mogul, that entity also falls under the principle of sharing benefits under the common heritage

---

[48] The International Space Station Intergovernmental Agreement. https://www.state.gov/documents/organization/107683.pdf

principle. One might ask why? Why is this entity, which is creating a sustainable space environment for human activity, to be charged for space activity on the heritage site? This is the reason why the common heritage principle hasn't been adopted as an expansion of the province of humankind. Joanne Gabrynowicz points out that province refers to the activities of state parties and nationals, while common heritage refers to the matter.[49] Current provisions of international space law are based on the principle of province of all humankind, thus an entity setting up a ground volatile extraction station gets to keep both the fuel produced, as well as any commodities fabricated or constructed on the Moon or in orbit. Those materials might be essential for the survival of lunar, LaGrange or deep-space habitats, interplanetary transports and so on. Besides commercial refuelling stations, most of those ISRU techniques would be used for meeting ongoing needs of station personnel and hardware. The more self-sufficient a habitat or spacecraft is, and the less reliant on resupply from Earth, the better. For those on site—who are maintaining the station, using the kaizen production/logistics methods and stockpiling excess materials for the future—the requirement to share the benefits is unreasonable. Their benefit is their well-being, whereas their parent space agency or company should benefit from better operation, lifespan and reduced maintenance and resupply launch costs. Putting additional taxation on sustainable technologies, to which ISRU spin-offs will contribute, is also unreasonable. If the international community is eager to impose taxes, they might think about creating a 5 percent space activity tax on every activity, from launching and mining to remote sensing. The tax revenue would go towards a space development fund for developing nations, yet the tax rate should be paid by all who benefit from space activity.

The model behind the common heritage principle was based on a fear that the rich nations would exploit the resources in international waters, as well as those in outer space, thus gaining an even greater advantage against the remaining countries—especially the developing nations of Africa and Asia. Furthermore, this model carried out the need for participation in space exploitation. Though it looks more like *lex talionis* in international policy than a reasonable approach to modern international relations in the context of future technologies. International law must withstand decades or centuries, thus must consider matters such as newly developing 'nations'. By 'nations', I

---

[49] Joanne Gabrynowicz "The 'Province' and 'Heritage' of Mankind Reconsidered: A New Beginning" in Lunar Bases & Space Activities 1988. http://www.nss.org/settlement/moon/library/LB2-805-ProvinceAndHeritage.pdf

mean the future communities in outer space, 'living off the land' or in the void in outer space, creating their own culture. As suggested before, this can be seen as a new form of colonialism, where space colonists are being exploited for the benefit of all mankind. So why is it that the United Nations is more concerned with direct benefits, rather than access to spin-off technologies, and incentives for private or public entities to provide access in developing nations to such technologies as sustainable water management or energy production and storage? Perhaps because such spin-offs weren't so visible during the initial proceedings on the Moon Treaty as they are today. Maybe it is due to the fear of losing any significance in the international arena to the developing states that had suffered colonial exploitation in their past, or those who are being exploited or kept in debt due to their natural resources. Addressing this issue, one must recall, that the reason they remain in debt and exploitation is the lack of feasible alternatives. On the other hand, if space miners were the breadwinners of the future economy, it might be that *they* should be paid accordingly by all nations of the world, as they would provide the means of sustainable development and changes in economic paradigms. Asteroid mining, along with other commercial space activities is a very risky endeavour, and as such, is costly. Burdening mining entities with additional taxation or principles of obligatory could very easily make them unsustainable, let alone not beneficial.

Duality of Legal Models

Asteroid-mining models are easier to create than lunar models, as most near-Earth asteroids (NEAs) are too small, or lack the proper composition and property, to be turned into a space station or a remote outpost. That said, scarcely anyone would apply the same laws to the lunar or Martian surface. This is due to the techniques used to acquire asteroid resources being different than those for surface and subsurface mining of larger celestial bodies. Therefore, mining asteroids would be governed by a different regime than mining the Moon, or gas mining Jupiter.

Although there is no doubt that both lunar and asteroid mining require governmental authorization, redirecting a handful of asteroids for ISRU and processing would have less political impact than tunnelling or strip-mining portions of the Moon. There are greater safety concerns when mining in the vicinity of any human habitation. Also, although the Moon is considered province of humankind, according to Article I of the Outer Space Treaty, active mining and reshaping of its landscape may still be seen as "other means of appropriation" in association with Article II.

Therefore, in order to harmonize larger-body mining with mining asteroids, and especially space settlement, there needs to be either a supervisory authority with a thoroughly studied 'outer space development plan' (where the Moon, Mars and asteroids are being sliced and partitioned into habitation sites, study sites, mining/industry sites and heritage sites, like the Apollo or Hayabusa or Rosetta/Philae landing sites), or there will be a need for major amendments in international space law. It can also boil down to assigning 'national lunar zones'—the same way that geostationary orbit is being divided between the nations of the world that are members of the ITU. At this point, any nation may order mining or settlement operations to be commenced in its national zone.

If the national zones are being shared with other nations, their needs would have to be addressed accordingly. That might lead to concerns regarding the grouping of nations (possibly developing nations with one space superpower per zone), the scarcity of resources in said zone, accessibility, and ultimately industrial monopolies. Alternatively, states and companies might pursuit a form of a space trade agreement, outlining the state's rights and obligations, as well as rights and obligations of non-state parties. One such solution might involve creating special forms of limited partnerships, between the companies and consortia and the members of the international community. In this case, states are offered purchase of specially created shares or investments and gain a title similar to that of limited partners. Purchase of those shares or investments by interested states on the one hand will bring more R&D, production, and operational capacity to the mining companies, and on the other, the company will be obliged to pay the distribution or dividend to the limited state partners who purchased their shares or investments. In this case, the limited liability of the state partners plays very well, as they participate in the benefit of the endeavour; yet their liability, should a mission be unsuccessful, is limited by those shares or investments. It is certainly easier to dodge taxes than shareholders. One could even create a whole new concept of lending money to the developing nations, so that they also can buy shares in space mining companies or consortia. The same can be said of space manufacturing companies, powersats/SBSP, interplanet-coms and other endeavours. We shouldn't be parasites in space, we should be partners.

Robots

Basically, outside of classic science fiction literature, all serious approaches to asteroid mining involve using robots.[50] Those robots are either teleoperated or autonomous. The issues with robots are as follows:

– Setting up the liability for damage inflicted by an autonomous robotic mining craft.[51]
– The economic implications of the 'robot tax'.[52]
– Dual-use equipment.

Addressing the issue of liability is crucial in order to create an actual framework for robotic mining/hauling ships.[53] While teleoperated robots create a possibility for human error to occur, more advanced autonomous AI/MI-based units might have less of a problem in colliding, infringing on others' safe work-zones or otherwise posing a threat to the safety or security of mining operations.[54] Although currently developed autonomous units still require human aid, future space robots might have legal and ethical principles embedded in their software.[55] That way, laws regarding robots would mostly work as guidelines, and standardized software would be a *sine qua non* condition for any asteroid-mining mission to be authorized by any government authority.

The second issue is the robot tax. The concept of universal basic income (UBI) is mostly discussed as a solution to the automated economy, whereas asteroid mining would actually provide more resource for a post-scarcity economy. However, in the current legal and political environment, where the

---

[50] https://www.nasa.gov/pdf/740784main_Cohen_Spring_Symposium_2013.pdf; Henryk Karaś "Robotics in mining". http://www.eumicon.com/images/EUMICON_2015/Robotics%20in%20 mining%20-%20Henryk%20Karas.pdf

[51] F. Patrick Hubbard, Ronald L. Motley "Regulation of and liability for risks of physical injury from 'sophisticated   robots'".   http://robots.law.miami.edu/wp-content/uploads/2012/01/Hubbard_ Sophisticated-Robots-Draft-1.pdf

[52] Richard B. Freeman "Who owns the robots rules the World". https://wol.iza.org/uploads/articles/5/ pdfs/who-owns-the-robots-rules-the-world.pdf

[53] Although the UNCOPUOS recognizes the issue of labour and human rights in an analogy to the conditions of terrestrial miners, that however will not be the case. https://static1.squarespace.com/ static/521b88b9e4b024f66a58adf9/t/5883c97517bffc09e3a47814/1485031800005/ COPUOS_+Mining+in+Space.pdf

[54] Gregor Fitzi, Hironori Matsuzaki "Legal regulation of autonomous systems and social acceptance in Japan". http://www.jura.uni-wuerzburg.de/fileadmin/_migrated/content_uploads/Legal_regulation_of_ autonomous_systems_and_social_acceptance_in_Japan_-_Fitzi_05.pdf

[55] David C. Vladeck "Machines without principals: liability rules and artificial intelligence". http://digital.law.washington.edu/dspace-law/bitstream/handle/1773.1/1322/89WLR0117.pdf?sequence=1

EU Parliament is working on a 'robot tax' and 'robot laws',[56] the former might be problematic for the new space industry, especially in mining and in-space manufacturing.

Essentially, the robot tax is a proposed form of taxation, where the fully automated company is obligated to pay an amount of its profits, which then would create the basis for the UBI. This UBI, or Basic Income Guarantee,[57] would provide citizens with the proper purchasing power; especially those whose jobs were liberated by automation. This, however, would provide an incentive for miners to register their fleet of space robots in states that provide sufficient legal support for their actions, and do not force additional taxation on them.[58] In the worst-case scenario, an asteroid-mining company would be taxed double, first by the possible common heritage of humankind regulation (models A–C, or analogous to the UNCLOS regulations and ISA practice), and afterwards for reaping profits of full automation. That would be an even greater incentive for companies to perform tax dodging or forum shopping. One has to take that into consideration when figuring out an adequate framework for asteroid mining to work in. As mentioned in above, a form of a limited partnership might be more reasonable than simple taxation.

The problem of dual use is the same as with every issue, including robotics and teleoperation, as well as Earth observation. The term dual use equipment is defined as products and technologies normally used for civilian purposes but which may have military applications". This applies to its capacity to be used as a means to build a weapon of mass destruction or gain military advantage, but also to be used as a weapon or means of defence.[59] Spacecrafts that are capable of accelerating a 1,000 metric tonne asteroid in a selected direction might be considered mass drivers, and pose a security threat to people and installations in outer space, as well as on Earth. Also, safety and security reasons should make the operators and manufacturers extremely cautious in

---

[56] Leonid Bershidsky "A Robot Tax Is a Bad Idea", Bloomberg 24 January 2017. https://www.bloomberg.com/view/articles/2017-01-23/why-benoit-hamon-s-idea-of-a-robot-tax-is-flawed; European civil law rules in robotics. http://www.europarl.europa.eu/RegData/etudes/STUD/2016/571379/IPOL_STU (2016)571379_EN.pdf

[57] Olli Kangas, Laura Kalliomaa-Puha "Basic income experiment in Finland" ESPN flash report 2016/13. ec.europa.eu/social/BlobServlet?docId=15135&langId=en

[58] A science-fiction fan could also add an option with the 'brain in a jar' concept. Creating a pseudo cyborg, which would officially run the machine as its prosthesis, would not only help the company dodge the automation tax, it would also secure government funding and tax exemptions for providing work for people with disabilities. The other option would be tricking legislators that their machines still require human authorization for their actions, so they place a 'George Jetson'-like figure, who only pushes one button during his workday.

[59] James C. Howe "Common ground: Asteroid Mining and Planetary Defense" Ad Astra, Summer 2015. http://www.nss.org/adastra/volume27/AsteroidMiningAndPlanetaryDefense.pdf

regards of software and hardware. Although no robotic spacecraft would go rogue and 'turn on its masters', hacking has been a serious threat in every field of industry.

Other Hazards and Concerns

As was mentioned earlier, asteroid-mining technology is of dual use. Yet there is another concern, regarding the radioactive isotopes that may be found on asteroids, such as thorium, uranium or helium-3.[60] The problem with mining those isotopes from space ores is in regard to their use or transport as a nuclear weapon grade material,[61] and possible use for space-based nuclear weaponry, as well as creating fusion generators and producing medical isotopes.[62] Article III point 2 of the 1968 Nuclear Non-Proliferation Treaty holds that "Each State Party to the Treaty undertakes not to provide: (a) source or special fissionable material, or (b) equipment or material especially designed or prepared for the processing, use or production of special fissionable material, to any non-nuclear-weapon State for peaceful purposes, unless the source or special fissionable material shall be subject to the safeguards required by this article".[63] This would clearly limit the free-market distribution of helium-3 or other radioactive materials extracted from outer-space resources. Also, radioactive or nuclear payloads making planetfall might cause hazard, or even become intercepted by a state party or terrorist organization. One might also think of a barter-based black market, where nuclear-grade materials are smuggled,[64] or traded in exchange for essential equipment and goods between space station crews or operators.

Also, jettisoning any 'overburden' from an asteroid mined in-situ should be considered illegal, as it creates additional 'man-made' space debris that is dangerous to systems and vehicles.

---

[60] E. N. Slyuta, A. M. Abdrakhimov, E. M. Galimov, V. I. Vernadsky "The estimation of helium-3 probable reserves in lunar regolith". Lunar and Planetary Science XXXVIII (2007). http://www.lpi.usra.edu/meetings/lpsc2007/pdf/2175.pdf

[61] G.L. Kulcinski "Using Lunar Helium-3 to Generate Nuclear Power Without the Production of Nuclear Waste". http://fti.neep.wisc.edu/presentations/glk_isdc.pdf

[62] David Buden "Atoms for space" U.S. Department of Energy Idaho Operations Office 1990. http://www.iaea.org/inis/collection/NCLCollectionStore/_Public/22/035/22035347.pdf

[63] Treaty on the Non-Proliferation of Nuclear Weapons. https://www.un.org/disarmament/wmd/nuclear/npt/

[64] Sam Dinkin, "Dividing up the spoils" Space Review, 6 June 2005. http://www.thespacereview.com/article/386/1

Finally, mining also changes the landscape, allowing future inhabitants to appropriate, in a non-legal meaning of the word, lava tubes, tunnels and caves, as well as former mining sites for habitation.

Conclusions

The problems of setting up international regimes and frameworks for asteroid mining requires a more open approach to the topic, as it involves geopolitical shifts (such as liberating developing countries from exploitation and poverty); affects the ecosystem (lessening the terrestrial mining operation and allowing for better 'green hi-tech' solutions); and represents a change in the economical paradigm (as automation frees humans from the necessity of enlisting to the workforce, abundance of resources should follow). There are more benefits to asteroid mining than there are threats. However, asteroid miners fear being overburdened with taxes and a forced sharing in the spirit of *res communis*. One must bear in mind that any models should provide means to fight market speculations or resource hoarding, yet at the same time, provide an incentive for those pioneers who take upon themselves the risk of failure, where multibillion dollar investments may burn on the launchpad, or drift helplessly into the deepness of outer space.

10

Potential Issues for Interplanetary and Interstellar Trade

John Hickman

If and when interplanetary and interstellar trade develops, it will be novel in two respects. First, the distances and time spans involved will reduce all or nearly all trade to the exchange of intangible goods. That threatens the possibility of conducting business in a genuinely common currency and of enforcing debt agreements incurred by governments. Second, interstellar trade suggests trade between humans and aliens. Cultural distance is a probable obstacle to initiating and sustaining such trade. Such exchange also threatens the release of new and dangerous memes.

Encountering extraterrestrial alien civilizations and colonizing other worlds are amongst the most powerful and enduring ambitions of space exploration. Realizing either of these objectives implicates the possibility of trade over the vast distances of outer space.

The impetus to engage in economic exchange appears to be a fundamental part of the human behavioural repertoire. Given even the remote possibility of advantageous trade between worlds in our solar system, or with worlds in other solar systems, it would be surprising if humans did not make an attempt. However, that trade is likely to be novel in two critical respects.

The salient difference between existing international trade and any hypothetical interplanetary or interstellar trade are the distances involved. Even the nearest worlds in outer space are much further from Earth than is any point

J. Hickman (✉)
Department of Government and International Studies, Berry College,
Mt. Berry, GA, USA
e-mail: jhickman@berry.edu

© The Author(s) 2018
T. James (ed.), *Deep Space Commodities*,
https://doi.org/10.1007/978-3-319-90303-3_10

on Earth from any other. The world nearest Earth is the Moon, and its distance from Earth varies between 216,000 and 252,000 miles. That is roughly 27 to 32 times the equatorial diameter of Earth. Mars' trajectory varies between 35 million and 62 million miles from Earth. Yet, if such distances are conceived in terms of the speed of communication, this is nothing new in human experience. Uncrewed interplanetary space exploration of Mars has been conducted at communication speeds of between roughly three and six minutes and at transportation speeds counted in months. Communication times of only minutes would have been perceived as extraordinarily fast, and transportation times of months would have been perceived as normal for Western European entrepreneurs sending written messages, or shipping goods to Asia and the Pacific in the fifteenth century through to the mid-eighteenth century.

Distances between stars are counted in light-years. Of those stars within 20 light-years of the Sun, only a very small number have been discovered to date to have 'extrasolar' planets. The nearest of these stars is 'Lalande 21185' and this is 8.3 light-years away. If communication ever bridges interstellar space, it will take years or decades for messages to arrive and any transportation across the void would probably take decades, if not generations or centuries, to complete.

Still, whilst the extraordinary travels of the Polynesians and Norse-speaking tribes never involved individual voyages of such time lengths, they do indicate our species' capacity for high-risk exploration and settlement over protracted periods.

So rather than the distances involved, interplanetary and interstellar economic exchange would be novel because of what would be traded and with whom. The first and more prosaic possibility is that such trade would involve economic exchange, either largely in intangible goods over interplanetary distances or entirely in intangible goods over interstellar distances.

The second, and by far the most exotic, is the possibility that interstellar economic exchange might be conducted between humans and an alien species. Admittedly, this is entirely unlikely within our lifetimes, but as our understanding of the galaxies grows exponentially, planets which support carbon-based life as we know it, or have entirely different genetic makeups, could surface. But not anytime soon … we'll be mining space before trading with extraterrestials.

Although projecting when interplanetary and interstellar trade might emerge lies beyond the horizon of useful prediction, economic history nonetheless offers useful insights when considering the effects of these two novel characteristics should it develop.

Trade Without Tangible Goods

Where the probable energy costs of transporting large amounts of tangible goods over interplanetary and especially over interstellar distances is likely to be prohibitive in the long-term future, the energy costs of communicating information, and thus of exchanging intangible goods over those distances, is likely to be acceptable. Recorded music and product designs are far more likely to be exchanged over such distances than musical instruments and manufactured products.

Conducting trade almost entirely or entirely in intangible goods has never been attempted before. Whilst the 'information economy' has grown as a share of economic activity on Earth, it has never been disconnected from, and remains dependent upon, the exchange of tangible goods. Interplanetary and interstellar trade would be moored to the exchange of tangible goods only on separate worlds.

To understand why such economic exchange would encounter unusual problems, consider the origins of large-scale international trade on Earth. Although humans have bartered goods across the boundaries of their different societies (since they recognized the advantage of economic exchange over coercion to obtain desired goods), the emergence of large-scale trade with foreigners required the introduction of money.

The convertibility, portability and divisibility of money meant that economic exchange need not be simultaneous, but instead could be separated in time, and that money itself could be a valuable commodity. The growth of international trade depended on the business dealings within the networks of merchant bankers; for example investment bankers, who would accept bills of exchange originating in the transfer of tangible goods transported across international borders.

Currency exchange and merchant banking eventually gave rise to other forms of high finance, but that all ultimately depended on economic exchange in tangible goods. Bills of exchange were accepted because they could be settled against imported tangible goods that could be sold in local markets.

Foreign currencies could be traded because they could be used to buy tangible goods in foreign markets. Bankers could make international loans because they were made in currencies that could buy tangible goods or other currencies that could buy tangible goods. That connection has never been broken. The prices of the currencies traded in international currency markets and used to price commodities are often explained as rough estimates of the strength of national or, in the case of the European Union, 'supranational economies'. Contemporary economic activity reflected in those currency prices involves both tangible and intangible goods. Crucially, the exchange of intangible goods in the 'information economy' cannot be divorced from the exchange of tangible goods in the traditional economy. For example, software designers and artists who earn their living selling intangible goods must still use their earnings to buy a range of tangible goods such as food and clothing. That's the mechanism.

Therein lies the problem for interplanetary and interstellar trade. An information economy involving only the exchange of intangible goods such as information between worlds would lack the basis for a common or convertible currency, one capable of being exchanged for tangible goods. And on first impressions, this appears to be no problem at all.

Why, for instance, could not buyers and sellers in separate planetary economies, who would normally employ money to exchange both tangible and intangible goods on their own worlds, exchange intangible goods in bargains struck at long distance? The answer is that they could exchange intangible goods through barter, but that attempts to monetize that trade would in turn suffer because it could not be conducted in a common or convertible currency.

Off-planet sellers of intangible goods who accept 'local' currency in exchange would have to search for 'local' intangible goods to buy if they want to repatriate their profits. Even if they deposited their local currency in a localized bank, or invested it in a local business, they would eventually need to buy some local intangible good for sale off-planet.

A repatriated local currency itself might find other off-planet buyers because it could be used to purchase local intangible goods, but that would not dispose of the problem of finding some local intangible good worth purchasing for sale off-planet.

It should be noted that this natural wrinkle in the fabric of interplanetary and interstellar trade does not occur in international trade, where money profits can always be used to buy local goods that may be shipped home. Although intangible goods exchanged between worlds would be as portable as a currency, because just information need only be transmitted, they would only be convertible and divisible into the local currency. So in effect, the problems associated with barter could not be eliminated because the divisibility of intangible goods could not be eradicated through monetization.

As such, the ancient dilemma of determining precisely how many 'milk cows' will buy a 'draft horse' may reappear in the future. As will be explained in the next section, the potential cultural distance and certain physical distance in interstellar trade, rather than interplanetary trade, would add significantly to the transaction costs of searching for intangible goods to purchase to repatriate profits.

The absence of trade in tangible goods would pose an even more profound problem for the development of the interplanetary or interstellar equivalents of international banking. Where private firms that are borrowing may be forced to honour their debts to foreign lenders in the courts of either the borrower's country or the lender's country, borrowing governments are a different matter. Their national courts are usually not available to foreign lenders to enforce loan agreements because default is deemed a political decision. That means they must resort to other means.

Demonstrations of military power were sometimes used to compel governments to honour their sovereign debts in the era of 'gunboat' diplomacy. Today, the primary means available for use against a defaulting government are moral suasion, political pressure and, most importantly, economic threats in the form of embargoes and so on.

To what extent could economic threats be used in enforcing the payment of interplanetary or interstellar loans? Consider the 'hypo-theoretical' situation in which the government of a human colony on Mars refuses to continue servicing its sovereign debt to a consortium of lenders on Earth. What means are available to compel the resumption of payments?

Remember that in this example nearly all of the trade between Mars and Earth consists of exchanges of intangible goods. Beyond refusal to make new loans to the Martian government (a sanction that would require the continuing cooperation of other lenders on Earth, who might wish to make loans to the Martian government in the future), it is likely that the consortium would have to resort to seizing and selling under court order any non-diplomatic assets of the Martian government it could locate on Earth.

Seizing and selling any intangible goods would be far more difficult than seizing tangible goods. As the ubiquity of gossip, espionage, broadcast propaganda and intellectual piracy all demonstrate, nothing is more difficult to control than the movement of information. Just as trade embargoes create opportunities for smugglers of contraband, efforts to establish information blockades between worlds within the same solar system would be difficult to enforce.

Trade with Non-humans

Communicating with a non-human civilization across the vast distances of outer space, if and when it has been detected or has detected us, is such a daunting prospect that it is unsurprising that there has been so little public discussion about how the discovery could be exploited.

For all the enthusiasm pertaining to the 'Search for Extraterrestrial Intelligence', or SETI, and the scientists and lay supporters with aspirations to detect an artificial signal indicating an alien civilization, other schools of thought are extremely sceptical of our ability to actually achieve any form communication anyway.

One scholar concluded that the "possibility of learning anything at all about the thoughts and behavior of alien beings is very remote". He continues, "We must find them, then establish communication, and finally engage in a prolonged exchange of ideas .... It may take years to acquire even the rudimentary facts about the psychological and social makeup of an alien being, even if it is of a cooperative disposition".[4]

If communication can be achieved with 'E.T.', why bother to continue communicating after introductions are made, curiosity about physical appearance and society satisfied and mathematics interrogated to confirm or disconfirm fundamental assumptions about the universe? The obvious and moreover the correct answer is to exchange useful and entertaining information. There are several problems with this muted solution.

Economic exchange itself might be 'alien' to the aliens. Members of an alien species may not experience the same intense sense-of-self that is exhibited in rationally self-serving economic exchange amongst humans.

Instead, a collective identity could be dominant. Money might not exist and without it neither would complex markets or banking. If they do engage in economic exchange, then it might take a form akin to 'potlatch' (a competitive gift giving for status solely amongst members of the same tribe, traditional amongst societies in Melanesia and the Pacific Northwest).

Moreover, an alien species might not live in separate societies and could thus have no conception of trade between different societies with different cultures. Even if an alien species did live in multiple societies with different cultures and engaged in monetized trade in tangible goods, it might not 'commodify' non-tangible goods.

Even amongst humans, with the bulk of the intangible goods distributed on the Internet, perhaps the closest model of interaction involving only exchange of non-tangible goods takes the form of gifts of information to strangers rather than of monetized sales of intellectual property.

All of that generous gift giving is possible because the information consists almost entirely of non-rival goods and is effectively free to distribute. Whether the intangible goods transmitted across interstellar space would be distributed as commodities or gifts, the energy and time costs of interstellar transmission would be high.

Energy and time costs involved in transmitting information within our solar system would be much lower than those for transmitting information between solar systems, simply because the distances involved are different orders of magnitude. The distance from the edge of our solar system at the outer boundary of the Kuiper Belt through past the Sun to the opposite outer boundary of the Kuiper Belt is 100 AU (Astronomical Units), or a mere 0.0016 of a light-year. The distance between the Sun and Gliese 581, a red dwarf star recently discovered to have a possibly Earth-like planet, is 20.5 light-years or 1,296,420 AU.[6]

Distance matters because it reduces the accuracy with which transmissions may be focused on target antennae; increased distance requires wider beamed transmissions to insure a transmission is received; radio transmissions are limited by the speed of light.

Hence, a hypothetical message sent between the most distant locations in the solar system would take only 84.5 minutes to arrive whilst a message sent from Earth to Gliese 581 C would take 20.5 years to arrive. The short distances within our solar system mean that verification a transmission had arrived would take minutes, whilst the longer distances between solar systems would mean that verification would arrive in years or decades.

Even if an alien species is more patient or has a greater longevity of life than humans, it is unlikely that the humans with whom they trade would be content to risk the passage of years or decades with narrow-beam transmissions that may miss the intended target to save energy costs. Therefore, in theory, humans are likely to insist upon 'wastefully' wider beam width and repetition of transmitted messages.

Private firms transmitting information over interstellar distances will probably want a return in the form of useful or entertaining information, which could be resold to pay for the original investment. Of course, government agencies might be willing to absorb these aforementioned energy costs to facilitate communication between solar systems, but they would probably employ a formula rationing access that might, or might not, reflect the economic demand for information.

This implies a third problem, namely that there may be little worth exchanging between societies, or that one society may have more intangible goods worth exchanging than another. Consider that most of the intangible goods that are actually purchased take the form of recorded entertainment, produced and purchased within a single society or within culturally similar societies.

Some works of entertainment have 'universal' appeal and correspondingly sales of global proportion, but most will likely fail to find large audiences outside the societies in which they are produced. US popular music finds a truly global market, but the same cannot be said of Chinese popular music. The cultural distance between humans and any non-human intelligent species is likely to be far greater than any encountered between human societies, and thus might radically restrict the range of intangible goods that would be worth exchanging.

The intangible goods most likely to have value for economic exchange with non-human, intelligent species, will probably be works on physical science and engineering. And these make up a surprisingly small portion of the total volume of intangible goods produced by us humans.

A final problem with economic exchange between humans and aliens is that of unforeseeable risks. The general risk that exposure to new ideas, and especially to new technology, can produce violent conflict is readily evident in our history. For example, the reinvention of the printing press in fifteenth-century Europe permitted mass publication of the Christian bible in the vernacular, thus facilitating the 'Protestant Reformation' and its associated wars.

Again, the introduction of the potato and firearms to the Maori as trade goods by the British in the early nineteenth century led to the eruption of New Zealand's Musket Wars. Pests and pathogens have also been spread through trade. The Norwegian rat and the bubonic plague are amongst the best-known examples of this.

If the introduction of new technology and new pathogens present palpable risks to society, the potential threat from exposure to new and unanticipated ideas might be even more profound. There is no evidence for or against the assumption that humans have already conceived in general terms everything that an alien species might have conceived. Or that members of an alien species have already conceived in general terms, of everything that humans have conceived.

A non-trivial risk exists that humans might receive or transmit new memes. That human societies as sophisticated as the Qing Dynasty of China and post-communist Russia suffered because of the re-release of such phenomena indicate the risk associated with unwitting openness to unfamiliar memes. The Taiping Rebellion in China was the bloodiest civil war in history, and is at least partially attributable to the exposure of China to evangelical Protestantism. Russia was exposed to pyramid schemes of gigantic proportions following the end of communism in the 1990s.

Conclusion

One possible public policy response to the problems outlined in this chapter would be to allow economic exchange between worlds to develop through private initiative. Laissez faire presents the path of least resistance and would be practical for interplanetary economic exchange, because the distances involved would slow the bartering of intangible goods only by minutes.

Perhaps the establishment of a solar system monetary union would permit the free flow of capital, but trade itself could be conducted even without the use of a common currency.

Much longer communication times and possible encounters with non-human species might mean increased state intervention in interstellar economic exchange. The public interest in encouraging acquisition of new and useful technology and interdicting dangerous memes, could be achieved by establishing a planetary clearinghouse for bartering intangible goods, overseen by the equivalent of customs officials empowered to stop the dissemination of potentially dangerous memes.

Interplanetary and interstellar economic exchange may be more than just a consequence of human space exploration. As on Earth, economic exchange might become one of the important motivations for the further exploration of space.

Notes

1. David S. Landes, *Bankers and Pashas: International Finance and Economic Imperialism in Egypt* (Cambridge, MA: Harvard University Press, 1979), pp. 3–14.
2. Robert Zubrin suggests that human colonists on Mars might support themselves by selling intangible goods. Robert Zubrin, *Entering Space: Creating a Spacefaring Civilization* (New York: Jeremy P. Tarcher=Putnam, 1999), pp. 106–107.
3. Diplomatic property is typically the easiest to locate but immune under international law from attachment to satisfy sovereign debts.
4. John C. Baird, *Inner Limits of Outer Space* (Hanover, NH: University Press of New England, 1987), p. 86. See also Stephen Webb, *Where is Everybody? Fifty Solutions to the Fermi Paradox and the Problem of Extraterrestrial Life* (New York: Copernicus Books, 2002), p. 120.
5. Alternatively, members of some alien species may present a more intense sense-of-self than humans and simply be too distrustful to engage in economic exchange.
6. Kerr Than, "Major Discovery: New Planet Could Harbor Water and Life". *Space.com.*, 24 April 2007, http://www.space.com/scienceastronomy/070424_hab_ex.planet.html (retrieved 28 April 2007).

7. Whether the printing press was first invented in China or in Korea is still disputed.
8. James Belich, *Making Peoples: A History of the New Zealanders* (Honolulu: University of Hawaii Press, 1996), pp. 156–164.
9. Melanesian cargo cults, such as the John Frum Movement in Vanuatu, is an example of the formidable power of foreign ideas and foreign things to generate social change.
10. Similar pyramid schemes were also perpetrated on unsuspecting Romanians and Albanians.
11. Ben R. Finney, "The Prince and the Eunuch", In, *Interstellar Migration and the Human Experience*, Ben R. Finney and Eric M. Jones, Eds. (Berkeley, CA: University of California Press, 1986), pp. 196–208.

11

Astropolitics and International Relations

Bleddyn E. Bowen

What does the world of Thucydides have in common with that of Wehrner von Braun or Sergei Korolev; of the realm of the trireme with the *Delta IV* rocket? Much like the popular misconception that satellites in orbit have 'escaped' the influence of Earth's gravity, there is a common perception that outer space is a politically different or separate realm to Earth. In truth, however, our affairs as a species in outer space have not escaped the influence of *homo politicus*; reaching outer space is not necessarily humanity's road to absolution. Astropolitics is what humans seek to make of it. So far, politics in space reflects some of the prevailing features of international relations in an anarchic system that dates back to antiquity. The major powers of any international system tend to act according to fear, honour and interest; and it should not be assumed that an expansion of a political economy to deep space will alleviate such motivations. There may be nothing politically new around the sun.

A foundational analogy that we can make between human behaviour on Earth and in space is Carl von Clausewitz's conception of war as a political, emotional and chaotic activity; space warfare is the continuation of Terran politics by other means. As satellites become crucial for modern military

This chapter originally appeared as a blog post on *Defence in Depth*, the Department of Defence Studies' blog at King's College London: https://defenceindepth.co/2016/09/26/from-sparta-to-space-astropolitics-and-ir-theory/. Their homepage can be found here: https://defenceindepth.co/. It has been edited and updated by the author for this book.

B. E. Bowen (✉)
University of Leicester, Leicester, UK
e-mail: bb215@leicester.ac.uk

power and socioeconomic activity on Earth, they become lucrative targets in any war planning involving spacepowers. This is evidenced by the spread of sophisticated anti-satellite weapons technology in the US, Russia, and China. Such satellites will not be targeted for their own sake however, whether or not they are worth shooting down or harassing will depend on their strategic value, and the political objectives of the war that ultimately determine whether an act is worth doing and if its costs are worth suffering.

By understanding space warfare and spacepower as the exploitation of a geography for ultimately political objectives in war and security, it opens one's mind to the conceptual (*but not historical*) analogies one can make between abstract conceptions from international relations into outer space. There will never be another Sparta and Athens, Rome and Carthage, or British and German Empires. But there may be a recurrence of the fear of attack, the credibility of one's honour, and competing material interests at stake between rival powers in an anarchic international system. They will manifest in new and unpredictable ways but the base concepts that animates war, peace and strategy will remain. Space is not a place that is uniquely free of humanity's fears and interests, though popular perceptions may give the impression that outer space is defined as a scientific frontier where the great scientific powers cooperate in manned exploration and interplanetary science. Rather, space is as varied a political environment as the sea where brute power politics, economic interests, rule-shaping and adherence to the norms of 'international society' happens all at once. The anarchic international system of states—where there is no superior authority able to impose order upon the most powerful states—has simply spread to include Earth orbit. The same will be true should humanity's political economy spread into cislunar and deep space. It is important therefore to consider economic activities in outer space, however briefly, in the context of scholarship on international relations and power politics.

Ideas and arguments across recorded history that examine and question the larger concepts of power, security and politics often contain some insights into new scenarios and locations. Extending terrestrial political experience to space is not merely an entertaining allegory one might make between the end of the Cold War in the early 1990s with the collapse of the fictional Klingon Empire in the early 2390s. Much astropolitical research is predicated on the conception that very little has changed in the core motivations of humans in dealing with politics, power and resources across time and geographies. Whether it is to check the growth of the power of Sparta or to match the prowess of the Soviets in space, it is the same base motivations that still influence, if not define, strategic behaviour and the pursuit of armaments. To do so requires booming and secure economies. If this extends to outer space with deep space mining, and if humanity's economy would become dependent upon it, there would be an increased premium on protecting and exploiting the command of space between Earth's major military and economic powers. In this scenario, the dicta of Everett Dolman's *Astropolitik* may be realized: "He who controls low-Earth orbit controls near-Earth space. Who controls near-Earth space dominates Terra. Who dominates Terra determines the destiny of humankind." Indeed, economic power is indivisible from military power and potential, as E.H. Carr noted in the *Twenty Years' Crisis*, and would-be tycoons of a space resource economy cannot distance themselves from the strategic and political consequences of their actions. Four examples in this chapter show how activities in space can be understood through some timeless concepts by applying Thucydides' core motivations of international behaviour.

Thucydides famously described the motivations for Greek empire building in the wake of the Persian retreat and the Peloponnesian War (431–403 BC) as being motivated by fear, honour and interest. He believed that, due to the unchanging nature of humans, these general parameters leading to war, or at least lenses guiding perceptions of insecurity, would recur in one way or another again *ad infinitum*. Indeed, it is not for nothing that many cite the growth of Athenian power and the fear it caused in Sparta whenever a rising power challenges the status quo. Though not comprehensive by any means in describing all of international relations, these three motivations certainly capture some fundamental drivers of strategic behaviour from the dawn of the Space Age to today and provide a useful starting point for power-political analysis. The US and the Soviet Union had invested heavily in space technology by the late 1950s as a result of their mutual fear, their competition over technological prestige and the pursuit of their own further interests as a result of their exploitation of outer space in the international system.

Without a long-range bomber force to strike in kind against the American homeland, the Soviet Union would always fear the possibility of nuclear blackmail. The American nuclear monopoly and decisive air superiority had to be negated and harnessing the physics of orbital mechanics and ballistic rocketry was a way to do so. In October 1957, it was America's turn to fear the technological prowess of the Soviet Union. Sergei Korolev, the Union of Soviet State Republic's (USSR) chief rocket scientist, had succeeded in launching humanity's first artificial satellite—Sputnik-1. This triggered a scare among the US population, who had taken American and democratic-capitalist society as the technological leader of the world. Yet there was a Red Moon in orbit. The Soviet Union had engineered a coup for its image as a communist technological powerhouse, which unsettled the US. Furthermore, and more importantly, this demonstrated to Eisenhower that the Soviet Union was on-track to developing the capability to deliver nuclear warheads to the continental US by developing heavy-lift rockets.

By the early 1960s, American fear—and no small desire to regain lost prestige—drove the simultaneous development of American rocket science (under the leadership of the former German SS officer Wernher von Braun) and satellite reconnaissance systems. McDougall, in *The Heavens and the Earth*, details how, working under the guise of the International Geophysical Year, the US was able to develop the first US orbital-capable rocket and the means to build spy satellites in secret, whilst also being able to claim contributions to scientific advancement. The Corona programme gave the US the means of spying on the closed Soviet Union. Lyndon Baines Johnson would later praise the American satellite reconnaissance programme for quelling the fears the US had in the so-called missile gap that was an election issue in 1960 between Nixon and Kennedy. Indeed, the missile gap existed—but US satellite reconnaissance had shown the American leadership that the gap was in their favour. This helped reassure Washington that Khrushchev's bark was worse than his bite, as far as the security of the continental US was concerned.

Despite the possibility that many in the Soviet Union and the US were genuine in their desire to open up space for peaceful exploration and a cooperative colonization of outer space, not least among von Braun and Korolev themselves, it is an oft-forgotten fact that humanity's entry into the cosmos is steeped in blood and political repression. This reality is at odds with the idealism that tends to accompany popular histories of space technology. Germany's V2 rocket, and the foundation of much subsequent American and Soviet rocketry, killed more people through its construction by slave labour in the Mittelwerk factory than bombing civilians in London. Korolev himself was toiling in a Soviet gulag before being drafted in to work on the space programme. Without the promise of reconnaissance satellites and nuclear weapons delivery, rocket science may never have enjoyed the investment it did in the 1940s and 1950s. Idealism in space has its place, and justifiably so as a motivating and inspiring force, but not at the expense of writing out—and forgetting—the darker side of humanity and power politics.

Following the Space Race, and the victory of the US in securing its prestige with American bootprints on the Moon, the US and the USSR continued to pursue varying interests in outer space. But by the 1970s more states were developing interests in orbit. In 1976, a coalition of equatorial states attempted to enshrine the recognition of their sovereignty from their airspace upwards to infinity in the Bogota Declaration. This would allow the equatorial states to control and set conditions for the use of the geosynchronous and geostationary orbital slots that were directly above their territories at an altitude of approximately 36,000 kilometres. The declaration failed. The two superpowers had supreme national interests in continuing to have unfettered access to their strategic communications and early warning satellites in geostationary orbit, and to recognize a spatial form of sovereignty—as opposed to platform-based one—would give too much influence to the equatorial states upon the space-faring states of the global North. Europe and Japan were beginning to develop their own space industries at this time as well, and they did not support the declaration through their own self-interests in using outer space for strategic and commercial purposes.

Also in the 1970s, Europe and the US demonstrated diverging interests in their pursuit of spacepower as detailed by Wang in *Transatlantic Space Politics*. The US was willing to launch European satellites on the condition that they were scientific satellites. This effectively barred European states from launching their own communications and reconnaissance satellites for both military and commercial purposes. Europe, under the leadership of France, West Germany and Italy, pursued the development of a European launcher, giving birth to the *Ariane* family of launchers. Early European rocket development was supported by the donation of the abandoned *Blue Streak* data and materials by the British. The US had not assisted European rocket development, and France even turned to the Soviet Union from 1974 onwards for the supply of unsymmetrical dimethylhydrazine (a crucial compound for rocket fuel). US interests were being threatened by the entry of European competition into the commercial satellite communications launch business, and an independent access to space would also allow European states to collectively follow a different strategic path to the US. Such concerns played out again in the Galileo satellite navigation negotiations between the US and the European Union. Only after extensive negotiations, and a flirtation with Chinese cooperation, did Europe and the US agree to make Galileo and GPS interoperable. Galileo, if integrated into European militaries, will allow greater freedom of action in tactical and operational terms than the American ubiquitous GPS service.

Today, India can be seen to be acting according to its fear, honour and interest in outer space. It fears being cut off from navigation signals in a regional war, and has therefore embedded itself in both GPS and GLONASS. Its regional GPS augmentation system, GAGAN, and regional navigation system, NAVIC, provide accurate signals for its military. Furthermore, as a full partner of GLONASS, Russia ensures India has another source of military-grade navigation signals. It is unlikely that India will face a scenario where *both* Russia and the US will seek to cut the subcontinent off from their navigation signals. This ensures that Indian precision warfare infrastructure is politically and strategically reliable. In terms of pursuing material interests, India has secured privileged access to GLONASS technology to develop downstream applications and services in its domestic economy, attempting to model America's success with downstream GPS applications, and increased technological development opportunities for Indian space research. Acting out of honour and prestige, India has 'beaten' China to Mars with a successfully orbiting satellite, and rightly gained an elevated profile and garnered prestige for pulling off such a difficult achievement.

For its part, China should not be interpreted as acting solely out of fear or a desire to threaten the US. True, it has developed a range of anti-satellite weapons capabilities and a comprehensive space infrastructure partly out of fear for its own security. But that is unremarkable in the context of similar developments in Russia and the US. China no doubt acts to pursue honour and prestige as well, as its human spaceflight and ambitious robotic programme demonstrates. China's economic modernization and development of a Space Information Corridor under its New Silk Road initiative shows a healthy appetite for material interests in outer space. Therefore, it is important to view astropolitics not from an unduly militaristic or paranoid lens, nor a blindly optimistic idealistic view of space exploration. Rather, fear, honour and interest capture the multifaceted motivations behind any spacepower and will continue to shape them if humanity develops a deep space economy.

Some of the core concepts of political life derived from the classical era can be just as useful to frame understandings of contemporary astropolitics, and makes the case for viewing outer space as just another place where human politics continues as it does on Earth. The choice of Thucydides to highlight this does not mean that astropolitics is *only* about fear, honour and interest—but that it is just as complicated, diverse and ambiguous as the politics of any other place on Earth. Outer space is not a place of unfettered cooperation or unrivalled competition. Astropolitics is not an aberration of political life. Space is used for military purposes because of the timeless motivations of fear, honour and interest. It has been since the dawn of the Space Age. In an anarchic international system, this is the context to any economic activity in outer space, especially if such economic activity becomes a source of military power. This understanding—that space is used for military purposes by all major powers—takes the hyperbolic sting out of contemporary official statements and denouncements in space arms control proceedings about the supposed doom facing peace on Earth if outer space is 'militarized' or 'weaponized.' For better and worse, humanity's use of outer space is shaped by Terran politics, and the solar system a rich vista waiting for the humanities to join the engineers and the scientists.

Bibliography

Aron, Raymond. 1966. *Peace and War: A Theory of International Relations*. Trans. Richard Howard and Annette Baker Fox. London: Weidenfeld & Nicholson.

Bowen, Bleddyn E. 2017. From the Sea to Outer Space: The Command of Space as the Foundation of Spacepower Theory. *The Journal of Strategic Studies* (Online Before Print). https://doi.org/10.1080/01402390.2017.1293531.

———. 2018. British Security Strategy and Outer Space: A Missing Link? *The British Journal of Politics and International Relations*. http://journals.sagepub.com/doi/abs/10.1177/1369148118758238

Bull, Hedley. 2012. *The Anarchical Society: A Study of Order in World Politics*. New York: Columbia University Press.

Carr, Edward H. 2001. *The Twenty Years' Crisis*. London: Palgrave Macmillan.

Dolman, Everett C. 2002. *Astropolitik: Classical Geopolitics in the Space Age*. London: Frank Cass.

Hilborne, Mark P. 2016. China. *Space Policy* 37: 1. https://doi.org/10.1016/j.spacepol.2016.10.004.

McDougall, Walter. 1985. ... *The Heavens and the Earth: A Political History of the Space Age*. Baltimore: Johns Hopkins University Press.

Pollpeter, Kevin. 2011. Upward and Onward: Technological Innovation and Organizational Change in China's Space Industry. *Journal of Strategic Studies* 34 (3). https://doi.org/10.1080/01402390.2011.574983.

Sagan, Carl. 1997. *Pale Blue Dot: A Vision of the Human Future in Space*. New York: Ballantine.

Sheehan, Michael. 2007. *The International Politics of Space*. London: Routledge.

Thucydides. 2009. *The Peloponnesian Wars*. Trans. Martin Hammond. Oxford: Oxford University Press

Wang, Sheng-Chih. 2013. *Transatlantic Space Politics*. London: Routledge.

Wendt, Alexander. 2011. *Social Theory of International Politics*. Cambridge: Cambridge University Press.

Further reading can be found at.: https://astropoliticsblog.wordpress.com/reading-list/

Bleddyn E. Bowen is a Lecturer in International Relations at the Department of History, Politics and International Relations, University of Leicester, England and holds a PhD on spacepower theory from the Department of International Politics, Aberystwyth University, Wales. Bleddyn's research specializes in spacepower theory, space warfare, space policy, modern warfare and classical military philosophy, and he has published in a variety of academic journals. Bleddyn is also a frequent contributor on BBC news and current affairs programming in both Welsh and English languages as an expert in modern warfare and security issues. Bleddyn also convenes *The Astropolitics Collective*, an informal network of astropolitical scholars mostly based within or affiliated with institutions in the United Kingdom.

12

The Economic Viability of Mars Colonization

Robert Zubrin

The economic viability of colonizing Mars has been extensively examined. It is shown that of all bodies in the solar system other than Earth, Mars is unique in that it has the resources required to support a population of sufficient size to create locally a new branch of human civilization. It is also shown that while Mars may lack any cash material directly exportable to Earth, its orbital elements and other physical parameters give it a unique positional advantage that will allow it to act as a keystone, supporting extractive activities in the asteroid belt and elsewhere in the solar system.

The potential of relatively near-term types of interplanetary transportation systems has also been researched and it is shown that with very modest advances on a historical scale, systems can be put in place that will allow individuals and families to emigrate to Mars at their own discretion. Their motives for doing so will parallel in many ways the historical motives for Europeans and others to come to America, including higher pay rates in a labour-short economy, escape from tradition and oppression, as well as freedom to exercise their drive to create in an untamed and undefined world.

Under conditions of such large-scale immigration, sale of real estate will add a significant source of income to the planet's economy. Potential increases in real-estate values after 'terraforming' will provide a sufficient financial incentive to do so. In analogy to frontier America, social conditions on Mars will make it a pressure cooker for invention. These inventions, licensed on

R. Zubrin (✉)
President Mars Society & President Pioneer Energy, Lakewood, CO, USA

© The Author(s) 2018
T. James (ed.), *Deep Space Commodities*,
https://doi.org/10.1007/978-3-319-90303-3_12

Earth, will raise both terrestrial and Martian living standards and contribute large amounts of income to support the development of the colony.

Introduction

A frequent objection raised against scenarios for the human settlement and terraforming of Mars is that while such projects may be technologically feasible, there is no possible way that they can be paid for. On the surface, the arguments given supporting this position appear too many to be cogent, in that Mars is distant, difficult to access, possesses a hostile environment and has no apparent resources of economic value to export.

These arguments appear to be ironclad, yet it must be pointed out that they were also presented in the past as convincing reasons for the utter impracticality of the European settlement of North America and Australia. It is certainly true that the technological and economic problems facing Mars colonization in the twenty-first century are vastly different in detail than those that had to be overcome during the colonization of the New World in the seventeenth century, or Australia in the nineteenth century. Nevertheless, it is my contention that the argument against the feasibility of Mars colonization is flawed by essentially the same false logic and lack of understanding of real economics. This has resulted in repeated absurd misevaluations of the value of colonial settlements (as opposed to trading posts, plantations and other extractive activities) on the part of numerous European government ministries during the 400 years following Columbus.

During the period of their global ascendancy, the Spanish ignored North America; to them it was nothing but a vast amount of worthless wilderness. In 1781, while Cornwallis was being blockaded into submission at Yorktown, the British deployed their fleet into the Caribbean to seize a few high-income sugar plantation islands from the French. In 1802, Napoleon Bonaparte sold a third of what is now the United States for two million dollars. In 1867, the Czar sold off Alaska for a similar pittance. The existence of Australia was known to Europe for 200 years before the first colony arrived, and no European power even bothered to claim the continent until 1830. These pieces of short-sighted statecraft, almost incomprehensible in their stupidity, are legendary today. Yet their consistency shows a persistent blind spot amongst policy-making groups as to the true sources of wealth and power. I believe that it is certain that 200 years from now, the current apathy of governments towards the value of extraterrestrial bodies, and Mars in particular, will be viewed in a similar light.

This chapter will return to historical analogies periodically; however, the arguments presented within are not primarily historical in nature. Instead, they are based on the concrete knowledge already derived from Mars itself—its unique characteristics, resources, technological requirements and its relationships to the other important bodies within our solar system.

The Phases of Mars Colonization

In order to understand the economics of Mars colonization it is necessary first to examine briefly the different phases of activity that will be necessary to transform the so-called Red Planet. There are four phases, which we will identify as exploration, base building, settlement and terraforming.

Exploration

The exploration phase of Mars colonization has been going on for some time now with the telescopic and robotic surveys that have been and continue to be made. It will take a quantum leap, however, for actual human expeditions to the planet's surface to begin. As has been shown in numerous papers about the planet, if the Martian atmosphere is exploited for the purpose of manufacturing rocket fuel and oxygen, the mass, complexity and overall logistics requirements of such missions can be reduced to the point where affordable human missions to Mars can be launched with present-day technology. Moreover, by using such 'Mars Direct' type approaches, human explorers can be on Mars within ten years of programme initiation, with total expenditure not more than 20 percent of NASA's existing budget.

The purpose of the exploration phase is to resolve the major outstanding scientific questions bearing on the history of Mars as a planet and a possible home for life in the past; to conduct a preliminary survey of the resources of Mars and determine optimum locations for future human bases and settlements; and to establish a modus operandi whereby humans can travel to and reside on the planet, and conduct useful operations over substantial regions of the surface of Mars.

Base Building

The essence of the base building phase is to conduct agricultural, industrial, chemical, and civil engineering research on Mars to master an increasing array of techniques required to turn Martian raw materials into useful resources.

While properly conducted initial exploration missions will make use of the Martian air to provide fuel and oxygen, in the base building phase this elementary level of local resource utilization will be transcended as the crew of a permanent Mars base learns how to extract native water and grow crops on Mars, to produce ceramics, glasses, metals, plastics, wires, habitats, inflatable structures, solar panels, and all sorts of other useful materials, tools and structures.

The initial exploration phase can be accomplished with small crews of about four members each, operating out of spartan base camps spread over vast areas of the Martian surface. The base building phase, however, will require a division of labour entailing a larger number of people, in the order of 50, equipped with a wide variety of equipment and substantial sources of power. In short, the purpose of the base building period is to develop a mastery of those techniques required to produce on Mars the food, clothing and shelter required to support a large population on the Red Planet.

The base building phase could begin in earnest about ten years after the initial human landing on Mars.

Settlement

Once the techniques have been mastered that will allow the support of a large population on Mars out of indigenous resources, the settlement of Mars can begin. The primary purpose of this phase is simply to populate Mars, creating a new branch of human civilization there with exponentially growing capabilities to transform the Red Planet.

While the exploration and base building phases can and probably must be carried out on the basis of outright government funding, during the settlement phase economics comes to the fore. That is, while a Mars base of even a few hundred people can potentially be supported out of pocket by governmental expenditures, a Martian society of hundreds of thousands clearly cannot. To be viable, a real Martian civilization must be either completely autarchic—very unlikely until the far future—or be able to produce some kind of export that allows it to pay for the imports it requires.

Terraforming

If a viable Martian civilization can be established, its population and powers to change its planet will continue to grow. The advantages accruing to such a society of terraforming Mars into a more human-friendly environment are manifest. Put simply, if enough people find a way to live and prosper on Mars, there is no doubt but that sooner or later they will terraform the planet. The feasibility, or lack thereof of terraforming Mars, is thus in a sense a corollary to the economic viability of the Martian colonization effort.

Potential methods of terraforming Mars have been discussed in a number of locations. In the primary scenario, artificial greenhouse gases such as halocarbons are produced on Mars and released into the atmosphere. The temperature rise induced by the presence of these gases causes CO_2 adsorbed in the regolith to be 'outgassed', increasing the greenhouse effect still more, causing more outgassing and so on. It has been shown that a rate of halocarbon production of about 1,000 tonnes per hour would directly induce a temperature rise of about 10 K on Mars, and that the outgassing of CO_2 caused by this direct forcing would likely raise the average temperature on Mars by 40–50 K, resulting in a Mars with a surface pressure over 200 mbar and seasonal incidence of liquid water in the warmest parts of the planet.

Production of halocarbons at this rate would require an industrial establishment on Mars wielding about 5,000 MW or power supported by a division of labour requiring at least (assuming optimistic application of robotics) 10,000 people. Such an operation would be enormous compared to our current space efforts, but very small compared to the overall human economic effort even at present. It is therefore anticipated that such efforts could commence as early as the mid-twenty-first century, with a substantial amount of the outgassing following on a timescale of a few decades.

While humans could not breath the atmosphere of such a Mars, plants could, and under such conditions increasingly complex types of pioneering vegetation could be disseminated to create soil, oxygen, and ultimately the foundation for a thriving ecosphere on Mars. The presence of substantial pressure, even of an unbreathable atmosphere, would greatly benefit human settlers, as only simple breathing gear and warm clothes (i.e. no spacesuits) would be required to operate in the open, and city-sized inflatable structures could be erected (since there would be no pressure differential with the outside world) that could house very large settlements in an open-air, shirt-sleeve environment.

Nevertheless, Mars will not be considered fully terraformed until its air is breathable by humans. Assuming complete coverage of the planet with photosynthetic plants, it would take about a millennia to put the 120 mbar of oxygen in Mars' atmosphere needed to support human respiration in the open. It is therefore anticipated that human terraformers would accelerate the oxygenation process by artificial technological approaches yet to be determined, with the two leading concepts being those based on either macro-engineering (i.e. direct employment of very large-scale energy systems such as terawatt-sized fusion reactors, huge space-based reflectors or lasers) or self-reproducing machines, such as Turing machines or nanotechnology.

Since such systems are well outside current engineering knowledge, it is difficult to provide any useful estimate of how quickly they could complete the terraforming job. However, in the case of self-replicating machines the ultimate source of power would be solar and this provides the basis for an upper bound to system performance. Assuming the whole planet is covered with machines converting sunlight to electricity at 30 percent efficiency, and all this energy is applied to releasing oxygen from metallic oxides, a 120 mbar oxygen atmosphere could be created in about 30 years.

Amongst extraterrestrial bodies in our solar system, Mars is unique in that it possesses all the raw materials required to support not only life, but a new branch of human civilization. This uniqueness is illustrated most clearly if we contrast Mars with Earth's Moon, the most frequently cited alternative location for extraterrestrial human colonization.

In contrast to the Moon, Mars is rich in carbon, nitrogen, hydrogen and oxygen, all in biologically readily accessible forms such as CO_2 gas, nitrogen gas, and water ice and permafrost. Carbon, nitrogen and hydrogen are only present on the Moon in parts per million quantities, much like gold in sea water. Oxygen is abundant on the Moon, but only in tightly bound oxides such as SiO_2, Fe_2O_3, MgO and Al_2O_3, which require very high energy processes to reduce. Current knowledge indicates that if Mars were smooth and all its ice and permafrost melted into liquid water, the entire planet would be covered with an ocean over 100 metres deep. This contrasts strongly with the Moon, which is so dry that if concrete were found there, lunar colonists would mine it to get the water out. Thus, if plants were grown in greenhouses on the Moon (a very difficult proposition, as will be explained), most of their biomass material would have to be imported.

The Moon is also deficient in about half the metals, for example copper, of interest to industrial society, as well as many other elements of interest such as sulphur and phosphorus. Mars has every required element in abundance. Moreover, on Mars, as on Earth, hydrologic and volcanic processes have occurred, which is likely to have concentrated various elements into local concentrations of high-grade mineral ore. Indeed, the geological history of Mars has been compared with that of Africa, with very optimistic inferences as to its mineral wealth implied as a corollary. In contrast, the Moon has had virtually no history of water or volcanic action, with the result that it is basically composed of trash rocks with very little differentiation into ores that represent useful concentrations of anything interesting.

But the biggest problem with the Moon, as with all other airless planetary bodies and proposed artificial free-space colonies (such as those proposed by Gerard O'Neill) is that sunlight is not available in a form useful for growing crops. This is an extremely important point and it is not well understood. Plants require an enormous amount of energy for their growth, and it can only come from sunlight. For example, a single square kilometre of cropland on Earth is illuminated with about 1,000 MW of sunlight at noon—a power load equal to a US city of one million people. Put another way, the amount of power required to generate the sunlight falling on the tiny country of El Salvador exceeds the combined capacity of every power plant on Earth. Plants can stand a drop of perhaps a factor of five in their light intake compared to terrestrial norms and still grow, but the fact remains that the energetics of plant growth make it inconceivable to raise crops on any kind of meaningful scale with artificially generated light. That said, the problem with using the natural sunlight available on the Moon or in space is that it is unshielded by any atmosphere. (The Moon has an additional problem with its 28-day light/dark cycle, which is also unacceptable to plants). Thus, plants grown in a thin-walled greenhouse on the surface of the Moon or an asteroid would be killed by solar flares. In order to grow plants safely in such an environment, the walls of the greenhouse would have to be made of glass 10 cm thick, a construction requirement that would make the development of significant agricultural areas prohibitively expensive. Use of reflectors and other light-channelling devices would not solve this problem, as the reflector areas would have to be enormous, essentially equal in area to the crop domains, creating preposterous engineering problems if any significant acreage is to be illuminated.

Mars, on the other hand, has an atmosphere of sufficient density to protect crops grown on the surface against solar flares. On Mars, even during the base building phase, large inflatable greenhouses made of transparent plastic protected by thin hard-plastic, ultra-violet and abrasion-resistant geodesic domes could be readily deployed, rapidly creating large domains for crop growth. Even without the problems of solar flares and a month-long diurnal cycle, such simple greenhouses would be impractical on the Moon as they would create unbearably high temperatures. On Mars, in contrast, the strong greenhouse effect created by such domes would be precisely what is necessary to produce a temperate climate inside.

Even during the base building phase, domes of this type up to 50 metres in diameter could be deployed on Mars that could contain the 5 psi atmosphere necessary to support humans. If made of high-strength plastics such as Kevlar, such a dome could have a safety factor of four against burst and weigh only about 4 tonnes, with another four tonnes required for its unpressurized

Plexiglas shield. In the early years of settlement, such domes could be imported pre-fabricated from Earth. Later on, they could be manufactured on Mars, along with larger domes (with the mass of the pressurized dome increasing as the cube of its radius, and the mass of the unpressurized shield dome increasing as the square of the radius: 100-metre domes would mass 32 tonnes and need a 16-tonne Plexiglas shield, and so on). Networks of such 50- to 100-metre domes could rapidly be manufactured and deployed, opening up large areas of the surface to both shirt-sleeve human habitation and agriculture. If agriculture-only areas are desired, the domes could be made much bigger, as plants do not require more than about 1 psi atmospheric pressure. Once Mars has been partially terraformed however, with the creation of a thicker CO_2 atmosphere via regolith outgassing, the habitation domes could be made virtually to any size, as they would not have to sustain a pressure differential between their interior and exterior.

The point, however, is that in contrast to colonists on any other known extraterrestrial body, Martian colonists will be able to live on the surface, not in tunnels, and move about freely and grow crops in the light of day. Mars is a place where humans can live and multiply to large numbers, supporting themselves with products of every description made out of indigenous materials. Mars is thus a place where an actual civilization, not just a mining or scientific outpost, can be developed. And significantly for interplanetary commerce, Mars and Earth are the only two locations in the solar system where humans will be able to grow crops for export.

Mars is the best target for colonization in the solar system because it has by far the greatest potential for self-sufficiency. Nevertheless, even with optimistic extrapolation of robotic manufacturing techniques, Mars will not have the division of labour required to make it fully self-sufficient until its population numbers in the millions. It will thus for a long time be necessary, and forever desirable, for Mars to be able to pay for import of specialized manufactured goods from Earth. These goods can be fairly limited in mass, as only small portions (by weight) of even very high-tech goods are actually complex. Nevertheless, these smaller sophisticated items will have to be paid for, and their cost will be greatly increased by the high costs of Earth-launch and interplanetary transport. What can Mars possibly export back to Earth in return?

It is this question that has caused many to deem Mars colonization intractable, or at least inferior in prospect to the Moon. After all, the Moon does have indigenous supplies of helium-3, an isotope not found on Earth and which could be of considerable value as a fuel for thermonuclear fusion reactors. Mars has no known helium-3 resources. Because of its complex geological history, Mars may have concentrated mineral ores, with much greater concentrations of ores of precious metals readily available than is currently the case on Earth, due to the fact that the terrestrial ores have been heavily scavenged by humans for the past 5,000 years.

It has been shown that if concentrated supplies of metals of equal or greater value than silver (such as germanium, hafnium, lanthanum, cerium, rhenium, samarium, gallium, gadolinium, gold, palladium, iridium, rubidium, platinum, rhodium and europium) were available on Mars, they could potentially be transported back to Earth at high profit by using reusable Mars-surface-based single-stage-to-orbit (SSTO) vehicles to deliver the cargoes to Mars orbit; and then transporting them back to Earth using either cheap expendable chemical stages manufactured on Mars or reusable cycling solar sail powered interplanetary spacecraft. The existence of such Martian precious metal ores, however, is still hypothetical.

Another alternative is that Mars could pay for itself by transporting back ideas. Just as the labour shortage prevalent in colonial and nineteenth-century America drove the creation of Yankee ingenuity's flood of inventions, so the conditions of extreme labour shortage combined with a technological culture and the unacceptability of impractical legislative constraints against innovation will tend to drive Martian ingenuity to produce wave after wave of invention in energy production, automation and robotics, biotechnology and other areas. These inventions, licensed on Earth, could finance Mars even as they revolutionize and advance terrestrial living standards as forcefully as nineteenth-century US invention changed Europe and ultimately the rest of the world as well.

Inventions produced as a matter of necessity by a practical intellectual culture stressed by frontier conditions can make Mars rich, but invention is not the only way that Martians will be able to make a fortune. The other way is trade.

To understand this, it is necessary to consider the energy relationships between Earth, the Moon, Mars and the main asteroid belt. The asteroid belt enters into the picture here because it is known to contain vast supplies of very high-grade metal ore in a low-gravity environment that makes it comparatively easy to export to Earth. Miners operating in the main belt, for reasons given above, will be unable to produce their necessary supplies locally. There will thus be a need to export food and other necessary goods from either Earth or Mars to the main belt. As shown in Table 12.1, Mars has an overwhelming positional advantage as a location from which to conduct such trade.

In Table 12.1, all the entries except the last two are based upon a transportation system using CH_4/O_2 engines with an Isp of 380 s and high-thrust ΔVs. These were chosen because CH_4/O_2 is the highest performing

Table 12.1 Transportation in the inner solar system

	Earth		Mars	
	ΔV(km/s)	Mass ratio	ΔV (km/s)	Mass ratio
Surface to low orbit	9.0	11.4	4.0	2.9
Surface to escape	12.0	25.6	5.5	4.4
Low orbit to lunar surface	6.0	5.1	5.4	4.3
Surface to lunar surface	15.0	57.6	9.4	12.5
Low orbit to Ceres	9.6	13.4	4.9	3.8
Surface to Ceres	18.6	152.5	8.9	11.1
Ceres to planet	4.8	3.7	2.7	2.1
NEP round-trip LO to Ceres	40.0	2.3	15.0	1.35
Chem to LO, NEP rt to Ceres	9/40	26.2	4/15	3.9

space-storable chemical propellant, and can be manufactured easily on either Earth, Mars or a carbonaceous asteroid. H_2/O_2, while offering a higher Isp (450 s) is not storable for long durations in space. Moreover, it is an unsuitable propellant for a cheap reusable space transportation system, since it costs more than an order of magnitude more than CH_4/O_2 (thus ruling it out for true cheap surface-to-orbit systems) and its bulk makes it very difficult to transport to orbit in any quantity using SSTO-type vehicles. The last two entries in the table are based upon nuclear electric propulsion (NEP) using argon propellant, available on either Earth or Mars, with an Isp of 5,000 s for in-space propulsion, with CH_4/O_2 used to reach low orbit (LO) from the planet's surface.

It can be seen that if chemical systems are used exclusively, then the mass ratio required to deliver dry mass to the asteroid belt from Earth is 14 times greater than from Mars. This implies a still (much) greater ratio of payload-to-take-off mass ratio from Mars to Ceres than from Earth, because all the extra propellant requires massive tankage and larger calibre engines, all of which requires still more propellant, and therefore more tankage and so on. In fact, looking at Table 12.1, it can safely be said that useful trade between Earth and Ceres (or any other body in the main asteroid belt) using chemical propulsion is probably impossible, while from Mars it is easy. It can also be seen that there is a five-fold advantage in mass ratio delivering cargoes to the Earth's Moon from Mars over doing it from Earth.

If NEP is introduced the story changes, but not much. Mars still has a seven-fold advantage in mass ratio over Earth as a port of departure for the main asteroid belt, which translates into a payload-to-take-off weight ratio nearly two orders of magnitude higher for Mars departure than for Earth.

A comparison of Earth to Ceres and Mars to Ceres for all chemical and chemical/NEP missions is shown in Table 12.2. Both missions deliver 50 tonnes of cargo. Tankage for both NEP and chemical systems is calculated at 7 percent of the mass of the propellant required. For surface-to-orbit vehicles, it is assumed that dry mass excluding tankage is equal to the payload. For chemical interplanetary systems, it is assumed that the dry inert mass excluding tankage is equal to 20 percent of the payload. The NEP versions in Table 12.2 are 10 MWe for delivery from Mars and 30 MWe for delivery from Earth, with each NEP system massing 5 tonnes/MW. The different power ratings give both systems about equal power/mass ratios; the system leaving Earth still burns 2.4 times as long. If it were desired to increase the power rating of the Earth-based NEP vessel so that its burn time were the same as the Mars-based system, the mass of the Earth-based mission would go to infinity. In Table 12.2, the mass numbers are for the total mission. It is understood that the total launch requirement could be divided up into many launch vehicles, as required.

It can be seen that the launch burden for sending the cargo to Ceres is about 50 times less for missions starting from Mars than those departing from Earth, regardless of whether the technology employed is all chemical propulsion or chemical launch vehicles combined with NEP for interplanetary transfer. If the launch vehicle used has a 1,000 tonne lift-off mass, if would require 107 launches to assemble the CH_4/O_2 freighter mission if launched from Earth, but only two launches if the departure is from Mars. Even if propellant and other launch costs were ten times greater on Mars than on Earth, it would still be enormously advantageous to launch from Mars.

The result that follows is simply this: anything that needs to be sent to the asteroid belt that can be produced on Mars will be produced on Mars.

Table 12.2 Mass of freighter missions to the main asteroid belt (tonnes)

Planet of departure	Earth		Mars	
Propulsion system	CH_4/O_2	Chem/NEP	CH_4/O_2	Chem/NEP
Payload	50	50	50	50
Interplanetary spacecraft	10	150	10	50
Interplanetary tankage	85	19	15	3
Interplanetary propellant	1,220	268	205	37
Total mass in low orbit	1,365	487	280	140
Launch vehicle inert mass	1,365	337	280	90
Launch vehicle tankage	6,790	1,758	88	28
Launch vehicle propellant	97,000	25,127	1,250	401
Total ground lift-off mass	106,520	27,559	1,898	609

The outline of future interplanetary commerce thus becomes clear. There will be a 'triangle trade', with Earth supplying high-technology manufactured goods to Mars, Mars supplying low-technology manufactured goods and food staples to the asteroid belt and possibly the Moon as well, and the asteroids and Moon sending metals and possibly helium-3 to Earth. This triangle trade, illustrated in Fig. 12.1 is directly analogous to the triangle trade of Britain, her North American colonies and the West Indies during the colonial period. Britain would send manufactured goods to North America, the American colonies would send food staples and needed craft products to the West Indies, and the West Indies would send cash crops such as sugar to Britain. A similar triangle trade involving Britain, Australia and the Spice Islands also supported British trade in the East Indies during the nineteenth century.

Populating Mars

This proposition being made publike and coming to the scanning of all, it raised many variable opinions amongst men, and caused many fears & doubts amongst themselves. Some, from their reasons & hopes conceived, laboured to stir up & incourage the rest to undertake and prosecute the same; others, againe, out of their fears, objected against it, & sought to diverte from it, aledging many things, and those neither unreasonable nor unprobable; as that it was a great designe, and subjecte to many unconceivable perills & dangers...

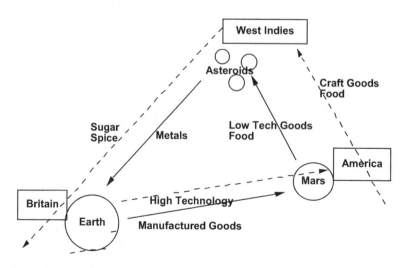

Fig. 12.1 The triangle trade: eighteenth century and twenty-first century

It was answered that all great & honourable actions are accompanied with great difficulties, and must be both enterprised and overcome with answerable courages. (Gov. William Bradford, "Of Plimoth Plantation", 1621)

The difficulty of interplanetary travel may make Mars colonization seem visionary. However colonization is, by definition, a one-way trip, and it is this fact which makes it possible to transport the large numbers of people that a colony in a new world needs to succeed.

Let us consider two models of how humans might emigrate to Mars: a government sponsored model and a privately sponsored model.

If government sponsorship is available, the technological means required for immigration on a significant scale are essentially available today. In Fig. 12.2 we see one version of such a concept that could be used to transport immigrants to Mars. A shuttle-derived heavy-lift launch vehicle lifts 145 tonnes (the Saturn V had approximately this capacity) to low-Earth orbit (LEO), then a nuclear thermal rocket (NTR, such as was demonstrated in the US in the 1960s) stage with an Isp of 900 s hurls a 70 tonne 'habcraft' onto a seven-month trajectory to Mars. Arriving at Mars, the 'habcraft' uses its

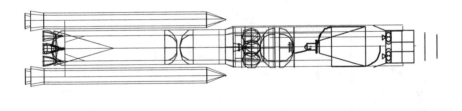

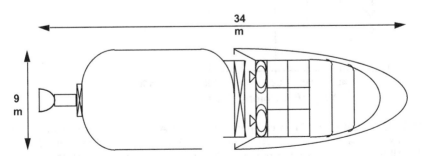

Fig. 12.2 An NTR-augmented heavy-lift launch vehicle, capable of transporting 24 colonists one-way to the Red Planet

'biconic shell' to aerobrake, and then parachutes and lands on its own sets of methane/oxygen engines.

The habcraft is eight metres in diameter and includes four complete habitation decks, for a total living area of 200 m², allowing it to adequately house 24 people in space and on Mars. Expansion area is available in the fifth (uppermost) deck after the cargo it contains is unloaded upon arrival. Thus in a single booster launch, 24 people, complete with their housing and tools, can be transported one-way from Earth to Mars.

Now let us assume that starting in the year 2030, an average of four such boosters are launched every year from Earth. If we then make various reasonable demographic assumptions, the population curve for Mars can be computed. The results are shown in Fig. 12.3. Examining the graph, we see that with this level of effort (and the technology frozen at late twentieth-century levels forever), the rate of human population growth of Mars in the twenty-first century would be about one-fifth that experienced by colonial America in the seventeenth and eighteenth centuries.

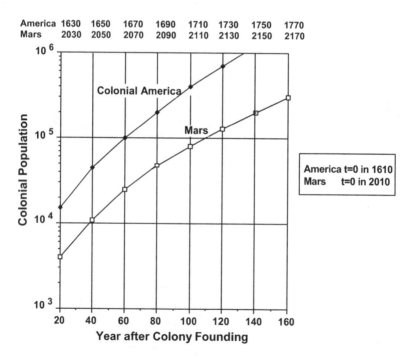

Fig. 12.3 Colonization of Mars compared to North America. Analysis assumes 100 immigrants per year starting in 2030, increasing at 2 percent annual rate, 50/50 male/female. All immigrants are aged between 20 and 40. Average of 3.5 children to an ideal Martian family. Mortality rates are 0.1 percent per year between ages 0 and 59, 1 percent between ages 60 and 79, 10 percent per year for those over 80

This in itself is a very significant result. What it means is that the distance to Mars and the transportation challenge that it implies is not a major obstacle to the initiation of a human civilization on the Red Planet. Rather the key questions become those of resource utilization, growing food, building housing, and manufacturing all sorts of useful goods on the surface of Mars. Moreover, the projected population growth rate, one-fifth of that of colonial America, while a bit slow, is significant on a historical scale, and assuming a cost of US$1 billion per launch, the US$4 billion per year programme cost could be sustained for some time by any major power on Earth that cared to plant the seeds of its posterity on Mars.

However, with a cost per launch of about US$1 billion, the cost per immigrant would be US$40 million. Such a price might be affordable to governments (for a time), but not to individuals or private groups. If Mars is ever to benefit from the dynamic energy of large numbers of immigrants motivated by personal choice to seek to make their mark in a new world, the transportation fee will have to drop a lot lower than this. Let us therefore examine an alternative model to see how low it is likely to drop.

Consider once again our CH_4/O_2 SSTO vehicles used to transport payloads from the surface of Earth to LEO. For every kilogram of payload delivered to orbit, about 70 kilograms of propellant are required. CH_4/O_2 bipropellant costs about US$0.20 per kilogram, so US$14 of propellant costs will be incurred for every kilogram lifted to orbit. If we then assume total system operation cost is seven times propellant costs (roughly double the total cost/fuel cost ratio of airlines), then the cost of delivery to LEO could be around US$100 per kilogram. If we assume that there is operating between Earth and Mars a cycling spacecraft which has the ability to recycle water and oxygen with 95 percent efficiency, then each passenger (100 kilograms with personal effects) will have to bring about 400 kilograms of supplies to provide themselves with food, water and oxygen during a 200-day outbound trip to Mars.

Thus 500 kilograms will need to be transported through a ΔV of about 4.3 kilometres per second to move the immigrant from LEO to a (two-year) cycling interplanetary spacecraft. The capsule mass, used to transport the immigrant from LEO to the cycler and from the cycler to the Martian surface, could be assumed optimistically to have a mass of 500 kg per passenger. Thus for each passenger a total of 1,000 kg needs to be delivered to the cycler orbit, which with an Isp of 380 s for the CH_4/O_2 propulsion system on the transfer capsules translates into 3,200 kg in LEO. At a delivery price of US$100 per kilogram to LEO, and assuming that the cost of the cycler itself is amortized over a very large number of missions, this in turn translates into a cost of US$320,000 per passenger to Mars.

Obviously, there are many assumptions in the above calculation that could be changed that would either raise or lower the calculated ticket price significantly. For example, use of air-breathing supersonic ramjet propulsion to perform a significant part of the Earth-to-orbit ΔV could cut orbit delivery costs by as much as a factor of 3. Using an electric propulsion LEO to L1 electric propulsion ferry, followed by a powered flyby through a LEO perigee using high-thrust chemical stage, would allow the cycler to be reached with a chemical ΔV of only 1.3 kilometres per second, thereby doubling payload and reducing costs yet again. If the cycler employs a magnetic sail instead of simply using natural ballistic orbits with gravity assists, the hyperbolic velocity departing Earth required to rendezvous with it can be essentially zero, thereby allowing the entire LEO to cycler delivery to be done by electric propulsion, or conceivably even solar or magnetic sails. Increasing the degree of closure of the life support system on the cycler would reduce the consumable delivery requirement for each passenger, thereby reducing passage costs still more. Thus, eventually Earth to Mars transportation costs could be expected to drop another order of magnitude, to US$30,000 per passenger or so. The cost impacts as each of these innovations is progressively introduced is displayed in Table 12.3.

Nevertheless, the order of magnitude of the US$320,000 fare cited for early immigrants—roughly the cost of an upper-middle-class house in many parts of suburban US, or put another way, roughly the life savings of a successful middle-class family—is interesting. It's not a sum of money that anyone would spend lightly, but it is a sum of money that a large number of people could finance if they really wanted to do so. Why would they want to do so? Simply this, because of the small size of the Martian population and the large transport cost itself, it is certain that the cost of labour on Mars will be much greater than on Earth. Therefore wages will be much higher on Mars than on Earth; while US$320,000 might be six years' salary to an engineer on Earth, it would likely represent only one or two years' salary on Mars. This wage differential, precisely analogous to the wage differential between Europe and America during most of the past four centuries, will make emigration to

Table 12.3 Possible cost reductions of Earth to Mars transportation system

	Baseline	Advanced	Reduction factor	Fare to Mars (US$)
Baseline mission	–	–	1.0	$320,000
Earth-to-orbit	Rockets	Scramjets	0.3	$96,000
Life support closure	95%	99%	0.7	$67,000
LEO escape propulsion	CH_4/O_2	NEP	0.6	$40,000
Cycler propulsion	Natural	Magsail	0.7	$28,000

Mars both desirable and possible for the individual. From the seventeenth through nineteenth centuries, the classic pattern was for a family in Europe to pool its resources to allow one of its members to emigrate to America. That emigrant, in turn, would proceed to earn enough money to bring the rest of the family over. Today, the same method of obtaining passage is used by Third World immigrants whose salaries in their native lands are dwarfed by current air-fares. Because the necessary income will be there to pay for the trip after it has been made, loans can even be taken out to finance the journey. It has been done in the past, it will be done in the future.

As mentioned before, the labour shortage that will prevail on Mars will drive Martian civilization towards both technological and social advances. If you're paying five times the terrestrial wage rate, you're not going to want to waste any of your workers' time with cheap labour tasks or filling out forms, and you will not seek to exclude someone who can perform some desperately needed profession from doing so just because they have not taken the trouble to run some institutional obstacle course to obtain appropriate certifications. In short, Martian civilization will be practical because it will have to be, just as nineteenth-century US civilization was, and this forced pragmatism will give it an enormous advantage in competing with the less stressed, and therefore more tradition-bound society remaining behind on Earth. Necessity is the mother of invention; Mars will provide the cradle.

A frontier society based on technological excellence and pragmatism, and populated by people self-selected for personal drive, will perforce be a hotbed of invention, and these inventions will not only serve the needs of the Martians but of the terrestrial population as well. Therefore, they will bring income to Mars (via terrestrial licensing) and at the same time they will disrupt the labour-rich terrestrial society's inherent tendency towards stagnation. This process of rejuvenation, and not direct economic benefits via triangle trade for main-belt asteroid mineral resources, will ultimately be the greatest benefit that the colonization of Mars will offer Earth, and it will be those terrestrial societies who have the closest social, cultural, linguistic and economic links with the Martians who will benefit the most.

Martian real estate can be broken down into two categories; habitable and open. By habitable real estate I mean that which is under a dome, allowing human settlers to live there in a relatively conventional shirt-sleeve, open-air environment. Open real estate is that which is outside the domes. It is obvious that habitable real estate is far more valuable than open real estate. Nevertheless, both of these can be bought and sold, and as transportation costs drop, both forms of Martian real estate will rise in value.

The only kind of land that exists on Mars right now is open. There is an immense amount of it—143 million square kilometres—but it might seem that that it is all completely worthless because it cannot currently be exploited. Not so. Enormous tracts of land were bought and sold in Kentucky for very large sums of money a 100 years before settlers arrived. For purposes of development, Trans-Appalachian America might as well have been Mars in the 1600s. What made it saleable were two things: (1) that at least a few people believed that it would be exploitable someday, and (2) that a juridical arrangement existed (in the form of British Crown land patents) which allowed Trans-Appalachian land to be privately owned. In fact, if a mechanism were put in place that could enforce private property rights on Mars, land on Mars could probably be bought and sold now. Such a mechanism would not need to employ enforcers, for example a 'space police', on the surface of Mars; the patent or property registry of a sufficiently powerful nation, such as the US, would be entirely adequate. For example, if the US chose to grant a mining patent to any private group that surveyed a piece of Martian real estate to some specified degree of fidelity, such claims would be tradable today on the basis of their future speculative worth (and could probably be used to privately finance robotic mining survey probes in the near future). Furthermore, such claims would be enforceable internationally and throughout the solar system simply by having the US Customs Office penalize with a punitive tariff any US import made anywhere, directly or indirectly, with material that was extracted in defiance of the claim. This sort of mechanism would not imply US sovereignty over Mars, any more that the current US Patent and Copyright Offices coining of ideas into intellectual property implies US government sovereignty over the universe of ideas. But whether it's US, NATO, UN or a Martian Republic, a government's agreement is needed to turn worthless terrain into real-estate property value.

Once that is in place, however, even the undeveloped open real estate on Mars represents a tremendous source of capital to finance the initial development of Martian settlements. Sold at an average value of US$10 per acre, Mars would be worth US$358 billion. If Mars were terraformed, these open land prices could be expected to grow hundred-fold, with a rough planetary land value of US$36 trillion implied. Assuming, as appears to be the case, that a method of terraforming Mars could be found with a total cost much less than this, then those who own Mars would have every reason to seek to develop their property via planetary engineering.

Of course, all open real estate on Mars will not be of equal value; those sections known to contain valuable minerals or other resources, or which are located closer to the habitable areas will be worth much more. For these reasons, as with land speculators on Earth in the past, the owners of open unexplored real estate on Mars will exercise all their influence to further the exploration of, and encourage the settlement of, land under their control.

Far more valuable than the open real estate will be habitable real estate beneath the domes. Each 100-metre diameter dome, massing about 50 tonnes (32 tonnes for the inflatable Kevlar pressure dome, 16 tonnes for the Plexiglas geodesic rigid shield dome, 2 tonnes for miscellaneous fittings), would enclose an area of about 2 acres. Assuming that dwelling units for 20 families are erected within it, and each family is willing to pay US$50,000 for their habitation land (a plot 20 metres on a side), then the total real-estate value enclosed by a single dome would be US$1,000,000. At this rate, the creation of habitable land by the mass production and erection of large numbers of domes to house the waves of immigrants should prove to be one of the biggest businesses on Mars and a major source of income for the colony.

In the twenty-first century, Earth's population growth will make real estate here ever more expensive, making it ever harder for people to own their own homes. At the same time, the ongoing bureaucratization of the former terrestrial frontier societies will make it ever harder for strong spirits to find adequate means for expressing their creative drive and initiative on Earth. Regulation to 'protect' what is, will become ever more burdensome to those who would create what is not. A confined world will limit opportunity for all and seek to enforce behavioural and cultural norms that will be unacceptable to many. When the frictions turn into inevitable revolts and wars, there will be losers. A planet of refuge will be needed, and Mars will be there.

Historical Analogies

[T]to the frontier the American intellect owes its striking characteristics. That coarseness of strength combined with acuteness and inquisitiveness; that practical, inventive turn of mind, quick to find expedients; that masterful grasp of material things, lacking in the artistic but powerful to effect great ends; that restless, nervous energy; that dominant individualism, working for good and evil, and withal that buoyancy and exuberance that comes from freedom – these are the traits of the frontier, or traits called out elsewhere because of the existence of the frontier. Since the days when the fleets of Columbus sailed into the waters of the New World, America has been another name for opportunity, and the people of the United States have taken their tone from the incessant expansion which has not only been open but has even been forced upon them. ... at the frontier, the bonds of custom are broken and unrestraint is triumphant. ...

and freshness, and confidence, and scorn of older society, impatience of its restraints and its ideas, and indifference to its lessons, have accompanied the frontier. What the Mediterranean Sea was to the Greeks, breaking the bonds of custom, offering new experiences, calling out new institutions and activities, that, and more, the ever retreating frontier has been to the United States directly, and to the nations of Europe more remotely. And now, four centuries from the discovery of America, at the end of a hundred years of life under the Constitution, the frontier has gone. (Frederick Jackson Turner, 1893)

The primary analogy to be drawn is that Mars is to the new age of exploration as North America was to the last. The Earth's Moon, close to the metropolitan planet but impoverished in resources, compares to Greenland. Other destinations, such as the main-belt asteroids may be richer in potential future exports to Earth, but lack the preconditions for the creation of a fully developed indigenous society; these compare to the West Indies. Only Mars has the full set of resources required to develop a native civilization. Only Mars is a viable target for true colonization.

As America had in its relationship to Britain and the West Indies, so Mars has a positional advantage that will allow it to participate in a useful way to support extractive activities on behalf of Earth in the asteroid belt and elsewhere. But despite the short-sighted calculations of eighteenth-century European statesmen and financiers, the true value of America never was as a logistical support base for West Indies sugar and spice trade, inland fur trade, or a potential market for manufactured goods. The true value of America was as the future home for a new branch of human civilization, one which as a combined result of its humanistic antecedents and its frontier conditions was able to develop into the most powerful engine for human progress and economic growth the world had ever seen. The wealth of America lay in the fact that it could support people, and that the right kind of people chose to go there. People create wealth. People create power. Ergo people *are* wealth and power. Every feature of frontier American life that acted to create a practical can-do culture of innovating people will apply to Mars a hundred-fold.

Mars is a harsher place than any on Earth. But provided one can survive the regimen, it is the toughest schools that are the best. The Martians will do well.

Conclusions

We have examined the prospects for colonizing Mars, addressing the question of its economic viability. We have shown that of all bodies in the solar system other than Earth, Mars is unique in that it has the resources required to support a population of sufficient size to create a new branch of human civilization. We have seen that despite the fact that Mars may lack any resource directly exportable to Earth, its orbital elements and other physical parameters give it a unique positional advantage that will allow it to act as a keystone, supporting extractive activities in the asteroid belt and elsewhere in the solar system.

This chapter has examined the potential of relatively near-term types of interplanetary transportation systems, and shown that with very modest advances on a historical scale, systems can be put in place that will allow individuals and families to emigrate to Mars at their own discretion. The motivation for people doing so will parallel in many ways the historical motives for Europeans and others to come to America, including higher pay rates in a labour-short economy, escape from tradition and oppression, as well as freedom to exercise their drive to create in an untamed and undefined world.

Under conditions of such large-scale and open immigration, sale of real estate will add a significant source of income to the planet's economy. However, the greatest source of Martian wealth, and the greatest benefit of its existence to the terrestrial world, will be as a pressure cooker for invention and innovation of every type. In analogy to frontier America, but going well beyond it, Mars will be a society of self-selected immigrants, operating in a harsh, labour-short environment in which practical innovation and technological acumen will be at a premium.

Licensing on Earth of the inventions created under conditions of necessity on Mars will bring vast amounts of income to support the development of the Red Planet, even as these same inventions continue to raise terrestrial living standards and destabilize tendencies that would otherwise exist on Earth towards technological and social stagnation.

What the Mediterranean was to the Greeks, what the New World was to the Western Europeans, Mars will be to the pioneering nations of the next several centuries: the engine of progress of the coming era. As the US showed in the nineteenth century, such an engine can pull far more than its own weight.

Bibliography

Baker, D., and R. Zubrin. 1990. Mars Direct: Combining Near-Term Technologies to Achieve a Two-Launch Manned Mars Mission. *JBIS* 43 (11): 519–526.

Cordell, B. 1984. A Preliminary Assessment of Martian Natural Resource Potential. AAS 84-185, Presented to the Case for Mars II Conference, Boulder, July.

Frederick Jackson Turner (1893) *America: A Narrative History*, 6th edition, Chapter 17. Inventing America. ISBN-13: 978-0393924268.

Fogg, M. 1993. Advantages of Terraforming for the Human Settlement of Mars. Presented to the Case for Mars V, Boulder, June.

Lewis, J., and R. Lewis. Resources from Space: Breaking the Bonds of Earth. ISBN-10: 0231064985 October 15, 1987.

O'Neill, G. 1977. *The High Frontier*. New York: William Morrow and Co.

Zubrin, R. 1992. Mars and Luna Direct. *Journal of Practical Applications in Space* 4 (1): 25–80.

Zubrin, R., and D. Andrews. 1991. Magnetic Sails and Interplanetary Travel. *Journal of Spacecraft and Rockets* 28 (2): 197–203.

Zubrin, R., and David Baker. 1990. Mars Direct: Humans to the Red Planet by 1999. IAF-90-672, 41st Congress of the International Astronautical Federation, Dresden, Acta Astronautica, October.

Zubrin, R., and C. McKay. 1993. Technological Requirements for Terraforming Mars. AIAA 93-2005, AIAA/SAE 29th Joint Propulsion Conference, Monterey.

Zubrin, R., and D. Weaver. 1995. Practical Methods for Near-Term Piloted Mars Missions. AIAA 93-2089 AIAA/SAE 29th Joint Propulsion Conference, Monterey, 1993, JBIS, June.

Robert Zubrin is president of Pioneer Astronautics, an aerospace research and development company located in Lakewood, Colorado. He is also the founder and president of the Mars Society, an international organization dedicated to furthering the exploration and settlement of Mars by both public and private means. Formerly a staff engineer at Lockheed Martin Astronautics in Denver, he holds a Master's degree in Aeronautics and Astronautics and a Ph.D. in Nuclear Engineering from the University of Washington. He also published the book, *The Case for Mars*. https://en.wikipedia.org/wiki/The_Case_for_Mars.

Index[1]

---

[1] Note: Page numbers followed by 'n' refer to notes.

© The Author(s) 2018
T. James (ed.), *Deep Space Commodities*,
https://doi.org/10.1007/978-3-319-90303-3

9783319903026